Shut Out

Shut Out

Low Income Mothers and Higher Education in Post-Welfare America

Valerie Polakow, Sandra S. Butler,

Luisa Stormer Deprez, and Peggy Kahn,

editors

State University of New York Press

Published by
State University of New York Press, Albany

For information, address State University of New York Press,
90 State Street, Suite 700, Albany, NY 12207

Production by Michael Haggett and Marilyn P. Semerad
Marketing by Fran Keneston

Library of Congress Cataloging-in-Publication Data

Shut out : low income mothers and higher education in post-welfare America / Valerie
    Polakow . . . [et al.], editors.
        p. cm.
    Includes bibliographical references and index.
    ISBN 0-7914-6125-4 (alk. paper) — ISBN 0-7914-6126-2 (pbk. : alk. paper)
        1. Welfare recipients—Education (Higher)—United States.   2. Poor women—Education
    (Higher)—United States.   3. Mothers—Education (Higher)—United States.   I. Polakow,
    Valerie.

HV699.S523 2004
378.1'9826941—dc22

                                                                                        2004041675

10   9   8   7   6   5   4   3   2   1

Contents

Introduction

Peggy Kahn, Sandra S. Butler,
Luisa Stormer Deprez, and Valerie Polakow

You can take anything from a person, but you can't take away their education.
... [My caseworker] actually told me, "We don't care about you going to
school, that is not what we want, Governor Engler wants ladies to work ..." I
was like, "Well, where is Governor Engler at, because he is obviously not trying to help me if he doesn't want me to further my education and get a stable
job. I mean this $6-an-hour job, I don't want that for the rest of my life. That's
why I'm in school, so I can have a better life for me and my child."

—Sandra, a single mother in Michigan struggling to stay in school

Some people could spend their entire five years going to college. Now that's
not my view of the importance of work and helping people become independent. And it's certainly not my view of understanding the importance of
work and helping people achieve the dignity necessary so that they can live a
free life, free from government control.

—President George Bush, Speech at West Ashley High School

Punitive and rigid Work First welfare policies and the ability of low income
mothers to pursue post-secondary education are on a collision course. The Work
First approach, enshrined in the 1996 Personal Responsibility and Work Opportunity Reconciliation Act (PRWORA) and reinvigorated in the Bush administration's reauthorization proposals, stigmatizes low income mothers as
undeserving of benefits, of time to parent their own children, of education, and
of general respect. The exclusive remedy prescribed for low income mothers—
variously stigmatized as work aversive, dependent, behaviorally disorganized,
and morally deficient—is escalating work requirements, now proposed as forty
hours per week. Many low income mothers, however, understand that their economic and social interests lie in post-secondary education, a far more realistic
pathway to independence and self-respect than the low-wage, insecure jobs into
which welfare recipients are driven by Work First policies. Such policies, as

1

framed by national and state legislation and implemented in the practices of social service and Work First agencies, have built a nearly insurmountable wall of
obstacles to student mothers' pursuit of two-year and four-year degrees as they
try to study while working and parenting in conditions of poverty. Remarkably,
some mothers have persisted, aided by their own fortitude and resilience, informal family networks, supportive advocates, or programs at educational institutions and in their communities. Only a handful of states have chosen to invest in
low income parents, viewing them as people with considerable developmental
potential rather than as malingerers who need to be booted into the workplace.

    *Shut Out: Low Income Mothers and Higher Education in Post-Welfare Amer-
ica* examines this confrontation between a welfare-to-work regime that coerces
single mothers into low-wage work, and women who have resisted, understanding that higher education is critical to their capacity to provide for their
family's long-term economic self-sufficiency and their ability to make autonomous decisions about their lives, their children's academic and social development, and their community's well-being. The book examines the general
issues of post-secondary education and low income mothers in the current welfare climate that equates personal responsibility with immediate engagement in
the low-wage labor market and exit from the welfare rolls, analyzing the actual
experiences of racially diverse low income mothers struggling to gain access to
meaningful education and training in a variety of geographic locations. The
formidable obstacles to their educational achievements include not only formal
work requirements in an unreformed labor market unfriendly to women with
children, but also restrictive, punitive, and inconsistent implementation of a
range of welfare-to-work provisions. Such policies and frontline delivery practices compromise student mothers' parenting, disrupt their educational progress
and disregard their work histories and aspirations, forcing independently
minded low income parents either to give up on college degrees or make
painful short-term sacrifices hoping they will make long-term gains. The book
also focuses on the policies and practices of educational institutions and higher
education financial aid policies as they affect low income mothers, and examines alternatives to Work First paradigms and practices. The voices, the struggles and the resistance of low income student mothers are presented, and
concrete organizational and policy alternatives are analyzed.

WORK FIRST POLITICS AND POST-SECONDARY EDUCATION

Preceded by political rhetoric that unremittingly denounced single mothers on
welfare as work aversive, personally disorganized, morally deficient, and patho-
logically dependent on public funds, the Personal Responsibility and Work Opportunity Reconciliation Act (PRWORA) of 1996 shifted U.S. welfare policy
decisively toward "immediate labor market attachment" or Work First welfare

policy. The new act abolished the major preexisting program for poor single mothers and their children, Aid to Families with Dependent Children (AFDC). AFDC was a federal entitlement program established by Title IVA of the 1935 Social Security Act, providing funds for single parents and their dependent children. During the initial decades of its operation, receipt of AFDC benefits often depended on caseworkers' assessments of claimants' moral virtues, need, and labor market opportunities, and the program plainly discriminated against African American women and their children, especially in southern states where Black women were expected to work in the fields and as domestics rather than care for their own children (Piven and Cloward 1993; Sidel 1986). Although AFDC was strengthened and standardized by the welfare-rights movement of the 1960s and 1970s, benefit levels continued to vary widely among the states, falling short of raising family incomes to an artificially low official poverty line, and generally leaving single-parent families with incomes less than half the average production wage (Piven and Cloward 1993; Sidel 1986; Kamerman 1984). Still, AFDC did entitle income-eligible poor, single mothers and their children to minimal benefits, thereby protecting most from abject destitution, and permitting some to enroll in training and educational activities.

From the mid-1960s, policy makers began to enact work requirements for benefit recipients: the Work Incentive Program in 1967, the mandatory job-search programs in the 1970s for mothers with children aged six or older, the Program for Better Jobs and Income during the Carter years, the work demonstration projects of the Reagan administration, and the 1988 Family Support Act's Job Opportunities and Basic Skills (JOBS) Program. However, although these programs focused on basic education and limited occupational skills training, there were also opportunities to pursue post-secondary education. The 1988 Family Support Act (FSA) is often described as marking a decisive shift in welfare policy from programs helping poor mothers care for their families to programs focused on reform of poor mothers, mandating employment or basic education and job training (Morgen 2001; Handler 1988). FSA required states to target education, training, and employment services to individuals most likely to become long-term AFDC recipients. Although most states funded education and job-training programs averaging six months in length (Riemer 2001, 73), states were also permitted to offer post-secondary education to welfare recipients, and a significant proportion of recipients took advantage of these education provisions (Kates 1996; Gittell 1991).

The Personal Responsibility and Work Opportunity Reconciliation Act not only dismantled the minimal federal entitlement to welfare assistance, but also decisively terminated post-secondary educational options. It replaced AFDC with conditional block grants called Temporary Assistance for Needy Families (TANF) and gave states the authority to design their own programs for poor mothers and children within the federal guidelines. The central condition of federal TANF funding is that recipients of cash benefits must not only

meet income tests but also must comply with new mandatory work requirements, enforced by harsh, often arbitrary, sanctions for noncompliance. With
benefits conditional on work and a five-year lifetime limit on TANF assistance,
the new law shredded the already thin and frayed safety net for single-parent
families. Passage of the act not only changed federal and state policy, but also
accelerated a transformation in the culture of social service agencies and their
private contractors. Such agencies had historically stigmatized and exercised
surveillance over clients, but post-1996 agency practices added a new focus on
reducing the welfare rolls through employment to well-established attitudes of
suspicion and denigration of clients in a de-legalized welfare environment
(Diller 2000; Brodkin 1997, 1996).

The Work First model contains sinister and derogatory assumptions about
low income women and education. Because it is based on the idea that welfare
clients are morally and socially deficient and that any job will reform and improve the behavioral problems and social disorganization, aimlessness, and lack
of discipline of poor mothers, Work First marginalizes education. The policy
impugns the motives of low income mothers pursuing education, framing education as a loophole and form of work avoidance, and denies women autonomy and self-determination about the care of their young children and their
right to pursue education. Although previous welfare legislation encouraged
some limited development of low income mothers' human capital, the 1996
legislation and its supporters have decried education as diverting recipients
from the development of a work ethic, self-sufficiency, and personal responsibility. More specifically, they have denounced any suggestion that education be
included in federal work requirements, claiming, like Wade Horn, Assistant
Secretary for Children and Families at the Department of Health and Human
Services, that such policy would amount to supporting generous financial aid
packages for poor mothers when many working people themselves could not
afford college. Robert Rector, policy analyst at the Heritage Foundation, argues
against legislative provisions allowing access to college on grounds it would
"discourage marriage and reward out-of-wedlock childbearing. . . . This sends a
dangerous message to women at risk of having children out of marriage: 'Have
a child out of wedlock and the government will support your family and put
you through college for free'" (Rector 2002).

Work First objectives of reforming the behavior of poor, deficient mothers are also aligned with the fiscally conservative objectives of cutting public
funds expended on poor women by cutting the benefits themselves, by cutting
back state personnel who support and render service to low income parents,
and by privatizing parts of the welfare system to lower costs. Such objectives
limit the willingness of states to provide short-term support to families while
parents attend school, even though such support would have lower costs than
benefits (Coalition for Independence Through Education [CFITE] 2002; see
also Gruber 1998). Such views of public expenditure also limit the ability of
welfare workers with high caseloads, complex program administration respon-

sibilities, and limited training to attend to issues of welfare, education policy, education, and labor markets (Morgen 2001; Kahn 2000).

Frances Fox Piven (2002a, b, 1998) has pointed out that Work First policy creates a pool of disciplined low-wage laborers—women who must work at any job that is available or see themselves and their children reduced to utter desperation. Such a workforce is in high demand as global restructuring expands the low-wage service sector. At the same time, it suits the interests of business and economic conservatives to blame low income mothers' personal irresponsibility for their own economic insecurity, diverting attention from the impact of corporate restructuring and managerial strategies and reassuring other working people that they are more deserving and less vulnerable than poor mothers. Gwendolyn Mink (2002, 1998) argues that Work First welfare and its coercive paternity-identification requirements punish women who have dared to have children out of wedlock by restricting their motherhood and family choices, and by coercing mothers with infants and very young children into the low-wage workforce so that "welfare law now forbids mothers who remain single to work inside the home caring for [their own] children" (Mink 1998, 30). The marriage remedies for poverty that have recently gained prominence once again reveal the deeply conservative social agenda that has driven this legislation, and which serves to obstruct meaningful self-sufficiency through post-secondary education.

In recent decades, women have entered not only the labor market but also post-secondary education in large numbers, and a strong consensus supports the argument that women's post-secondary education is critical to their ability to succeed in the labor market. Yet the 1996 legislation essentially revokes such post-secondary options and de-emphasizes skills training, while focusing on shaping participants' attitudes to work, forcing them to search for the low-paid jobs for which they are already qualified, in which they have often already worked, and which have been responsible for their resort to public assistance in the first place (Lafer 2002a, b).

In fact, public policy treats single mothers as if they are unencumbered male breadwinners, disguising the different and subordinate position of women on assistance. Mothers on assistance are caregivers responsible for dependents; they are poor women with few resources and many responsibilities; and they are often women of color who face disproportionate poverty and racism in labor markets and public and private institutions (Albelda 2002; Burnham 2002; Neubeck and Cazenave 2002, 2001; Albelda and Tilly 2001; Schram 2000).

WORK REQUIREMENTS AND THEIR IMPACT ON POST-SECONDARY EDUCATION

Two key work requirements in the PRWORA legislation have an impact on low income mothers' ability to access and persist in post-secondary education: a work requirement imposed on individual recipients and an aggregate work-participation rate requirement imposed on the state. First, each welfare recipient must work in exchange for receiving benefits, and PRWORA lets each state decide which activities satisfy the individual work requirement. Under these provisions, it is possible for states to determine that college attendance meets the work requirement, but few states have done so. If recipients do not meet these requirements, they are sanctioned; that is, their benefits are reduced or completely withdrawn. PRWORA specifies that individuals must work a minimum of twenty hours per week, rising to thirty-five over time unless the parent has a child under the age of six. These work requirements for single parents represent a forced absence from the home even in families with multiple young children. Some states such as Michigan, New York, Massachusetts, Ohio, and Wisconsin have required that mothers with infants twelve weeks and over enter the work force, and an acute crisis of unmet child care needs has resulted (Children's Defense Fund 2000). The need to comply with such long work hours while providing the intensive caregiving required of a single parent, all in the context of limited resources, is a primary barrier to post-secondary education.

In addition, there is a required percentage of the state's overall caseload that must meet federal definitions of work, "the aggregate work-participation rate requirement," and the federal definitions of work in relation to this requirement exclude post-secondary education. If states fail to meet their aggregate work-participation rate, they face loss of federal funding. This caseload work requirement has escalated from 25 percent of the caseload in 1997 to 50 percent in 2002. Some education and training activities may be counted toward overall participation rates in the 1996 legislation. Vocational educational training may count toward the first twenty hours and in excess of the first twenty hours for up to twelve months, but no state may count more than 30 percent of its caseload as fitting into this category of work participation; arguably some post-secondary education fits into this category. However, caseload-reduction credits allow reduction of the required work-participation rates proportionate to the reduction in the caseload.

States may make use of the initial twenty-four months of welfare assistance to include post-secondary education because the aggregate work-participation rate is applied to clients in the caseloads after the first twenty-four months. States may structure program funding so that federal money is used to fund those in federally sanctioned work activities, while the state's expenditures under PRWORA, the so-called maintenance-of-effort grant, might be used to fund recipients in education, partly to protect them from using up their lifetime TANF time limit because they are pursuing education. By maintaining restrictive definitions of work and failing to offer post-secondary education options, states continue to direct recipients into low-wage labor markets, and avoid the political hazards of granting benefits to politically devalued welfare mothers.

In fact, only a handful of states have taken advantage of the limited flexibility accorded them in the 1996 legislation. Maine, Illinois, Kentucky, Wyoming, and California are five states that are often cited as having made substantial provision for post-secondary education for TANF-eligible clients. Maine's Parents as Scholars program is perhaps the most innovative and comprehensive program providing access to TANF-eligible mothers. It is a separate program, funded with state-only money, that provides cash assistance at the same level as the state's TANF program for low income parents in approved two-year and four-year educational programs (see Deprez, Butler, and Smith, this volume; Maine Equal Justice Partners at www.mejp.org). By October 1999, only twenty-two states permitted some limited options for post-secondary education, but these were strictly circumscribed by the federal guidelines—education must be vocational (directly tied to employment, as defined by the state and its agencies) and limited to twelve months—and did not allow full-time education to count as meeting work requirements in full (Greenberg, Strawn, and Plimpton 2000).

The Bush administration's current proposal for reauthorization further tightens these already coercive work requirements. The Bush proposal requires recipients to work forty hours a week to retain benefits, a workweek that exceeds the average 24.5 hours per week worked by all mothers and the 34–35-hour workweek for production and non-supervisory workers on private payrolls (Institute for Women's Policy Research [IWPR] 2002; Pear 2002), but without additional child care funding. The Bush administration also proposes that only twenty-four hours would have to be paid market work and that sixteen hours may involve other "constructive activities" such as job training. But post-secondary education is clearly not considered such a "constructive" option. The proposal also requires states to have 70 percent of the workforce meeting work-participation requirements by 2007. The alternative bill sponsored by the late Patsy Mink (D-Hawaii) would have redefined work activities to include four years of college, care of children under age 6, and various other activities such as mental-health counseling and substance-abuse treatment.

By insisting that low income mothers take any job and exit cash assistance quickly, regardless of their human capital, their educational aspirations or abilities, or other circumstances, PRWORA has pulled hundreds of thousands of low income mothers out of education and pushed them into low-wage work and off the welfare rolls. Although about three-quarters of a million recipients, mainly single mothers, were in college in 1996, decreases in their college enrollments after 1996 ranged from 29 to 82 percent (IWPR 1998, 2; Wright 1997). The City University of New York (CUNY) alone reported a rapid decline from 27,000 students on assistance in 1994 to 14,000 in 1997 and 5,000 in 2002, a drop steeper than the fall in New York City welfare rolls (Phillips-Fein 2002). The Center on Law and Social Policy (CLASP) cites a dramatic drop in recipients in post-secondary and vocational education reported by the states to the federal government under the JOBS program of the 1988 FSA and TANF, from 3.9 percent of the caseload in 1996 to 1.8 percent in 1998. Although some policy analysts dismiss these data as simply showing that single mothers are staying in college but leaving the welfare rolls, or that low income mothers in college have simply found family-supporting jobs, there is considerable evidence that such policies have ejected single mothers from college as they scrambled to keep benefits for their children, that barriers to enrollment for those on assistance are very high, that dramatic declines across many states can be tracked to escalating mandatory work hours, and that some determined and resourceful poor mothers have left welfare in order to stay in school but live with terrible economic and social stress.

THE EDUCATIONAL ASPIRATIONS AND NEEDS OF LOW INCOME MOTHERS

Ranged against the towering obstacles erected by Work First are low income mothers who are determined to pursue their education. Student mothers and other welfare clients who aspire to two- and four-year degrees perceive post-secondary education as their path out of poverty to self-sufficiency. Although welfare rolls have plummeted, falling over 50 percent, from five million families in 1994 to four million in 1996, and then to just over two million families in 2002 (U.S. Department of Health and Human Services, 2002), large proportions of leavers continue to struggle with low-paid work, and many low income mothers know that without education, sub-poverty wages, vulnerability, and dependence on public assistance are their fate. Welfare-leaver studies tend to show that between two-thirds and three-quarters of adult leavers are employed at jobs paying about $7.50 per hour with few, if any, health-care benefits, paid sick days, or paid time off. However, the evidence also indicates that for a variety of reasons, leavers may not retain their jobs for long, becoming unemployed and returning to welfare. Average incomes remain at or near the poverty line, and household income overall does not increase with increased earnings and the earned income tax credit, as public assistance is withdrawn and expenses grow (Albelda 2002; Albelda and Tilly 2001; National Campaign for Jobs and Income Support 2001; Loprest 1999; Parrott 1998). Many leavers report extraordinary hardships, including housing and food insecurity (Burnham 2002; Boushey and Gundersen 2001; Children's Defense Fund 2000; Sherman et al. 1998).

Although many policy makers assume that post-secondary education is beyond the capabilities of women now on assistance, there is a constant turnover of the caseload, and welfare clients are not simply a static set of hard-to-serve clients with devastating barriers to employment and self-sufficiency. Research using data from the early 1990s has shown that a third to a half of welfare clients have pursued post-secondary education and that at least 15 percent have some college experience (Carnevale and Desrochers 1999; Spalter-Roth et al. 1995; Kates 1992).

Studies of welfare recipients who have completed two- and four-year degrees indicate that post-secondary education has enormous benefits for women and children on assistance. Such women work more steadily, find jobs related to their fields of study, earn higher wages, receive more post-employment training and report higher levels of family well-being after graduation (Boldt 2000; Alexander and Clendenning 1999; Reeves 1999; Seguino and Butler 1998; Karier 1997; Gittell et al. 1996; Gittell and Covington 1993; Gittell, Gross, and Holdaway 1993; Kates 1991; Gittell, Schehl, and Fareri 1990). Despite this evidence, policy makers remain unconvinced by, or uninterested in, such demonstrably positive effects. Because education is now essentially disallowed under the hegemonic Work First model and perhaps because the poverty-research industry has accepted the assumptions of the legislation (O'Connor 2001), there has been little new large-scale research on this issue, although the innovative large-scale California study reported in this volume is an important exception.

The findings regarding the importance of post-secondary education for single mothers is consistent with other findings about the importance of college degrees for women. Women's earnings and income increase dramatically when they have college degrees (McCall 2000; Blau 1998; Mishel, Bernstein, and Schmitt 1997; Spalter-Roth and Hartmann 1991), and completing a four-year college degree sharply reduces women's chances of being poor, from 16.7 percent to 1.6 percent compared with those with only high school education (U.S. Department of Labor, Bureau of Labor Statistics 1997). Generally, there are increasing earnings differentials based on education for both women and men in the economy; economic downturns have the worst impact on those with the least education, and, although historically men have enjoyed greater returns on education, women have most needed such returns to earn above-poverty wages (Kennickell, Starr-McCluer, and Surette 2000; Gruber 1998; Lerman 1997; Mishel, Bernstein, and Schmitt 1997; Kane and Rouse 1995).

Post-secondary education not only increases women's income but also increases parental expectations of children's achievement and children's own educational aspirations (Nichols 2001; Gittell, Gross, and Holdaway 1993). Higher levels of parental education lead to early development of language and literacy skills and increase the likelihood that children will be successful in school (Federal Interagency Forum on Child and Family Statistics [FIFCFS] 1997). Increased mandated hours at low-wage work, on the contrary, may endanger parents' ability to pursue education and read to their young children, undermining children's educational success.

Recognizing their own developmental potential even as public policy denies it, single mothers want to pursue education to permanently transform themselves and their families. Whereas public policy makers refuse to think in these terms, low income mothers understand that education is an investment in their social capital, and that increased social capital results in increased autonomy over their lives. Women's increased independence means far more than independence from public benefits; it extends to their psychological well-being, their capacity for family self-sufficiency, and their power to exercise some choices over their children's care and development. Although the dominant ways of discussing the benefits of education in relation to poor women are framed in terms of individual economic outcomes, many low income women, as demonstrated in this volume, also use their education to become articulate activists who work to transform their communities.

ORGANIZATION OF THE BOOK

Shut Out examines the economic, educational, and existential struggles that single mothers confront as they fight back against a Welfare-to-Work regime that attempts to strip them of their educational rights. The book does not purport to develop a theorized analysis of low income women's position within a broader feminist framework, nor does the book address the politics of the various women's organizations such as the National Organization for Women (NOW) and their political engagement (or lack thereof) in the struggles of low income women for post-secondary education. Rather, we have attempted to create a policy analysis grounded in the lived educational experiences of women in poverty across the states, documenting the confrontation between harsh and punitive public policies that are designed to keep poor women trapped in low-wage work, and the actions of those who have resisted, and who continue to do so, inspired by dreams of a world made possible by education and an exit from chronic poverty.

Chapter 1, "Debunking the Myth of the Failure of Education and Training for Welfare Recipients: A Critique of the Research," argues that policy makers frequently justify their restrictions on education and training by pointing to flawed research that appears to show that education and training have failed to help recipients. This research, much of it conducted prior to 1996, is flawed in its assumptions, methodologies, and definitions of success, and Kates argues that the dominant research institutions conducting such studies and releasing mainstream reports are "circumscribed by the fact that they do not draw on the scholarship of a parallel stream of research that has paid close attention to education and training, particularly post-secondary, options for over two decades."

Chapters 2–4 examine low income mothers' experiences of trying to go to school in conditions of poverty under work-first policy regimes and depicts the existential realities of "Work First, Education Last" public policy. In chapter 2, "Failing Low Income Students: Education and Training in the Age of Welfare Reform," Lizzy Ratner presents compelling portraits of four mothers who have struggled to receive an education in New York City, where college enrollment has fallen precipitously. In chapter 3, "That's Not How I Want to Live: Student Mothers Fight to Stay in School under Michigan's Welfare-to-Work Regime," Peggy Kahn and Valerie Polakow show the actual impact of work requirements and work-first policies on the lives of a group of student mothers in Michigan. The authors weave together the narratives of African American, White, and biracial student mothers struggling to complete four-year degrees into the context of Michigan's welfare-to-work policies and practices, illuminating the nexus of obstacles they confront: active discouragement and harassment of their post-secondary educational aspirations, acute child care crises, concealed information and denied access to benefits to which they are entitled. Frances Riemer's "Connecting and Reconnecting to Work: Low Income Mothers' Participation in Publicly Funded Training Programs," chapter 4, portrays the experiences of low income mothers in public training programs and examines the assumptions that traditionally underlie training for low income African American mothers. She argues that job-training programs for poor women have traditionally diverted them from post-secondary education and family-supporting jobs, temporarily preempting but ultimately not crushing their desires or need for more education.

Chapters 5–7 focus on post-secondary educational institutions and higher-education policy. In chapter 5, "Supporting or Blocking Educational Progress? The Impact of College Policies, Programs, and Practices on Low Income Single Mothers," Sally Sharp draws on three case studies to examine what programs, policies, services, and people at post-secondary institutions support or block welfare-reliant mothers' educational progress and whether and how institutional arrangements can make a difference given the high barriers erected by welfare policy. Chapter 6, Don Heller and Stefani Bjorklund's "Student Financial Aid and Low Income Mothers," questions whether the current financial aid system serves the needs of low income parents and recommend how it might be transformed. They point out that low income student mothers use the financial aid packages available to them to absorb educational costs and defray living expenses, but that they have considerable unmet need because financial aid does not include even basic family expenses, including child care costs. Such students face a variety of other barriers to receiving financial assistance when they attend school part time or participate in noncredit programs. In chapter 7, "Credentials Count: How California's Community Colleges Help Parents Move from Welfare to Self-Sufficiency," Anita Mathur et al. show, on the basis of an extensive new study of California community college students, that welfare recipients who complete a significant amount of courses work more hours and increase their earnings substantially in one to three years after exiting college; those who obtain an associate's degree or vocational certificate experience the most substantial increases.

In the final chapters of the book, contributors depict legislative and programmatic alternatives to work-first, education-last policies. In all of these cases, low income women and their allies have mobilized to fight for education. Christiana Miewald, in " 'This Little Light of Mine': Parent Activists Struggling for Access to Post-Secondary Education in Appalachian Kentucky," chapter 8, analyzes the intersection of welfare reform, post-secondary education, and political activism in Kentucky, illustrating how women in Appalachian Kentucky mobilized with other groups to transform state legislation and create opportunities for new social relationships in areas of rural poverty. Deborah Clarke and Lynn Peterson, in chapter 9, "College Access and Leadership Building for Low Income Women," describe a college-access and leadership program in Boston and portray the experiences of four of its graduates. The program is a clear example of how women use education as a resource for transforming themselves and their low income urban communities. In chapter 10, "Transcending Welfare: Creating a GI Bill for Working Families," Julie L. Watts and Aiko Schaefer write about the efforts of advocates to create a policy in Washington State that transforms welfare-to-work and opens up post-secondary education for all low-wage working women, a project with potential for crossing class and racial barriers. The concluding chapter, "Securing Higher Education for Women on Welfare in Maine," by Luisa Stormer Deprez, Sandra S. Butler, and Rebekah J. Smith, examines the Parents as Scholars program in Maine, showing how Maine resisted the national trend to restrict higher education for welfare recipients and constructed a program that allowed student parents receiving assistance to attend either a two-year or four-year institution. They document how returning to school was an overwhelmingly positive transformative experience for low income parents, leading to increased feelings of personal independence and empowerment, better jobs, increased pay, more stable employment, and better relationships with their children.

Throughout the book, there is an attempt to juxtapose the lived experiences and struggles of low income women against the harsh and discriminatory public policies that restrict their educational opportunities and threaten their autonomy, their children, and their economic self-sufficiency. Post-secondary education emerges as a major source of low income women's empowerment, shaping their futures and that of their children, instilling dignity and self-respect and rectifying the larger injustices of indoctrinated inferiority and severe economic inequality.

REFERENCES

Albelda, Randy. 2002. Fallacies of welfare to work policies. In *Lost ground: Welfare reform, poverty and beyond*, ed. Randy Albelda and Ann Withorn, 79–94. Cambridge, Mass.: South End Press.

Albelda, Randy, and Chris Tilly. 2001. Moving beyond "Get a job": What real welfare reform would look like. In *Squaring up: Policy strategies to raise women's incomes in the*

United States, ed. Randy Albelda and Ann Withorn, 15–45. Ann Arbor: University of Michigan Press.

Alexander, Michelle, and Dodie Clendenning. 1999. *The state of Maine's Parents as Scholars program: Executive summary of early findings.* Orono: University of Maine, Center for Community Inclusion.

Blau, Francine. 1998. Trends in the well being of American women, 1970–1995. *Journal of Economic Literature* 36:112–165.

Boldt, Nancy. 2000. From welfare to college to work: Support factors to help students persist and succeed and the economic and social outcomes of college degree attainment. Ph.D. diss. University of Vermont.

Boushey, Heather, and Bethney Gundersen. 2001. *When work just isn't enough: Measuring hardships faced by families moving from welfare to work.* Washington, D.C.: Economic Policy Institute.

Brodkin, Evelyn Z. 1996. *The false promises of administrative reform: Implementing quality control in welfare.* Philadelphia: Temple University Press.

———. 1997. Inside the welfare contract: Discretion and accountability in state welfare administration. *Social Service Review* 71(1):1–33.

Burnham, Linda. 2002. Welfare reform, family hardship and women of color. In *Lost Ground*, ed. Randy Albelda and Ann Withorn, 43–56. Cambridge, Mass.: South End Press.

Bush, George. 2002, 29 July. Speech. West Ashley High School.

Carnevale, Anthony P., and Donna M. Desrochers. 1999. *Getting down to business: Matching welfare recipients' skills to jobs that train.* Princeton, N.J.: Educational Testing Service.

Children's Defense Fund (CDF). 2000. *Families struggling to make it in the workforce: A post welfare report.* Washington, D.C.: CDF.

Coalition for Independence Through Education (CFITE). 2002. Access and barriers to post-secondary education under Michigan's welfare to work policies: Policy background and recipients' experiences. Available at http://www.umich.edu/~cew/pubs.html.

Diller, Matthew. 2000. The revolution in welfare administration: Rules, discretion and entrepreneurial government. *New York University Law Review* 75:1121–1220.

Federal Interagency Forum on Child and Family Statistics (FIFCFS). 1997. *America's children: Key national indicators of well being.* Washington, D.C.: Federal Interagency Forum.

Gittell, Marilyn. 1991. Women on welfare: Education and work. In *Women, work and school: Occupational segregation and the role of education*, ed. Leslie R. Wolfe, 168–180. Boulder, Colo.: Westview Press.

Gittell, Marilyn, and Sally Covington. 1993. *Higher education in JOBS: An option or an opportunity? A comparison of nine states.* New York: Howard Samuels State Management and Policy Center.

Gittell, Marilyn, Jill Gross, and Jennifer Holdaway. 1993. *Building human capital: The impact of post-secondary education on AFDC recipients in five states.* A report to the Ford Foundation. New York: Howard Samuels State Management and Policy Center.

Gittell, Marilyn, Margaret Schehl, and Camille Fareri. 1990. *From welfare to independence: The college option.* A report to the Ford Foundation. New York: Howard Samuels State Management and Policy Center.

Gittell, Marilyn, Kirk Vandersall, Jennifer Holdaway, and Kathe Newman. 1996. *Creating social capital at CUNY: A comparison of higher education programs for AFDC recipients.* New York: Howard Samuels State Management and Policy Center.

Greenberg, Mark, Julie Strawn, and Lisa Plimpton. 2000. *State opportunities to provide access to postsecondary education under TANF.* Washington, D.C.: Center for Law and Social Policy.

Gruber, Andrew. 1998. Promoting long-term self sufficiency for welfare recipients: Post-secondary education and the welfare work requirement. *Northwestern University Law Review* 93:247–299.

Handler, Joel. 1988. The transformation of Aid to Families with Dependent Children: The Family Support Act in historical context. *Review of Law and Social Change* 16:457–533.

———. 1995. *The poverty of welfare reform.* New Haven, Conn.: Yale University Press.

Institute for Women's Policy Research (IWPR). 1998. Precipitous declines in college enrollment among welfare recipients. Welfare reform and postsecondary education: Research and policy update. *Welfare Reform Network News* 2(1):2.

———. 2003, June. Forty hour work proposal significantly raises mothers' employment standard. Briefing paper. Washington, D.C.: IWPR.

Kahn, Peggy. 2000. "Governor Engler wants ladies to work": Single mothers, work-first welfare policy and post-secondary education in Michigan. *Journal of Poverty* 5(3):17–38.

Kamerman, Sheila. 1984. Women, children and poverty: Public policies and female-headed families in industrialized countries. In *Women and poverty,* ed. Barbara C. Gelpi, Nancy C. M. Hartsock, Clare C. Novak, and Myra H. Strober, 41–64. Chicago: University of Chicago Press.

Kane, Thomas, and C. E. Rouse. 1995. Labor market returns to two- and four-year college, *American Economic Review* 85(3): 600–614.

Karier, Thomas. 1997. *Welfare graduates: A study of welfare recipients who graduated from a comprehensive university.* Available at http://www.class.ewu/ECON/karier.

Kates, Erika. 1991. *More than survival: Access to higher education for low income women.* Washington, D.C.: Center for Women Policy Studies.

———. 1992. *Women, welfare and higher education: A selected bibliography.* Washington, D.C.: Center for Women Policy Studies.

———. 1996. Colleges help women in poverty. In *For crying out loud: Women's poverty in the United States*, ed. Diane Dujon and Ann Withorn, 341–348. Boston, Mass.: South End Press.

Kennickell, Arthur B., Martha Starr-McCluer, and Brian J. Surette. 2000. Recent changes in U.S. family finances: Results from the 1998 survey of consumer finances. Available at http://www.federalreserve.gov/pubs/bulleting/2000/0100lead.pdf.

Lafer, Gordon. 2002a. Job training for welfare recipients: A hand up or a slap down? In *Work, welfare and politics*, ed. Frances Fox Piven, Joan Acker, Margaret Hallock, and Sandra Morgen, 175–196. Eugene: University of Oregon Press.

———. 2002b. *Let them eat training: The false promise of federal employment policy since 1980.* Ithaca, N.Y.: Cornell University Press.

Lerman, Robert I. 1997. Meritocracy without rising inequality? Wage rate differences are widening by education and narrowing by race and gender. Paper no. 2, in the Series *Economic restructuring and the job market*. Washington, D.C.: Urban Institute.

Loprest, Pamela J. 1999. *Families who left welfare: Who are they and how are they doing?* Washington, D.C.: Urban Institute. Available at http://www.urban.org/url.cfm?ID=310290.

Maine Equal Justice Partners. 2003. Available at http://www.mejp.org.

McCall, Leslie. 2000. Gender and the new inequality: Explaining the college/noncollege wage gap. *American Sociological Review* 65:234–255.

Mink, Gwendolyn. 1998. *Welfare's end.* Ithaca: Cornell University Press.

———. 2002. Violating women: Rights abuses in the welfare police state. In *Lost Ground: Welfare reform, poverty, and beyond*, ed. Randy Albelda and Ann Withorn, 95–112. Cambridge, Mass.: South End Press.

Mishel, Lawrence, Jared Bernstein, and John Schmitt. 1997. *The state of working America 1996–1997.* Armonk, N.Y.: M.E. Sharpe.

Morgen, Sandra. 2001. The agency of welfare workers: Negotiating devolution, privatization and the meaning of self-sufficiency. *American Anthropologist* 103(3): 747–761.

National Campaign for Jobs and Income Support (NCJIS). 2001. *Leaving welfare, left behind: Employment status, income and well being of former TANF recipients.* Washington, D.C.: NCJIS.

Neubeck, Ken, and Noel Cazenave. 2001. *Welfare racism: Playing the race card against America's poor.* New York: Routledge.

———. 2002. Welfare racism and its consequences: The demise of AFDC and the return of the states' rights era. In *Work, welfare and politics*, ed. Frances Fox Piven, Joan Acker, Margaret Hallock, and Sandra Morgen, 35–54. Eugene: University of Oregon Press.

Nichols, Adriana. 2001. Making sense of the puzzle: The intergenerational impact of educating welfare mothers. Ph.D. diss. Center for the Study of Higher and Post-secondary Education, University of Michigan.

O'Connor, Alice. 2001. *Poverty knowledge: Social science, social policy and the poor in twentieth century U.S. history.* Princeton, N.J.: Princeton University Press.

Parrott, Sharon. 1998. *Welfare recipients who find jobs: What do we know about their employment and earnings?* Washington, D.C.: Center on Budget and Policy Priorities.

Pear, Robert. 2002, 4 April. Study by governors calls Bush welfare plan unworkable. *New York Times.* Available at http://www.nytimes.com.

Phillips-Fein, Kim. 2002. The education of Jessica Rivera. *The Nation* 25 November: 20–23.

Piven, Frances Fox. 1998. Welfare and Work. *Social Justice* 25(1):67–81.

———. 2002a. Globalization, American politics and welfare policy. In *Lost ground: Welfare reform, poverty and beyond*, ed. Randy Albelda and Ann Withorn, 27–42. Cambridge, Mass.: South End Press.

———. 2002b. Welfare policy and American politics. In *Work, welfare and politics*, ed. Frances Fox Piven, Joan Acker, Margaret Hallock, and Sandra Morgen, 19–34. Eugene: University of Oregon Press.

Piven, Frances Fox, and Richard A. Cloward. 1993. *Regulating the poor.* New York: Vintage Books.

Rector, Robert. 2002. "Work" bill would cripple welfare reform. Available at http://www.heritage.org/Research/Welfare/ed092302.cfm.

Reeves, Angela. 1999. *An analysis of economic achievement experienced by graduates of a Perkins funded single parent and displaced homemakers' program.* Flint, Mich.: Mott Community College.

Riemer, Frances Julia. 2001. *Working at the margins: Moving off welfare in America.* Albany: State University of New York Press.

Schram, Sanford. 2000. *After welfare: The culture of postindustrial society.* New York: New York University Press.

Seguino, Stephanie, and Sandra Butler. 1998. *Struggling to make ends meet in the Maine economy: A study of former and current AFDC/TANF recipients.* Augusta, Maine: Women's Development Institute and Maine Center for Economic Policy.

Sherman, Arloc, Cheryl Amy, Barbara Duffield, Nancy Ebb, and Deborah Weinstein. 1998. *Welfare to what? Early findings on family well being and hardship.* Washington, D.C.: Children's Defense Fund and National Coalition for the Homeless.

Sidel, Ruth. 1986. *Women and children last: The plight of poor women in affluent America.* New York: Penguin Books.

Spalter-Roth, Roberta, Beverly Barr, Heidi Hartmann, and Lois Shaw. 1995. *Welfare that works: The working lives of AFDC recipients.* A report to the Ford Foundation. Washington, D.C.: IWPR.

Spalter-Roth, Roberta, and Heidi Hartmann. 1991. *Increasing working mothers' earnings*. Washington, D.C.: IWPR.

U.S. Department of Health and Human Services. 2002. *Temporary assistance for needy families total number of families and recipients July–September 2002*. Available at http://www.acf.dhhs.gov.

U.S. Department of Labor, Bureau of Labor Statistics. 1997. *A profile of the working poor 1996*. Washington, D.C.: Government Printing Office.

Wright, Scott. 1997. Despite Sallie's success story . . . Welfare reform expected to restrict college access. *Black Issues in Higher Education* 6 March:12–14.

Chapter 1

Debunking the Myth of the Failure of Education and Training for Welfare Recipients

A Critique of the Research

Erika Kates

INTRODUCTION

For millions of mothers receiving welfare benefits in 1996, the Personal Responsibility and Work Opportunity Reconciliation Act (PRWORA) changed access to education and training as they had known it.[1] PRWORA substituted a labor force attachment (LFA) approach, commonly referred to as "Work First," for a human capital development approach (HCD) that emphasized education and training. Work First signified a major reversal from the previous welfare policy, the Family Support Act (FSA) enacted in 1988.

Why this dramatic policy reversal occurred is puzzling because PRWORA superseded—and reversed—a policy whose effects were not yet fully known, but which seemed to be widely accepted and used. First, there were no reliable data showing that entry-level jobs led, through successive wage increases, to a salary that allowed a single mother to sustain her family. On the contrary, pre-reform data showed that former welfare recipients' hourly wages increased only from $6.07 to $6.72 per hour after twelve years (Strawn 1998). Second, there had been no major objections or resistance to the policy by state welfare administrators. By 1993, when FSA was fully implemented, forty-seven states had adopted the voluntary post-secondary education option (U.S. House Ways and Means Committee 1996). Third, throughout the country a substantial infrastructure existed in educational institutions—public and private, two-year and four-year, women's and coeducational—to provide a supportive environment for low income single mothers (Kates 1996). One reason for this reversal was a belief in some quarters that education programs had failed to help recipients, a position supported by researchers such as Gueron and Pauley (1991) working for the influential Manpower Demonstration Research Corporation (MDRC):

> A review of the research literature indicates there is currently little solid evidence that education programs for adult welfare recipients can improve their educational attainment or achievement. In fact, there is little research of any kind on the adult JOBS population, on mandatory education programs for adults, or on the relationship between mandatory participation in adult education and subsequent employment success. (219)

Their conclusion referred primarily to mandatory educational programs. However, it was often construed to be a rejection of education in its entirety, and it became highly influential, especially given the conservative political mood of the time. Although the MDRC studies were one of many factors influencing policy makers (many of whom had already made up their minds based on other considerations), such an acknowledgment of the "failure" of education provided grist for the Work First mill.

This chapter argues that access to substantive education and training options is essential for welfare recipients, and it examines the role that MDRC and other research institutions have played and continue to play—wittingly and unwittingly—in perpetuating the myth that access to education for welfare recipients has been a failure. With the reauthorization of PRWORA on the horizon as this book goes to press, this issue takes on particular significance. While the Bush administration is pressing to increase the work requirement to forty hours a week, others who originally ignored or downplayed the importance of substantive education and training are coming to recognize the critical importance of skills development, not only for low income mothers but for the workplace as a whole. In addition, liberals and centrists are reframing the goal of welfare reform. They are now more focused on policies that assist families in escaping from poverty rather than just leaving the welfare rolls. This new position provides a window of opportunity to craft policies that provide better access to substantive education and training for low income mothers.

Policy suggestions currently offered in mainstream reports are circumscribed by the fact that they do not draw on the scholarship of a parallel stream of research that has paid close attention to education and training—particularly post-secondary—options for over two decades. This chapter defines these respective approaches as "traditional" and "nontraditional," and suggests that the strengths of each should be combined to create a more expansive view of policy options that can assist families in moving out of poverty.

RATIONALE FOR EXPANDING ACCESS TO EDUCATION AND TRAINING

A fundamental premise of this chapter is that the underlying problem that needs to be addressed is the growing income inequality in the United States, and its disproportionate effects on female-headed families with dependent children, particularly women of color and immigrants. For two decades the income gap between the richest and poorest income groups has grown steadily in all but four states. The disparities are particularly great among households in the top 5 percent and lowest 5 percent income groups (Bernstein et al. 2002), and in child poverty rates. Although child poverty declined slightly from 1996 to 2001, the number of children living in deep poverty (below half of the official poverty guideline) has grown, mostly in families with female heads of household.

The median income of female-headed households remains roughly half that of two-parent households in all cultural groups (Table 1.1). This income gap is exacerbated for immigrants. In Massachusetts, which has the second highest rate of immigrant growth in the United States, the median income of the households of women immigrants is half that of their native-born counterparts and almost one-fourth that of two-parent immigrant families (Table 1.2).

As might be expected from these data, the poverty rates for female-headed households, especially for female-headed immigrant households, are substantial (Kates and Curley 2002). Sixty percent of households headed by native-born women live in poverty, compared to 80 percent of immigrant female-headed households (Table 1.3).

Public assistance benefits (TANF) are not enough to pull families out of poverty. In fact, their value has declined over the past two decades, a trend that was intensified with PRWORA, when several states decreased their TANF benefits. Even the most generous states do not provide cash benefits sufficient to bring families up to half of the official poverty level. In 2001, the federal poverty guideline for a family of three (a mother with two children under the age of 18) was $14,630, compared to TANF benefits ranging from $2,400 per annum in some southern states to approximately $7,200 in California, Hawaii, and Alaska.

TABLE 1.1
National Median Incomes by Family Type and Cultural Background, 2001

Family Type	All	White	Black	Hispanic
Two-parent	$61,000	$61,000	$52,000	$41,000
Female-headed	$28,000	$31,000	$22,000	$24,000

Source: U.S. Bureau of the Census 2001.

TABLE 1.2
Median Income by Family Type and Nativity, Massachusetts, 1995–97

Family Type	Median Income Native-Born	Median Income Immigrant
Two-parent	$64,700	$45,000
Female-headed	$26,000	$12,800

Adapted from Sum and Fogg 1999, p. 82.

TABLE 1.3
Massachusetts Poverty Rates by Family Type and Nativity, 1996–97

Family Type	% Native-Born in Poverty	% Immigrants in Poverty
Two parent	2	11
Female-headed	60	80

Adapted from Sum and Fogg 1999, p. 85.

TABLE 1.4
Median Earnings for Males and Females, 25–64 Years, Full-Time Workers, 1998

| Level of Education | Median Earnings | |
	Men	Women
Below HSD	$21,800	$15,300
HSD/GED	$30,900	$22,000
A.A.	$38,400	$28,400
B.A.	$50,000	$35,400

Source: U.S. Bureau of the Census 2000.

The rationale for focusing on the importance of access to education and training for low income mothers becomes readily apparent when one examines the relationship between educational attainment and income level. As Table 1.4 shows, education levels and earnings are closely correlated. The median earnings for women without high school diplomas are about $15,000, compared to $35,000 for those with bachelor's degrees.

Again, there are income differentials between women of color and immigrants. Black and Hispanic women earn less than White women at each educational level, except for Black women with less than a high school diploma (HSD) (Table 1.5). It is also clear that mastering the English language is a prerequisite for immigrants—for those who have degrees as well as for those with little education—if they are to be able to support their families. Moreover, because women

TABLE 1.5
Median Earnings of Females, 25–64 Years, Full-Time Workers, 1998

Level of education	Median Income of Women		
	Black	Hispanic	White
Below HSD	$14,800	$13,900	$15,100
HSD/GED	$19,400	$19,800	$22,500
A.A.	$27,000	$27,400	$28,800
B.A.	$35,300	$32,300	$35,400

Source: U.S. Bureau of the Census 2000.

earn less than their male counterparts at each level of education, it is especially important that they have access to substantive educational opportunities.

In summary, these data show that some post-secondary education is necessary if women are to achieve earnings of $12–$15 an hour. Even with these earnings, families in many parts of the country would likely still need subsidized housing, child care, food stamps, and the Earned Income Tax Credit (EITC) to reasonably support a family of three.

Access to education for low income mothers does more than improve the families' income levels. It also contributes to child and family well-being and to workforce development. Mothers are better able to care for their children and provide positive role models when they can help them with their homework and speak to their children's teachers and doctors. From the perspective of economic development—where it is estimated that most of the job growth to 2005 will be in jobs requiring at least a bachelor's degree—it is important that low income women not be left behind in gaining access to the necessary skills (Silvestri 1995). Yet, in many Work First states, women participate in structured job searches and two to four weeks of soft-skills training before they must begin to look for work; they are denied the opportunity to gain even basic skills and to learn English. Thus PRWORA has effectively denied women the chance to progress along a continuum of education, leaving them with little hope of being able to support their children without the aid of cash benefits when their time limits expire. The widening gap between public assistance policies and workforce development needs is alarming (Kates 1999).

A CRITIQUE OF THE RESEARCH

A myth is not necessarily a fiction; the term signifies a widely accepted belief that gives meaning to events and that is socially cued, whether or not it is verifiable. (Edelman 1977)

In light of the previous discussion, it is puzzling why researchers have not given more serious consideration to education and training. For example, when MDRC researchers concluded that mandatory basic education programs were ineffective (although they recognized that families would be left in poverty if mothers could not increase their skills), they focused more on programmatic costs than on policy and programmatic changes. MDRC is singled out here because of its predominance in the field,[2] its numerous ongoing studies, and its ability to attract millions of research dollars from government sources, a phenomenon that Alice O'Connor refers to as the poverty industry (O'Connor 2001). One reason for MDRC's credibility is its use of "gold standard" research designs, that is, experiments using the random assignment of welfare recipients to either experimental or control groups.[3] But it is certainly not the only major research center to give short shrift to these concerns. As the following analysis shows, a broad range of studies that were released from 1996 to 2002 have contributed to the belief that education has "failed." They do so in a variety of ways—through omission (education is not mentioned), simplification (the broad range of educational options is ignored), lack of awareness (no knowledge of how programs work "on the ground"), and indifference (the importance of education is minimized).

A conceptual model was developed to structure this critique. It divides the research into two ideal types—traditional and nontraditional—based on their respective assumptions and definitions. The traditional approach makes strict claims on objectivity and on scientific rigor. The nontraditional approach, on the other hand, is more grounded in the realities of women's lives and experiences (Table 1.6). The purpose of the model is heuristic: to explicate these embedded assumptions and to broaden the dialogue concerning policies affecting families in poverty. Although these approaches are represented as dichotomous, there are many variations in each. The purpose here is not to emphasize the differences between them, but rather to promote a dialogue among researchers and policy makers.

Although the traditional model makes strong claims of objectivity, the analysis that follows assumes that research is rarely neutral and that although

TABLE 1.6
Nontraditional and Traditional Research Models

NONTRADITIONAL	TRADITIONAL
Pragmatic research designs	Rigorous research designs
Research based on small samples	Research based on large samples
Broad definitions of education and success	Narrow definitions of education and success
Grounded in women's lives	Removed from women's lives
Focus on structural, circumstantial barriers	Focus on personal barriers
Challenges current policy constraints	Adapts to current policy constraints
Subjective	Objective

partiality is often unintentional, it can be inferred from the language that is used. As Murray Edelman states, "It is only in naming situations or characteristics that they are conceived, communicated and perceived" (Edelman 1977, 12). Thus, in the sense that language structures the problem that is addressed, including technical and legal language, it is political. Therefore, the following critique of a sizable number of studies explores their methodologies, assumptions, and definitions.

THE NONTRADITIONAL APPROACH

If we don't have the skills to go into the working force we're not going to come out of poverty; we're always going to be in poverty.[4]

—Kates and Boston Outreach Group 2000, 35

The scholarship on low income women and post-secondary education emerged in the mid-1970s due to a growing awareness of the first wave of older students (over age twenty-four and mostly women) on college campuses. It continued as successive waves of older women entered colleges. The first and second waves (known as reentry students) were mostly White, married, middle-class women with grown children whose initial goal of self-fulfillment was eventually replaced by a desire to improve their career prospects as a buffer against rising divorce rates. The third wave consisted of less prosperous and more culturally diverse women who had to support their families, and therefore were more likely to enter college while their children were still at home. Often referred to as displaced homemakers, they became eligible for Job Training Partnership Act (JTPA) and Carl Perkins funding. Their numbers grew rapidly and by the mid-1980s, 2.5 million women over age twenty-four were attending college and, of these, one million were over the age of thirty-five. Thus, although they were often referred to as nontraditional students, they had become a sizable minority in many colleges. Colleges responded in turn by providing resources through either direct services—child care slots, housing, and emergency grants— or by developing links with community-based agencies, employers, volunteer groups, and welfare agencies.

The fourth wave of students consisted of welfare recipients. Although they had overlapped with the earlier waves since the late 1960s, they remained largely "invisible" (Kates 1991). The first studies of welfare recipients in post-secondary education emerged in the 1980s as researchers examined women's motivations, documented the obstacles they encountered, and highlighted existing policy conflicts between financial aid and other state and federal benefits and the factors that aided enrollment and retention (Thompson 1993; Wolfe 1991; Ackelsberg, Bartlett, and Buchele, 1988; Moran 1986). Some low income student mothers wrote "survival guides" to help other women (Riley

1991; Mendelsohn 1989; Deem 1978). In spite of the various obstacles these women encountered, researchers found evidence that education paid off in many ways. Researchers in California found that attendance at community colleges increased women's earnings by 10 percent, even for those who did not graduate, and resulted in larger increases in earnings for welfare recipients compared to other students (Bryne 1997; Kane and Rouse 1995). Similar findings emerged from a study conducted in Washington (Karier 1998). Although few follow-up data were available, it appeared that the overwhelming majority of these students achieved substantial income gains within three years, their satisfaction with life increased, and their education and training experiences had positive effects on their children (Gittell, Gross, and Holdaway 1993; Kates 1990).

> My education was having a residual effect on my children. For the first time, they were considering college as an option for themselves. . . . There is no doubt in my mind that had I not entered college myself, they would not have had the desire to do so themselves.[5]

NONTRADITIONAL POST-PRWORA STUDIES

Collecting data on low income students has always been problematic because of the strict confidentiality of a student's financial status, but prior to PRWORA the aggregate number of AFDC recipients attending college could be obtained by counting the number of student financial aid forms that listed AFDC as an income source. For example, before the financial aid forms were changed, it was possible to estimate that the population of welfare recipients attending the fifteen community colleges in Massachusetts declined on average by almost 50 percent within the first two years of welfare reform (Kates 1998). Data collection in the post-PRWORA era is hampered by the elimination of this line item from student financial aid forms in 1997. Students now provide information on their total income but not on each source of income. The data collected from welfare caseworkers is unreliable because self-initiated education activities are not recorded. However, researchers at the Center for Law and Social Policy (CLASP) estimated that the percent of TANF recipients in college fell from about 5.8 percent in 1996 to about 2.7 percent in 1999 (Greenberg, Strawn, and Plimpton 2000). Although it is possible to obtain a proxy count by conducting a search in financial aid records for women students with dependent children and incomes below a specific amount, this is an onerous task for most colleges (Kates, McPhee, and Solomon 2002).

Another form of data collection is tracking state policies and noting how many make midcourse corrections—decide to grant extensions, or stop the time clock—so women can participate in education and training (Greenberg, Strawn, and Plimpton 2000; Pandey et al. 2000).

Other forms of analysis were undertaken by academics familiar with low income students. Rebekah Smith, Luisa Stormer Deprez, and Sandra Butler conducted research on women attending the Parents as Scholars program in Maine. This program provides a stipend equivalent to the TANF benefit—paid out of state Maintenance of Effort funds—to women attending college. The data show that women earn a median wage of over $11 per hour on graduation, compared to $7.50 per hour before entering college. In addition, 75 percent receive employer-sponsored health insurance, 61 percent have paid sick leave, and 68 percent have paid vacations (Smith, Deprez, and Butler 2002). In Vermont, where a waiver allowed a Job Opportunities and Basic Skills (JOBS) program to continue at the University of Vermont, a follow-up study of graduates revealed similar success (Boldt 2000). In New York, which has a less friendly policy, women dropped out of school, even when they were doing well academically, because of child care problems and employment commitments (Adair 2001). In California, a study of 1,500 recipients showed that their level of education at the first interview was positively and directly correlated with leaving TANF at the time of the second interview two years later. Fifty-three percent with a college degree had left TANF, compared to 30 percent with some college, 25 percent with a high school diploma (HSD) and 15 percent with no HSD. Conversely, two years later, two-thirds of the women with less than an HSD were still without an HSD and only 12 percent of those who had some college had been able to complete their degrees. "The long odds of being off AFDC increase 20 percent per year of education" (Mathur 1998, 17).

Other forms of studies have used interviews with women who have experienced the effects of welfare reform. A study in Boston, conducted by low income mothers, found that 80 percent of the women who were interviewed had improved their educational levels since leaving high school despite experiences of homelessness, chronic children's diseases, and their own health problems (Kates and Boston Outreach Group 2000). In another study, participants in fifteen focus groups in three cities discussed how difficulties with transportation, housing, and child care made it difficult to keep children's school and health appointments, look for housing, apply for food stamps, and find jobs. They also expressed frustration with their limited educational access (Angel et al. 2002). It is interesting that, despite these barriers, both studies found that many low income women make time to volunteer in hospitals, child care centers, churches, and schools, and to stay connected with family and community.

It is not only researchers in academic settings who demonstrate an interest in access to education and training for low income mothers. Since the mid-1980s, researchers at policy centers such as the Center for Women Policy Studies (CWPS), Institute for Women's Policy Research (IWPR), CLASP, Wider Opportunities for Women (WOW), and the National Organization for Women's Legal Defense and Education Fund (NOW-LDEF), have taken a consistent interest in post-secondary education access for welfare recipients.

They have convened conferences, conducted analyses of state policies, and advocated for better access. Recently, the Educational Testing Service published the results of tests designed to determine welfare recipients' educational skills. Defining competency levels as minimal (below high school), basic (high school completion), competent (beyond high school), and superior (degree level), they found that about one-third of the welfare recipients in their sample tested at minimal, one-third at basic, and one-third at superior competency. They also examined the disparities between tested competency and achieved grade levels, and found that almost half of the women who had less than a high school education tested higher, and almost 40 percent with a high school education tested higher. The researchers calculated that it would take nine hundred hours of classes to bring someone with minimal skills up to basic competency; 200 hours to move someone from basic to competent skills; and 200 hours to move someone from competent to superior skills. This work is significant not only because an objective rating was used, but also because the researchers' assumption was that women's skill levels are dynamic, that is, they can be improved (Carnevale and Desrochers 1999).

To summarize, the nontraditional approach is grounded in the lives and experiences of low income mothers and is designed to collect information directly from low income women and people close to them. Often the data are obtained through in-depth interviews, surveys, and participant observation and include direct quotes to bring the woman's experience closer to the reader. The language is respectful and specific, referring to research subjects as women and mothers rather than as "experimentals and controls." Perceptions of women are less bounded by stereotypes, and they are seen as aspiring to, and capable of achieving, long-term and advanced educational goals. Barriers are defined more in terms of lack of resources and structural barriers rather than personal deficiencies; research questions are framed to provide information on women's educational experiences and aspirations; and the definitions of a policy's success focus on the long-term policy effects on family life, rather than on short-term income increases and welfare caseload reduction. Finally, policy recommendations focus more on changing current policies than on adapting to existing policies, and women are often perceived as important actors in creating such changes.

THE TRADITIONAL APPROACH

> It is the authoritative status of the source of a categorization that makes his or her definition of the issue more readily acceptable for an ambivalent public called upon to react to an ambiguous situation.
>
> —Edelman 1977

This section discusses the research conducted by influential policy institutes that, in the view of this author, is seriously flawed in terms of its lack of attention to substantive education as an option for welfare recipients. The flaws occur by using narrow criteria for success and limited definitions of education; depersonalizing women by referring to them as "experimentals" and the hard-to-place, and implying a universality of low skill levels; focusing on personal deficiencies rather than structural and policy constraints as major barriers; and adapting to existing policy constraints rather than focusing on changing those policies.

The following analysis organizes the traditional research into four major themes: impact, leaver, retention, and skill advancement. Impact studies examine the relative effectiveness of "employment" versus "education" policies; leaver studies examine how families that have left welfare fare; retention studies explore welfare leavers' job stability and barriers; and skill advancement studies explore program models to build workers' skills within the context of Work First.

Impact Studies

The National Evaluation of Welfare-to-Work Strategies (NEWSS) and the Greater Avenues for Independence (GAIN) evaluation in California are two of the best-known and most influential studies to have explored the impact of employment relative to education. NEWSS involved the random assignment of welfare recipients to eleven welfare-to-work programs in seven locations. Most participants were assigned to programs that offered either employment or education, or a mix of the two.[6] In the six GAIN sites, welfare recipients were assigned to mixed employment/education programs, although the mix varied among sites. The initial assignment of controls and experimentals occurred in 1991–1994 for NEWSS, and in 1988–1990 for GAIN.

Beginning as JOBS evaluations, both studies were conducted by MDRC. The primary criteria used to measure success at each site were women's earnings, employment, and families' continued use of cash assistance. The initial research findings for GAIN were based on program participation in 1991–1993, and for NEWSS in 1993–1995. NEWSS data were also collected for participation in 1995–1997, and will continue to 2005. The first round of results concluded that differences between education and employment effects were marginal. The initial earnings increases of the employment group had diminished by the end of the two-year period while the relatively lower initial earnings of the education group increased slightly after two years. The four-year analysis concluded that participants in education-focused programs worked slightly less (8.1 quarters compared to 8.5 quarters) and started jobs slightly later (after 3.6 quarters compared to 2.9 quarters) than those in employment-focused programs, although "more hours, rather than higher pay, may have contributed to higher quarterly earnings" (Martinson 2000, section B, 1).

On examination, the term "success" rings hollow. Although the "most successful" 25 percent of the participants worked for 75 percent of the four-year period, and the "least successful" worked for less than 25 percent of the period, the earnings differential between the two groups was small ($6.34 per hour compared to $6.76 per hour). In fact, most participants earned less than $2,500 per quarter, and almost one-third earned less than $1,000 per quarter. The notion that annual earnings of $10,000 to support a family would constitute a "success" is difficult to reconcile with reality because this amount is well below the federal poverty level for a family of three. The fact that most women earned less is particularly sobering. Moreover, 60 percent of the families continued to rely on cash benefits (U.S. House Ways and Means Committee 2001, 1409). The definition of "failure" that was applied is also questionable. For example, self-initiated participants in education programs were recorded as "failures" because they extended their period of "welfare dependency," as did women living in states with higher earnings disregards[7] and in states with transitional benefits, that is, the comparatively generous states.

Whereas the researchers focused on comparing the effects of employment and education options, education was limited to basic education. Moreover, the type of basic education—GED, high school diploma, basic ESL, or ESOL— was not specified. Yet these differences in educational options are significant because they meet different educational needs, and vary considerably in curricula and pace. For example, in one program Spanish-speaking women were expected to become proficient in English within fifteen weeks by attending a part-time program. As one expert commented, "The gap between [their] needs and the scope of the program is sometimes breathtaking" (Grubb 1996, 93).

Additional methodological problems occurred because of loose control over program options. For example, although women in the experimental groups were assigned to an option, they might not have participated in it; and women in the control groups could have participated on their own initiative in either education- or employment-focused programs. In fact, education and employment were not clear-cut categories. For example, some employment programs included education prior to job placement; and employment often referred to job searches and not necessarily job placement. Moreover, when positive results might have been attributed to education, they remained unexplored. For example, although the most successful group in NEWSS had a higher GED achievement than the least successful group (75 percent compared to 55 percent), the researchers were unclear whether the program had helped them to reach their GED. This limitation is the result of the "black box" effect, because impact studies are rarely able to provide information on which component of the program explains the documented success or failure.

None of the studies explored the impact of additional education options—such as community college attendance—although they acknowledged that such enrollments existed, and researchers did not compare women's current and previous employment and earnings. It is highly likely that the employment "programs" help women find the types of jobs they would have found on their own because 60–70 percent of adult recipients have employment experience—some of it is extensive—and a quarter consistently combine welfare and work (Spalter-Roth, Hartmann, and Andrews 1994). Indeed, the lack of distinguishing effects between experimentals and controls may well have reflected these experiences.

Finally, a particularly worrisome flaw is the researchers' assumption that the results obtained from program options that were implemented prior to PRWORA were also valid in the post-PRWORA era because they included similar programmatic elements (Gueron and Hamilton 2002, 3). Even if the interventions—basic education and job placement—were the same, the larger context in which they are situated is very different. Participation in FSA/JOBS programs was often voluntary, cash benefits were always available as a fallback option (the so-called safety net), and child care was not as significant an issue because the participants' children were more likely to be of school age. None of these conditions apply in the post-PRWORA era. Participation is mandatory, with a high price for noncompliance, as witnessed by the sizable proportion of families leaving welfare because of sanctions (Friedman 1998; U.S. House Ways and Means Committee 1996). The 60 percent of NEWSS participants who relied on AFDC during times of unemployment (Martinson 2000) would not have had access to those benefits today because of time limits and lack of child care. This critique is not limited to the NEWSS and GAIN studies. Of the forty-one experimental sites covered by the twenty-six studies reviewed in the 2001 Green Book, welfare recipients' earnings declined in two programs, increased in twelve, and underwent no change in twenty-seven. Yet these conclusions have been used to demonstrate that education makes almost no difference to welfare recipients.

Leaver Studies

Once PRWORA was implemented, the Department of Health and Human Services allocated $200 million to document its effects. Some of this money went to the Census Bureau, some was allocated to study the longitudinal effects on children, and a substantial amount went to several large research companies—the Urban Institute, MDRC, the Center for Budget and Policy, CLASP, and the State University of New York at Albany—to assess the effects of forty-three state waivers (U.S. House Ways and Means Committee 1996, 1774).

As the following analysis of forty-three leaver studies in thirty-six states shows, most studies used administrative data from state welfare departments and follow-up surveys, and focused initially on leavers' earnings and employment. When the rapid declines in caseloads surfaced, researchers studied why families were leaving; when the high number of returns to welfare became evident, researchers examined employment conditions and the hardships that families experienced.

The initial leaver studies, documenting employment and pay, were conducted from 1996 to 1999. The findings revealed that wages averaged $6.60 per hour (Loprest 1999), and higher earnings were more likely to be the result of women working more hours (sometimes in two or three jobs) rather than higher earnings (Parrott 1998). The average annual earnings of a former welfare recipient working full time were between $8,000 and $10,000, an improvement over some states' welfare benefits, but certainly well below the poverty level for a family of three. Some studies alarmingly observed that 25–33 percent of families appeared to have no sources of income (Massachusetts Department of Transitional Assistance 1999).

Welfare caseloads declined rapidly after PRWORA's enactment, with an average decline of over 40 percent by 1999. At first, the booming economy of the late 1990s was the primary explanation for this trend: women were finding jobs. In addition, some researchers speculated that entry effects—families being discouraged from applying for benefits—contributed to this decline. Other researchers documented that a sizable number of families were leaving welfare because of an increase in administrative sanctions (Friedman 1998).

However, jobs were often temporary. As a result, nearly 30 percent of the families that left welfare between 1995 and 1997 were receiving benefits again by 1997 (Loprest 1999, 5). These figures tend to be low estimates because they generally excluded the "churning" factor, that is, the families that cycle on and off TANF within a one- or two-month period, often due to the imposition of sanctions. Several studies referred to families that returned to welfare as recidivists, a term typically used to refer to repeat criminal offenders.

As it became clear that even mothers who were employed could not support their families on a minimum wage, analysis shifted to families' use of transitional benefits. Studies found that nearly two-thirds of families had ceased to collect noncash benefits such as food stamps (Zedlewski and Brauner 1999) and Medicaid (Guyer and Mann 1999), although they qualified for them. Other surveys documented how families often went without food, were evicted, and had their utilities cut off. Some also focused on the effects of increased work participation on children (Cauthen and Knitzer 1999). Thus, these studies show that many families were worse off. Not only were their incomes lower, but they also experienced a loss of income security.

Although these studies provide valuable information, they too have important methodological limitations. The first is the unevenness of the data. Initially, the forty-three states that were granted waivers by the federal government were required to conduct evaluations, a requirement that was later removed. As a result, wide variations—of data availability and content—existed within and between states. Second, many surveys had very low return rates, either because current and former recipients moved, were evicted, or had their phones cut off, or because the surveys were regarded with suspicion because they came through welfare-department mailings.

Third, as with some impact studies, a number of researchers (Loprest 1999; Parrott 1998) made the highly questionable assumption that data collected from women who left welfare under FSA/JOBS policies were valid in the post-PRWORA era. Most important, however, in light of the dramatic change from HCD to LFA, is the fact that none of these studies document women's participation in education and training programs. As previously stated, PRWORA permitted twelve months of vocational education, and states adopted a wide range of education and training policies. Yet none of these studies examined how the twelve-month vocational guideline was being applied.

Retention and Barrier Studies

The leaver studies revealed that although finding a job in the booming economy was not a problem, keeping a job was. Retention is important, not only because it provides income stability for families, but also because it can be used to leverage additional resources. For example, annual earnings of $12,000–$14,000 a year can yield an extra $2,000–$3,000 from the Earned Income Tax Credit if employment is sustained for one year. As Holzer and Stoll (2001) state:

> The need to improve retention and reduce absenteeism among at least some current or former welfare recipients in the workplace remains strong. Improved access to reliable transportation and childcare will certainly help deal with these problems. But local workforce boards and agencies need to focus more broadly on retention issues, rather than simply job placements for recipients. (p. 82)

The following analysis draws on four types of retention studies. The first is the Post Employment Services Demonstration (PESD), an experimental follow-up study of former recipients; the second is a case study of a large and well-implemented training and job-placement program; the third is an analysis of business practices; and the fourth examines the types of barriers experienced by welfare recipients.

The PESD study examined whether intensive case management helped to reduce the percentage of ex-recipients who returned to welfare within one year. The findings were inconclusive. "The counseling and morale-boosting services the PESD case managers provided may not have been sufficient to help these clients through the welfare-to-work transition" (Rangarajan and Novak 1999, 17). PESD shows how poor implementation may affect research findings. Intensive case management was not tested because case managers were unclear about their roles, did not adhere to selection criteria, and women participants avoided case-management services because they distrusted the caseworkers and balked at the burdensome paperwork. Although the researchers noted that participants with relatively high rates of retention were those with a GED or HSD, they were unable to document whether women came with this credential or achieved it through program participation.

One landmark case study is Felice Perlmutter's (1997) detailed analysis of Blue Cross/Pennsylvania's attempts to recruit welfare recipients. Her study showed that despite a year of planning and expert training assistance, the program's success depended heavily on flexible work hours so women could take their children to doctors and school appointments, a willingness to intervene on behalf of trainees with the local welfare department, and a supervisor's efforts to "go the extra mile," for instance, to pick women up for work if their transportation failed:

> The more I became involved with the clients, and I saw situations and different environments they came from, the more I became committed, and the more I didn't want any of these students to fail, ever. . . . I found out that they are just as capable as anybody else given the chance and the encouragement. (p. 72)

In contrast to the in-depth analysis of Perlmutter's study are two reports providing an overview of the characteristics of twenty-three businesses claiming very high rates (67–100 percent) of retention for welfare recipients. The firms' practices included such a wide range of responses—the number of women hired ranged from 3 to 8,000; the period of training ranged from two to twenty-six weeks—that it is difficult to highlight the practices that might have been responsible for the high retention rates. In addition, the retention rates sometimes included interns (often unpaid) as well as those who were hired. More important for this discussion, they included no data on either the types of training that were offered before employment or the extent to which women had access to post-employment education and training (Stillman 1999; Hogan and Argentieri 1998).

Certainly, employers identify access to transportation and child care as the most prevalent barriers to both hiring and retention, but there are almost always multiple barriers. From the employers' point of view, these include a lack of soft skills such as reliability, problem-solving, verbal communication, ability to work in a team, understanding the unwritten rules of the workplace, and anger management (Houghton and Proscio 2001; Proscio and Elliot 1999). Other studies have estimated that 40–60 percent of women who receive welfare have experienced domestic violence (Tolman and Rosen 1999), and employer inflexibility on work hours, work conflicts, and discrimination are also problematic (National Partnership for Women and Families 1999). One study of self-reported barriers revealed that the most prevalent barriers were lack of transportation (47 percent), low skills (31 percent), and major depression (25 percent) (Danziger et al. 2000). Almost 60 percent of the women surveyed had between one and three barriers, and over 25 percent contended with more than four. Only 15–20 percent of the mothers in the survey did not experience significant barriers to employment. The study also found that many women attempted to work regardless of these obstacles, with two-thirds of the women with one to three obstacles reporting that they worked at least twenty hours per week.

These data help to explain why retention is erratic, but this study is interesting in that it also reframes low skill levels as a barrier instead of as a personal deficiency. Once "low skills" are defined as a barrier rather than as a fixed demographic variable, the implication is that they can be changed. This small shift in perception is important, because how the barriers are framed shapes the type and scope of potential policy solutions. If absenteeism and tardiness are perceived to be the lack of a work ethic, that is, as a personal deficiency, then the solution lies in behavioral change. However, if they are perceived to result from external factors such as a late school bus, a sick child, or a meeting with a child's teacher, then the solution lies in changing the environment or adjusting expectations. Personal barriers are obviously significant factors and should be addressed, but so should the lack of resources and the constraints imposed by current policies.

These studies also confirm the view of some scholars early on that PRWORA's 20-percent exemption policy was unrealistic, and that 40 percent would have been a more realistic rate (Pavetti 1997). They also draw attention to the possibility that it might be necessary to have "sheltered workshops for those who might never be able to support their families through their earnings" (Holzer and Stoll 2001, 82). More recently, two MDRC analysts admitted that relying on data from pre-PRWORA programs had led to an underestimation of the barriers faced by women (Gueron and Hamilton 2002).

Skills Advancement Studies

> Within the constraints of Work First approaches that are at the heart of the welfare-to-work programs, post-employment education and training services represent one potential avenue for individuals placed in low-paying jobs to transition gradually over time to higher-paying career-type jobs.
>
> —Trutko, Nightingale, and Barnow 1999, 16

As researchers became more aware of the numerous barriers that affect job retention and advancement, they turned their analysis to addressing those problems and to identifying strategies that could be applied within the Work First context (Kramer 1998). They identified an array of resources that went beyond minimum-wage jobs to include health and vacation benefits; housing; child care; transportation; mental health and career counseling; and skill development, including soft skills. Initially, support for such mix-and-match strategies focused mostly on post-employment skills development. One model cited frequently as providing the necessary mix of supports is in Portland, Oregon, where recipients gained a GED (in a six-week course) and benefited from individualized counseling prior to job placement and learning prior to entering the workplace. Researchers also began to address the need to find ways for welfare recipients to upgrade their skills before they were employed as well as after they were employed. Such ideas include open enrollments to eliminate long waiting periods for courses (important when families are facing time limits), "chunking" training into shorter blocks and modules, changing financial aid regulations to permit Pell grants for students taking three credits (instead of the current six-credit minimum), working with employers to design courses to fit training needs, and offering courses at convenient sites in neighborhoods and at workplaces (Strawn and Martinson 2000). These strategies typically involve considerable discussion between personnel in colleges, welfare departments, one-stop career centers, and businesses; they do not address the underlying assumption that they fit into the Work First framework.

Although researchers have conceded the importance of post-secondary education opportunities—"It is widely recognized that for welfare recipients and other low income workers to advance in today's economy, they need to acquire technical skills or post-secondary credentials" (Golonka and Mattus-Grossman 2001, ES-1)—the assumption that this would be *in addition to the work requirement* of twenty or thirty hours employment is not challenged (at least in these reports), despite the recognition that the number of hours of education outside employment can have negative effects on performance.

"Traditional age students without dependents did better if they worked less than fifteen hours in addition to outside work. . . . Given that just 14 percent of those in the study had dependents, the effects of full-time work on educational outcomes for single parents could be even more negative" (Strawn and Martinson 2000, 84). This prediction was borne out in an interim report from the New Vision demonstration program (Fein et al. 2000). The program requires participants to work for twenty hours a week, provides access to support services, and encourages participation at Riverside Community College, California, a site that has demonstrated its commitment to innovation in training programs. Participants were monitored to ensure that their participation reached the full thirty-two hours required by California's welfare policy. The interim results showed that recruitment is problematic and the retention rate is low. Despite intensive efforts that have included hiring celebrities and a marketing firm to boost the program, it has been almost impossible to "convince welfare recipients that they can handle school on top of already significant work and family responsibilities. . . . As a result, 41 percent of women who enrolled in order to get a college degree will be disappointed" (Fein et al. 2000, 5). The interim results show that education conflicts with time limits, the work requirement, and family responsibilities.

One assumption that appears to be unquestioned is that "traditional postsecondary education programs are often ill-suited to working individuals with families" (Golonka and Mattus-Grossman 2001, ES-1). This notion negates the 20–30 years of experience of many post-secondary institutions—in admitting a great many older women with family responsibilities, building supportive infrastructures, and developing linkages with businesses and community-based organizations—that were outlined earlier. It also minimizes the continuing efforts of colleges to adapt their entrance requirements, curricula, and resources to facilitate enrollment and retention. The typical complaint heard at many colleges now is that welfare policies limit an essential option and welfare caseworkers have little interest in explaining how women can take advantage of a few remaining windows of opportunity (Kates and Boston Outreach Group 2000).

Often, when researchers (Roberts 2002; Golonka and Mattus-Grossman 2001; Carnevale and Reich 2000) suggest that welfare caseworkers and college personnel should "work closely with," "consult with," and "adapt to," they are not grounded in the reality of efforts that colleges have made, and continue to make, in the face of welfare policies that impede such access. As a result, they underestimate the differences in culture between welfare, education, and business institutions, and the difficulties of modifying entrenched perceptions and practices. Many employers are either unwilling or unable to offer basic education at the workplace; many presidents of community colleges are unwilling to compromise that part of the schools' mission that offers low income students a pathway to academic degrees; educators are unwilling to whittle down their courses; welfare personnel are unwilling to refer recipients to educational programs; and workforce-development workers are unaware that such options exist. Although researchers now increasingly recognize the importance of better access to education and training for low income mothers, to the extent that they continue to focus on post-employment options rather than to challenge current restrictions on pre-employment options, they perpetuate the Work First ideology.

CONCLUSIONS

Community-based and ethnographic research, while eclipsed by the nationally representative survey, continues to offer a model not only for challenging the atomized vision of analytic poverty knowledge, but also for making research a more genuinely collaborative enterprise.

—O'Connor 2001, 294

We have amassed a great deal of immensely valuable information about PRWORA and its effects, and we are beginning to think beyond narrow policy boundaries to explore the interconnection between employment, wages, and educational opportunities. It is time that researchers recognize the value of a wide range of research designs and methods, and realize that ethnographic and exploratory, in-depth studies have their standards of rigor, and make valuable contributions to our knowledge base. Indeed, successful projects exist where researchers have combined different research designs and methods to yield rich findings. The MDRC's New Chance evaluation is a prime example of such an approach; it is an ethnographic study that provides important insights into the aspirations, experiences, and barriers faced by young low income women (Quint, Musick, and Ladner 1994). We need to continue to reach across the research divide and share the strengths of different methods and perspectives, so that we frame policy options that are more grounded in reality and offer more promise for the future.

Certainly, access to education and training for low income, low-wage women should become a viable option, one that is regarded as an investment in, and not a drain on, the rest of society. Further, we need to recognize that although most mothers would benefit immediately from access to education, training, counseling, and support services, others, affected by domestic abuse, homelessness, and illness, might need more time, and others might never be able to completely support their families. A systematic welfare and workforce-development framework that would apply to all low income families and not just to welfare recipients should include a comprehensive safety net of income support, tax credits, subsidized child care and housing, medical coverage, and opportunities for skill advancement.

The reauthorization debates divide those who think welfare reform has been a success because it has halved the welfare caseload from those who are concerned about families that remain in poverty. It divides those who want to increase the mothers' work requirements from those who want to ensure better access to education. It divides those who maintain that mothers should rely on the workplace for education and training opportunities from those who think handling family responsibilities and education are a sufficient workload and a good investment in future family and workforce development. If we wish to make education and training accessible to low income women, we need to take some important first steps. First, we need to think in more connected terms about women and their families. Second, we need to pay attention to their experiences, listen to their opinions, and acknowledge their family responsibilities. We should direct our attention to policies that create better access to substantive education and training opportunities—both as pre- and post-employment options—rather than limiting such access. We can begin by initiating new dialogues: between traditional and nontraditional scholars, employers and low income women, and community-based organizations and community colleges. We also need to craft policies— Workforce Investment Act (WIA), PRWORA, and others—that complement one another to create positive, long-lasting impacts for families, communities, and workforce development in the twenty-first century.

NOTES

1. This is a reference to President Clinton's promise to "change welfare as we know it."

2. In an analysis of impact studies on welfare-to-work, the Greenbook 2001 lists MDRC as the author of one-half of the twenty-six studies reviewed in the report. Other studies mentioned include those by Abt Associates (9), Mathematica, Inc. (3), and the Urban Institute (1).

3. The experimental group is exposed to the intervention being tested (an education program, for example), while the control group is not. If all other circumstances are the same for both groups, then any differences in outcomes that cannot be explained by chance must be attributed to the intervention.

4. An African American mother in her thirties, living in Boston with children ages six and fourteen.

5. A mother who attended a four-year college in Massachusetts. Personal communication.

6. The employment- and education-focused options were subsequently renamed labor-force attachment (LFA) and human capital development (HCD) respectively.

7. The amount of earnings that are not counted against families' cash benefits.

REFERENCES

Ackelsberg, Martha, Randall Bartlett, and Robert Buchele, eds. 1988. *Women, welfare and higher education: Towards comprehensive policies.* Northampton, Mass.: Smith College.

Adair, Vivian. 2001. Poverty and the (broken) promise of higher education. *Harvard Educational Review* 71(2):217–238.

Angel, Ronald, Linda Burton, P. Lindsey Chase-Lansdale, Andrew Cherlin, Robert Moffitt, and William Julius Wilson. 2002. Welfare, children and families: A three city project. Interim report. Baltimore: Johns Hopkins University.

Bernstein, Jared, Heather Bushey, Elizabeth McNichol, and Robert Zagradnick. 2002. *Pulling apart: A state-by-state analysis of income trends.* Washington, D.C.: Center on Budget and Policy Priorities.

Boldt, Nancy. 2000. From welfare to college to work: Support factors to help students persist and succeed and the economic and social outcomes of college degree attainment. Ph.D. diss. University of Vermont, Champlain.

Bryne, William. 1997. Community college courses raise earnings for California recipients. *Employment and Training Reporter* 14 May: 753–754.

Carnevale, Anthony P., and Donna M. Desrochers. 1999. *Getting down to business: Matching welfare recipients' skills to jobs that train.* Princeton: Educational Testing Service.

Carnevale, Anthony P., and Kathleen Reich. 2000. *A piece of the puzzle: How states can use education to make work pay for welfare recipients.* Princeton: Educational Testing Service.

Cauthen, Nancy K., and Jane Knitzer. 1999. *Beyond work: Strategies to promote the well being of children and families in the context of welfare reform.* Children and Welfare Reform brief 6. New York: National Center for Children in Poverty.

Danziger, Sandra, Mary Corcoran, Sheldon Danziger, Colleen Heflin, and Ariel Kalil. 2000. Barriers to the Employment of Welfare Recipients. In *Prosperity for all? The economic boom and African-Americans,* ed. R. Cherry and W. M. Rodgers, 245–278. New York: Russell Sage Foundation.

Deem, Rosemary. 1978. *Women and schooling.* London: Routledge & Kegan Paul.

Edelman, Murray. 1977. *Political language: Words that succeed and policies that fail.* New York: Academic Press.

Fein, David, Erik Beecroft, David Long, and Andree Catalfamo. 2000. *The New Visions evaluation—College as a job advancement strategy: An early report on the New Visions Self-Sufficiency and Lifelong Learning Project.* Cambridge, Mass.: Abt Associates.

Friedman, Donna. 1998. *Massachusetts (T)AFDC closings, October 1993–August 1997.* Boston: University of Massachusetts.

Gittell, Marilyn, Jill Gross, and Jennifer Holdaway. 1993. *Building human capital: The impact of post-secondary education on AFDC recipients in five states.* A report to the Ford Foundation. New York: Howard Samuels State Management and Policy Center.

Golonka, Susan, and Lisa Mattus-Grossman. 2001. *Opening doors: Expanding educational opportunities for low-income workers.* New York: Manpower Demonstration Research Corporation.

Greenberg, Mark, Julie Strawn, and Lisa Plimpton. 2000. *State opportunities to provide access to postsecondary education under TANF.* Washington, D.C.: Center for Law and Social Policy.

Grubb, Norton. 1996. *Learning to work: The case for reintegrating job training and education.* New York: Russell Sage Foundation.

Gueron, Judith M., and Gayle Hamilton. 2002. *The role of education and training in welfare reform and beyond.* Policy Brief #20. Washington, D.C.: Brookings Institution.

Gueron, Judith M., and Edward Pauley. 1991. *From welfare to work.* New York: Russell Sage Foundation.

Guyer, Jocelyn, and Cindy Mann. 1999. *Employed but not insured: A state-by-state analysis of the number of low-income working parents who lack health insurance.* Washington, D.C.: Center on Budget and Policy Priorities.

Hogan, Lyn A., and Marco Argentieri. 1998. *The road to retention: Reducing employee turnover through welfare to work.* Washington, D.C.: Welfare to Work Partnership.

Holzer, Harry, and M. Stoll. 2001. *Employers demand for welfare recipients: The effects of welfare reform in the workplace.* San Francisco: Public Policy Institute of California.

Houghton, Ted, and Tony Proscio. 2001. *Hard work and soft skills: Creating a culture of work in workforce development.* New York: Public/Private Ventures.

Kane, Thomas. J., and Cecilia Eleanor Rouse. 1995. Labor market returns to two and four year college. *American Economic Review* 85(3):600–614.

Karier, Tom. 1998. *Welfare graduates: College and financial independence.* Annandale: Jerome Levy Economics Institute.

Kates, Erika. 1990. A follow-up study of low-income women who attended college. *Proceedings of the Second Annual Women's Policy Conference,* 251–255. Washington, D.C.: Institute for Women's Policy Research.

———. 1991. *More than survival: Access to higher education for low-income women.* Washington, D.C.: Center for Women Policy Studies.

———. 1996. Educational pathways out of poverty: Responding to the realities of women's lives. *American Orthopsychiatric Association* 66(4):548–556.

———. 1998. *Closing door: Declining opportunities in education for low-income women.* Waltham: Brandeis University.

———. 1999. Public assistance and workforce development: A growing divide. *Connection: New England's Journal of Higher Education and Economic Development* 14(1):52–54.

Kates, Erika, and Boston Outreach Group. 2000. *Boarding up the windows: The effects of welfare reform on twenty low-income families in Boston.* Waltham: Brandeis University.

Kates, Erika, and Alexander Curley. 2002. *The effects of welfare reform in Massachusetts: Immigrant mothers and access to education and training.* Waltham: Brandeis University.

Kates, Erika, Sylvia McPhee, and Cate Solomon. 2002. *Declining enrollment of low-income mothers in sixteen Massachusetts colleges: The effects of the 1995 Massachusetts welfare policy.* Waltham: Brandeis University.

Kramer, Frederica. 1998. *Job retention and career advancement for welfare recipients.* Washington, D.C.: Welfare Information Network.

Loprest, Pamela. 1999. *Families who left welfare: Who are they and how are they doing?* Washington, D.C.: Urban Institute. Available at http://www.urban.org/url.cfm?ID=310290.

Martinson, Karin. 2000. *The national evaluation of welfare-to-work strategies: The experiences of welfare recipients who find jobs.* Washington, D.C.: U.S. Department of Health and Human Services Administration for Children and Families.

Massachusetts Department of Transitional Assistance. 1999. *Status of TAFDC recipients one year later.* Boston: Department of Transitional Assistance.

Mathur, Anita. 1998. *Welfare reform and opportunities for higher education.* M.A. thesis, University of California, Berkeley.

Mendelsohn, Pam. 1989. *Degrees of success: The stories of women who transformed their lives by going back to college.* Princeton: Peterson's Guides.

Moran, Mary. 1986. *Student financial aid for women: Equity dilemma?* ASHE-ERIC higher education report no. 5. Washington, D.C.: Association for the Study of Higher Education.

National Partnership for Women and Families. 1999. *Obstacles facing low-income women: Findings from a national survey of job trainers and others.* Washington, D.C.: National Partnership for Women and Families.

O'Connor, Alice. 2001. *Poverty knowledge: Social science, social policy, and the poor in twentieth century U.S. history.* Princeton: Princeton University Press.

Pandey, Shanta, Min Zhan, Susan Neely-Barnes, and Natasha Menon. 2000. The higher education option for poor women with children. *Journal of Sociology and Social Welfare* 27(4):109–170.

Parrott, Sharon. 1998. *Welfare recipients who find jobs: What do we know about their employment and earnings?* Washington, D.C.: Center on Budget and Policy Priorities.

Pavetti, LaDona. 1997. Personal and family challenges to the successful transition from welfare to work. Paper presented at the Odyssey Forum, Welfare to Work: Is It a Viable Policy? Baltimore, Md.

Perlmutter, Felice Davidson. 1997. *From welfare to work: Corporate initiatives and welfare reform.* New York: Oxford University Press.

Proscio, Tony, and Mark Elliot. 1999. *Getting in, staying on, moving up: A practitioner's guide to employee retention.* New York: Public/Private Ventures.

Quint, Janet C., Judith S. Musick, and Joyce Ladner. 1994. *Lives of promise, lives of pain: Young mothers after new chance.* New York: Manpower Demonstration Research Corporation.

Rangarajan, Anu, and Tim Novak. 1999. *The struggle to sustain employment: The effectiveness of the post employment services demonstration.* Princeton: Mathematica Policy Research, Inc.

Riley, Julia. 1991. *Living the impossible dream: The single parent's guide to college success.* Boulder: Johnson Books.

Roberts, Brandon. 2002. *The best of both: Community colleges and community-based organizations partner to better serve low-income workers and employers.* Philadelpia: Public/Private Ventures.

Silvestri, George. 1995. Occupational employment to 2005. *Monthly Labor Review* November:60–61.

Smith, Rebekah J., Luisa Stormer Deprez, Sandra S. Butler. 2002. *Parents as Scholars: Education works.* Augusta: Maine Equal Justice Project.

Spalter-Roth, Roberta, Heidi Hartmann, and L. Andrews. 1994. *Combining work and welfare: An alternative anti-poverty strategy*. Washington, D.C.: Institute for Women's Policy Research.

Stillman, Joseph. 1999. *Working to learn: Skills development under work first*. New York: Public/Private Ventures.

Strawn, Julie. 1998. *Beyond job search and basic education: Rethinking the role of skills in welfare reform*. Washington, D.C.: Center for Law and Social Policy.

Strawn, Julie, and Karin Martinson. 2000. *Steady work and better jobs: How to help low-income parents sustain employment and advance in the workforce*. A how-to guide. New York: Manpower Demonstration Research Corporation.

Sum, Andrew M., and Neal W. Fogg. 1999. *The changing workforce: Immigrants and the new economy in Massachusetts*. Boston: Massachusetts Institute for a New Commonwealth.

Thompson, Joanne. 1993. Women, welfare and college: The impact of higher education on economic well-being. *Affilia* 8:425–441.

Tolman, Richard M., and Daniel Rosen. 1999. *Domestic violence in the lives of welfare recipients: Implications for the Family Violence Option*. Ann Arbor: University of Michigan.

Trutko, John, Demetra Nightingale, and Burt Barnow. 1999. Post-employment education and training. Paper prepared for the U.S. Dept. of Labor, Employment and Training Administration. Washington, D.C.: Urban Institute.

U.S. Census Bureau. 2000. Current Population Survey. Table A.

———. 2001. Current Population Reports.

U.S. House Ways and Means Committee. 1996. *Green Book: Overview of Entitlement Programs*. Washington, D.C.: Government Printing Office.

———. 2001. *Green Book: Overview of Entitlement Programs*. Washington, D.C.: Government Printing Office.

Welfare-to-Work Partnership. 1998. *The road to retention: Reducing employee turnover through welfare-to-work*. Washington D.C.: Welfare-to-Work Partnership.

Wolfe, Leslie R. 1991. *Women, work and school: Occupational segregation and the role of education*. Boulder: Westview Press.

Zedlewski, Sheila R., and Brauner, Sarah. 1999. *Declines in food stamp and welfare participation: Is there a connection?* Washington, D.C.: Urban Institute.

Chapter 2

Failing Low Income Students

Education and Training in the Age of Welfare Reform

Lizzy Ratner

Within the tangle and fracture of today's public discourse, education is hailed as one of the few universal goods. From the politician's stump to the PTA floor, from the church pulpit to the social science lectern, Americans wave it with the fervor of the flag; it is an ideal to be encouraged, a dream to be pursued, the bedrock of democracy, the foundation of equality. True, the public might argue about how to educate its students, and politicians might squabble over who should pay, but most still agree that education is necessary. Or they say they agree that education is necessary. To suggest otherwise would be to risk being called antidemocratic, unjust, lacking compassion. Eager to prove his "compassion," President Bush adopted a pro-education stance during the 2000 race for president. "I refuse to leave any child behind in America," he declared in stump speech after stump speech. Later, as president, he added, "When it comes to our children, failure is simply not an option" (Bush 2001).

But if failure is not an option (if only at the rhetorical level) for the nation's children, and the Bush administration supposedly refuses to let any fall behind, the story is altogether different for certain of their parents. For a whole class of adults—for women and men who receive public assistance—education is neither lauded nor encouraged. Instead, it is roundly discouraged. For welfare recipients, education—particularly post-secondary education—is a dream they are seldom allowed to pursue.

Until a few years ago, the fact that an adult received welfare would have made little difference in his or her ability to pursue an education. At least as far as the law was concerned, there was nothing to stop him or her from going to college or earning a certificate in computer technology. Since the passage of PRWORA in 1996, however, going to school has become increasingly difficult for low income adults. Because of statutes that limit their access to education and training, particularly at the post-secondary level, millions of would-be students have been blocked from these programs, making welfare one of the few contexts in modern American life in which education is explicitly discouraged.

Nowhere is there is a better illustration of this situation than in New York City, where college enrollment among welfare recipients has declined by more than 80 percent (Lane 2003). Determined to "lead the nation in innovation" (Human Resources Administration 1998–2001), New York City has launched an aggressive welfare-to-work campaign that goes far beyond what the federal law demands. Whereas PRWORA has been tough on the nation's welfare recipients, New York City's Human Resources Administration (HRA) has been even tougher. PRWORA, for example, requires states to place at least 50 percent of able-bodied welfare recipients in thirty-hour-per-week work assignments; in dramatic excess, HRA insists that all able-bodied recipients perform work assignments for no fewer than thirty-five hours a week.[1] And HRA allows for few exemptions, particularly where students are concerned. Rather than acknowledge the few rights that exist for would-be students, the agency routinely, and often illegally, ignores these protections in the law.

Under PRWORA, states may allow recipients a twelve-month exemption from the work requirement to pursue vocational education and training. But in New York City, many caseworkers disregard this clause, telling students instead they have no right to school and must withdraw to perform "work activities." When students have protested, HRA caseworkers have been known to lie, telling students that their post-secondary programs are not approved when in fact they are. In so doing, HRA has funneled thousands of recipients into simulated work assignments and become the largest welfare-to-work initiative in the entire country[2] (Human Resources Administration 2002). It has also become something of a model, a prototype that other states and cities seek to emulate.

The credit for New York City's welfare "reforms" belongs primarily to former Mayor Rudolph Giuliani and his controversial welfare chief, Jason Turner. Together, the two men set about to "end dependency," save city dollars, and clear New York of its reputation as the "welfare capital of the nation." In numeric terms they succeeded. In 1995, the year the city began its welfare overhaul, New York City was home to more than one million welfare recipients (Human Resources Administration 1995). Six years later, this number had dropped by half, to some five hundred thousand (Human Resources Administration 2001).[3]

But at what social and moral price? To this day, no one knows exactly what has happened to those who have left welfare, and there is little evidence that many have escaped poverty. As for those who have remained on the rolls, the evidence that they are still struggling, that life has become even more precarious and difficult, is overwhelming. The number of recipients seeking help from food pantries has skyrocketed (New York City Coalition Against Hunger 2001), as has the number reporting wrongful case closings and sanctions

(Human Resources Administration 2002; Casey 1998). At the same time, lawyers for the poor have brought a storm of lawsuits against New York City, accusing the Human Resources Administration of everything from discrimination to human rights violations.

Among the most famous of these lawsuits is *Reynolds v. Turner*, a 1998 class action that accused HRA of deceitfully and recklessly preventing people from applying for public assistance. In an effort to shrink the welfare rolls, HRA began converting welfare centers to "job centers" and embarked on a conscious policy of lying to applicants about their right to welfare, food stamps, and Medicaid. They routinely told applicants there was no more welfare, lecturing them instead to go home and get a job; they regularly and improperly turned down applications for emergency benefits; and they forced applicants to go through days of job-search activities before they would even look at their application. At one job center, 84 percent of prospective applicants left without filing formal applications; at another center, this number was 69 percent (Welfare Law Center 1998). The result was that countless desperate New Yorkers went without food, medical care, and benefits for months at a time.

On December 16, 1998, seven of these New Yorkers filed suit against New York City and the Human Resources Administration. One month later, U.S. District Judge William J. Pauley issued a preliminary injunction barring the creation of additional welfare centers and ordering HRA to process applications and issue benefits in a timely manner. Four years later, most of the terms of this injunction still hold—and HRA continues to violate them (Cohan 2002).

At the heart of New York's welfare policy is the city's commitment to the principle of Work First. "It's work that sets you free"—or so said Jason Turner (1998), ominously echoing the motto posted over the entrance to Auschwitz, the Nazi death camp. Toward this end—freedom—New York has enacted the Work Experience Program (WEP), which aims to "help individuals and families to achieve their highest level of self-reliance" by placing them in mandatory work assignments. Although this program does not pay a salary, it is nonetheless rigorous and demanding, intended to communicate the value of work along with a few basic skills. Assignments can last up to thirty-five hours a week and might include sweeping the parks, scrubbing the courthouses, or organizing the files at a neighborhood nonprofit. They do not, as a rule, include postsecondary education. For that, able-bodied welfare recipients have to carve out their own time, perhaps in the evenings after WEP or else during the weekends. Alternatively, if they insist on going to school and foregoing their WEP, they must give up part of their welfare checks. Either way, however, they cannot win. They must choose between two flawed alternatives: either continue in school but lose all or part of their benefits or abandon school (along with their hopes) but keep their benefits. For many, especially mothers with children, it is a choice that pits future opportunity against present necessity; it is a choice, judging by the statistics, that lands frequently, and often sadly, on the side of necessity.

The City University of New York (CUNY) is a twenty-campus public university long known for providing vital education services to low income New Yorkers, including welfare recipients. But in the five years since welfare reform came to New York, the school lost more than 80 percent of its welfare-receiving students. According to Maureen Lane, co-director of community and legislative advocacy at the Welfare Rights Initiative, the number of students who receive welfare dropped from nearly 27,000 in 1995 to just over 5,000 in 2002 (Lane 2003)—a grave loss, both to students and taxpayers, because research has shown that 87 percent of all four-year graduates move permanently off welfare (Gittell, Schehl, and Fareri 1990). Neither the city nor the university can accurately say what has happened to those who have disappeared.

But even these statistics, dramatic as they are, do not tell the whole story. They might hint at a trend, they might shock or surprise, but they reveal little of what education really means to people, or of how New York's policies have derailed the dreams and reshaped the reality of students who receive welfare. For this, for meaning, the students themselves are the truest source.

I began speaking with some of these students and collecting their stories shortly after I finished college. I was working as a welfare rights advocate at a legal services organization in northern Brooklyn, and seeing woman after woman whose lives had been turned further upside down by the city's work rules. I was outraged by the stories these women told and frustrated that no one seemed to be noticing. Occasionally a reporter would venture into a job center or housing project, bringing back stories like Orpheus from the underworld, but these forays tended to be the exception, not the norm. Moreover, they rarely allowed the women to speak for themselves in their own voice. So I began collecting interviews, asking colleagues, organizers, friends, and clients if they knew of women who might be interested in a conversation. With my tape recorder in hand, I traveled from job centers in Brooklyn to apartments in the Bronx to a college on Staten Island.

Most of the women I met with were eager to talk. "I'm really happy that you came and talked to me," a woman named Latesha volunteered at the end of her interview. "I'm glad somebody could try to understand what I'm going through, because I really was starting to lose hope."

Among the trends I noticed was the number of women who dreamed of going to school or were trying to go to school or had tried to go to school but failed because of arduous work requirements. So many women felt the world of living-wage jobs was closed to them because they did not have enough schooling. I therefore decided to weave some of their stories together into a single powerful account, to edit and combine them into a statement on the way the welfare system is failing low income students. My goal was not so much statistical truth as a living, breathing, speaking compilation of people's experiences.

After five years of welfare "reform," I felt the time had more than come to heed the words of low income students.

Here are some of their stories.

....

LATESHA

AROUND AND AROUND AND AROUND

I want to make sure people totally understand what's going on, so they could see what I'm going through. If they was in my position, what would they do? And I think of it and I know for a fact they would not be able to take it. I know it would be really stressful and then they'd probably wind up in the hospital, too.

The bedroom that Latesha shares with her four-year-old son is windowless and hot. Toys and scraps of paper are everywhere, bursting out of a broken dresser, strewn across Latesha's bed, scattered across the floor. She seems self-conscious about this at first, apologizing for the mess while clearing a place at the foot of her bed. There are no chairs in her room, and she does not seem to have many visitors. Taped to the wall is the following quote:

> It is Human Nature
> to think Wisely
> and Act Foolishly.
> —Anatole France

Latesha is a short-haired, slender woman of medium height and clear brown eyes. She wears glasses with plastic black frames, and has a broad, all-embracing smile, which she shares only infrequently at first. When the interview begins, her voice is flat—a monotone almost—but she grows more and more animated as the afternoon wears on.

I initially went on public assistance when I was pregnant. The reason why I went on is *because* I was pregnant. I knew I didn't have anything to offer my child. I was eighteen years old, and I didn't have a high school diploma. I didn't have anywhere to live. I was staying with one of my friends because I couldn't get along with my mother.

So here I am pregnant in somebody else's house and I don't have anything. I didn't have no money, no job. I mean, I didn't finish school so what was I supposed to do, you know?

When you're young, sometimes you make the wrong decisions because you don't know right from wrong. Now, I was young. I wanted to have a baby because I felt not loved. I felt not appreciated. I felt just a lot of feelings that made me want to just have a baby. I told my boyfriend when I wanted to have a baby, and I thought that he was going to be there for me, because I'm pretty sure he knows what happens when you have sex, you know what I mean? We hope that he knew! So I got pregnant. *He* left. He ran off when he found out that he had to take care of his child.

So that's the reason why I got on. Other than that, I probably would have found some other way to get something. [But] I don't think it was a mistake. I'm not even ashamed to say that I'm on welfare, because I don't want to be on there. I'm doing everything I can to get off. So what's there to be ashamed of?

I learned to cook a long time ago, because my mother has a lot of kids—*a lot* of kids—and I was the oldest. My mother worked two jobs, and when I was about twelve years old, I started really cooking for everybody. I kind of liked it at first, the responsibility of having to make sure everybody got to eat and everything like that, and I liked to surprise my mother, like with the stuff that I could cook. My mother used to always praise me on this. She used to brag about me and say, "Oh, my daughter can cook! My daughter can cook!" So it was always a passion.

You know how when you're young and somebody asks you what you want to be? I was like, "A chef! I can cook, I'm creative. I want to do it. You know?" And I went to school. It was a natural course.

It's like I knew that I would have to start off slow, but I was doing so good. I mean, all my classes I passed great. It wasn't no problem because I really wanted to do it.

When I was in that school, it's so inspirational because everybody is different but everybody is still doing their thing. It's even people there that never even cooked nothing before and they be cheffing it up. Even the men! It's beautiful. It's such a positive atmosphere. I really wanna go back . . .

Right now I'm not in school. I haven't been in school since maybe April, because it was kind of stressful trying to stay in school with them pressuring me not to go—they meaning the WEP program. They were constantly like sending me letters and appointments to come into them and bring them proof and stuff that I was in school.

I started school—I wanted to start in October of 1998. And I went to an appointment at the WEP center and they explained to me that I had to participate. So me being the person that I am, I went to school and I changed my whole schedule around so that I could accommodate the WEP program. I changed my schedule from the morning full time to the evening full time. That meant that I was going to be going to the WEP program from 9:00 to 1:00 and then I was going to be in school from about 3:00 to 10:00. No problem, as long as I get to go to school.

Then they [WEP] changed it. I go back [to WEP] and they said, "Well, no, it's from 9:00 to 5:00 now."[4] I said, "Oh, my goodness." I was so hurt, you know? I was like, well maybe I could figure out *something* to do. So I went back to the school and I asked them, "Could I go part time?" They said there's no way. There was no way they could accommodate me, because if I went part time, I wouldn't get the full grants and everything like that. I would have to wind up paying for it and I can't afford to pay for it. So I was like, "My goodness, I can't do that. I'm already in a bad position as it is. I don't know what to do; I really want to go to school." So I just decided to keep going and hope that they would leave me alone.

They didn't.

They sent me more appointments. I kept going, and they kept sending me appointments to come down to the WEP program: "Please participate in our program, we're going to cut you off if you don't participate." I went down, and one of the workers, you know what he said to me? He said—because I told him I was in a *degree* program—he said, "We don't want you to get a degree. We only need you to get a GED. And that's it. If you have a GED or a high school diploma, that's good." I said, "How are you going to tell me what I should do with myself? This is my life." But they kept sending me to appointments. I had to keep missing days of school.

I tried to talk to them, but they don't care. I told them I wanted to speak to a supervisor because I can't understand why this was happening to me. [But] they don't listen! They were very nasty with me. They speak to me like I'm a child. They make you feel very, very small, and I'm not the type of person that takes that very easy. I don't take that, you know?

I did get to the point where I was like enough is enough. I got to that point when they cut me off. They cut my case in half; they cut my rent down to where it was like only $250 . . . and then they cut down my food stamps. Do you know what they gave me for two months? They gave me $16 or something like that. For me and my son! I was very hurt by it. I was like, "Is that what they're doing? They're reprimanding me so they're going to let me starve. They're going to let my baby starve!"

[That's when] I went into the hospital. I went to the hospital because it seemed like every time something happens to me, it's very hard for me to handle because I'm doing it by myself. And it just so happens that I was a little frustrated about the gas bill because they didn't tell me that they was going to cut off the gas. They just cut off my gas. And that kind of made me depressed and that kind of made me break down because I knew I had to go to the system and ask them to help me and I just hate that. But I had no choice because what am I going to do, you know? How am I going to feed my son? So that kind of made me really depressed and really sad. It's not just that one thing made me really depressed; it's the build-up.

It's like the whole thing is a big circle. Here it is, my rent is not being paid. Why is my rent not being paid? Because I didn't participate in the program. Why I didn't participate in the program? Because I was in school and I didn't want to stop going to school. Why was I going to school? Because I *wanted* to get a job, I *wanted* to get off public assistance so I wouldn't *need* them to pay the rent. It's a big circle. It's like around and around and around and it's really aggravating and it's really stressful. And, I kind of got admitted. I was in Woodhull Hospital. They gave me Paxil and they told me that would bring me out of my depression. They said it would help me to be able to deal with everyday things like everybody else. I thought that was a good idea.

And I was talking to one of the doctors and I told the doctor, "Look, I'm not crazy"—because I was there with crazy people, and I didn't feel like I was crazy. I just was depressed. So I tried to tell her. And she was like, "What could possibly be depressing you?"

I told her about the welfare. I said, "Look, they really are going to drive me crazy. They put so much pressure on me." And I told her how they had cut me off and how I only had $16 to feed my [son]—and she said, "Are you kidding me? They gave you that little bit of money to feed your baby?" I said, "That's it—they give you the kind of ultimatum that you cannot turn down. You have no choice to take it. Either you be hungry or you be homeless." She couldn't believe it. She was like, "Look, we need you to get better because you have to be able to go at them and let them know *this is not a joke.* You're in a hospital, you're sick because of what they're doing to you. You have to get strong and you have to be able to go and tell them, *'Look!'*"

I was in the hospital for maybe like five days. About five days. I actually signed myself out, and the only reason I signed myself out is because I knew I had to get the gas cut back on. It was like I couldn't even relax in the hospital to actually get better the way I needed to be better. I knew nobody else could do it but me. . . .

I really do want to go back [to school]. They send me a letter just about every semester, asking when I'm coming back. I had promised that I would finish, and I kind of feel bad now because I knew that I would. Everybody knew. All my friends around me, they was like, "I think you're going to do great." Everybody was always so happy for me. Even the lady that admitted me there, she was like, "I want you to come back. Call me, talk to me." They all so positive there. They all so want-you-to-do-great type attitude. And that's good. That makes you want to be there. That makes you want to stay.

I felt so good about myself because I knew I was doing something good. I knew that when I finished, I was going to get a great job. I was going to be able to say, "Look, I'm a chef," or "I'm a restaurant manager. I have a degree." And they just snatched it from me. They was like, "So what? You don't need to get a degree." What kind of thing is that to say to somebody? Who are you to tell me that? It's like, so it's OK for you to get whatever *you* want but. . . . [her voice trails off]

They make it seem like we have another alternative here. If I can go out and fill out a application and get a job tomorrow and I knew that I was going to have this job I would be glad to have that job. But it doesn't happen overnight, you know? That's what I was trying to do. I was trying to make it happen but it can't happen overnight.

Sometimes I think about it and I want to cry. I mean I can understand why people just sit around and don't want to do nothing. Because look what they do to us. They kill our self-esteem. They kill everything that we even have or hope or dream for. It kind of killed my spirit a little bit because I'm tired. I'm really tired. I feel like a old woman and I'm twenty-four years old. And I've been thinking so hard about going back in the hospital because there's so much for me to deal with by myself. I can't really depend on my mother because she's on public assistance. Do you know that just about everybody that I know is on welfare? Just about everybody I know is on public assistance.

And right now, I really do feel stuck. Because I'm running out of things to do, I'm running out of ideas. It's very demoralizing. And I mean that's the worst thing that you could do to anybody, because then you feel like you can't really do nothing. You feel stuck.

POSTSCRIPT: STILL STUCK

It has been more than two years since Latesha spoke these words, offering them hesitantly at first but falling quickly into a rhythm that lasted more than three hours. Since that day, Latesha has tried several times to go back to school, but she has never had much success; each time, WEP or child care or the raw fact of life has gotten in the way.

It is hard to say where Latesha will go from here or in what direction her future lies. Once she spoke excitedly about a job she had applied for at a local Rite Aid. With some work experience and a GED, she felt confident she had a decent chance of getting it. After waiting several weeks, however, and hearing no answer, she finally called the store, only to find that she had not been hired.

Latesha would like few things more in her life than to leave her welfare days behind her. She is young, smart, and has dreams that she writes in a note-book filled with poetry. But Latesha has few resources and endless responsibil-ities, which she takes very seriously: a small son she has to take care of, a teenage sister she has decided to raise, a grandmother she has agreed to look after. Above all, Latesha is part of a system that makes it impossible for her to strive for something better. As one caseworker sneered when Latesha was pe-titioning to go to school, "What do *you* need a degree for?" It is a question that all too many women who receive public assistance have been asked.

Though welfare "reform" alone did not put Latesha in the hospital, it cer-tainly helped get her there. The anxiety she felt in the face of approaching time limits, the hopelessness in escaping poverty, the voicelessness in the midst of a controlling system—all these feelings helped push Latesha toward breakdown. And while they may not have pushed others into the hospital, they have led all too many women to a place of depression and defeat.

....

MICHELLE

THE WELFARE LADY

> And I tell you, I came on this campus, I didn't want to know nothin'
> about politics. I just wanted to get on, get off. For once I didn't want to
> be a loudmouth. I wanted to mind my business. But of course, sooner
> or later, you know. . . . Like, if you're here during the week or somethin'
> like that and you ask, "Have you seen Michelle?" Most of the people
> would say, "Oh yeah, I saw the welfare lady. That way." Okay?

It is a Monday afternoon toward the end of January, and the College of Staten Island (CSI) is a ghost town of snow and ice. The new semester has not yet started, and only a few students can be spotted on the walkways. At forty-two years old, Michelle is one of these students. Although it is vacation, she still has work to do for several of the student organizations to which she belongs. One of these, Students Against WEP (SAW), she founded herself in 1998: "Basi-cally, I try to help women not go through what I went through, let them know what their rights are. You know, stand up to Giuliani."

Michelle began her career in campus activism at an early age, when her mother brought her along for the takeover of the administration building at Brandeis University in the late 1960s. By the time she was eighteen, and she her-self was beginning college, however, an abusive boyfriend and mounting drug problem shifted her focus away from the campus. She soon left school and began an odyssey that took her from New Jersey to Boston, McDonald's to the military and ultimately to New York. Many years and dozens of struggles later, she is finally back on campus, organizing and agitating as she did when she was small.

Michelle has four children. They range in age from preschool to late teen. She lives with three of them in an apartment on Staten Island.

I don't pride myself on being the most intelligent, but I try to read. I started watching the turning of the tide, and when they were talkin' about they were gonna make people go work sweeping the streets and stuff like that, I knew it would be a matter of time before they tell me I had to go. I said, "Pretty soon, watch, you're gonna have your baby and a couple of weeks later you're gonna be out there shovelin' or whatever-whatever." So I decided, well, I'm gonna go back to school.

The first year nobody bothered you. It was cool. I was doin' work-study and I had a 3.59 my first semester. I was *so* proud [laughs]. My second semester I failed a course, so I just went down a little bit because I didn't know then that you should drop it. But I've learned since then. Then the second year, they started to say crazy stuff like—they were telling me I had to do WEP.

That's what they told me. Overnight the law changed! I was there [at the welfare center] the day before. I remember, they had me literally come back twenty-four hours later to tell me that my work-study didn't count anymore and I *must* do WEP. In twenty-four hours the rules changed that much! So I demanded to see what's governing me. And [the caseworker] says to me, "You're not allowed to see that." I said, "I spent eight years in the military and they let me see what governed me. Why can't I see it here?"

Then I remember the lady telling me, "You're gonna be able to still go to school but your work assignment is at the Welfare Office." I said, "Come on, *please!*" 'Cause see, what they were going to do was, you have to average thirty-five hours a week [in WEP], so I would be workin' in between classes. And there was no way I could get from the ferry in Staten Island—from the welfare office—to where we at at the College of Staten Island. That's a thirty-minute bus ride on a *good* day. On a bad day, we don't know.

I said, "When am I supposed to go school? I go to school in between this."

"Well, you could *run* . . ."

"No, I can't do that!" So then she tells me, then she tells me, "Well, we're gonna put you down as refusing." I said, "So be it. 'Cause you can't tell me I can't go to school." So then she went and got her supervisor: "We got one that won't comply!"

That year it seemed like I went to over a hundred fair hearings. And there was one officer, he laughed so much, he just gave me a job application and told me I might as well come get a job. He said, "You're down here enough. Every time you leave outta here you got a smile on your face. You're winning. Why don't you just come get a job when the baby gets older?" [Laughing] I had been there over a dozen times.

Then they said that they were counting work-study,[5] so as long as I had the work-study I was WEP exempt. Then I don't know what happened. I have twenty-one hours of classes; I'm gonna do a twenty-hour internship; plus I'm going to work twenty hours a week. That's sixty-one hours. Do you know what the deputy director of Center 99[6] asked me on the ninth of January, year 2001? "Well, do you think you could make room to do WEP?" I said, "So, did you ever read *Oliver Twist*?"

When do you expect to finish school?

Hopefully in another year-and-a-half. But the answer that I give the welfare workers when they ask me that, "When you get done calling me out my classes. When you get done making me half-ass. When you get done making me have incompletes. Then I'll be done with school." Right now I'm working on two incompletes and I'm trying to get out of here in the next year-and-a-half, but if it takes me two years, look, I'm forty-two years old, it will take me what I need to take. Like I tell them, "You leave me alone. If you would have left me alone, I would have been out here much quicker."

You understand? I get penalized because I miss a class. You got to go in for appointments, you miss classes, and they hold that against you here. Then my grades go plummeting. 'Cause welfare pulls you out of class so damn much—to prove that you live in Staten Island; maybe four to five times just to get child care straight; to go to a face-to-face;[7] to prove to them that you are in school. And they have all the papers, they know you're in school, but they're gonna make you miss a day to prove to them you're in school. And it's never on that one day when I got one class. It's on that day when I have to choose, and they won't postpone it.

So that's the little tortures that Jason Turner[8] puts in front of us. It's very stressful. You fail courses when you're stressed out, when you can't think. I love science, and when I got here—I always was a straight-A student in science and math. Got here, they tell me I can't add two and two, I'm so stressed.

Welfare is supposed to be here to help me, not to discourage me. I should be the kind of recipient they say, "Oh yeah, she wants to get the hell off this damn roll. Let us pay for graduate school for her." You know? I deserve to go to school. I should have the same opportunity as everybody else. If this is the land of opportunity, why don't I have the same opportunities as everybody else?

You see my friend here? She's gonna have the opportunity 'cause she's not on welfare. She's gonna have the opportunity where she can take whatever she wants to take in school, take *however* long she wants to take in school and spend whatever time she wants to study. But I'm a welfare recipient. I gotta take what they say that I can take in order for my child care to get paid. I got to pray that they don't want me to work for the Parks Department. Because tell me, you want me to work thirty-five hours a week for $216 dollars and 50 cents?

Basically, Jason Turner came here with one thing in mind. Jason Turner says that he wants to put us through very nice tiny tortures so we leave the system in shock. I say let's shock him and let him leave the system. Okay? 'Cause I'm not going to leave in shock. I'm a tax-payer. I pay taxes. I was in the military. I gave the military eight years, I'm not good for six? Six to seven?

So it's time for everybody just to look at this. Because I'm tired of the, "because I'm on welfare I shouldn't go to school, I can't go to school, I shouldn't have that desire." So twelfth grade was good enough for me? I need no more schooling?

Because I want to go to school. I want to get ahead. They don't want me to. Know why? 'Cause it teaches you how to think. Teach you how to think too much. Makes you want to fight back, get angry and fight back. And I learned from the political science head of the department that no matter what anybody does to me, once I get the education, that's the one thing they can never take away from me. And it got to be something good 'cause they're trying to keep me from having it.

POSTSCRIPT: DOWNSIZED DREAMS

By the standards of many would-be welfare students, Michelle is a success story. Despite numerous threats and orders to do WEP, she managed to stay in school and pursue an associate's degree. She did this—was able to do it—because she had the support of a legal aid attorney, the will to fight, and a strong knowledge of her welfare rights. For example, unlike many of her sister students, Michelle knew about the New York State Work Study/Internship Bill, a significant yet poorly implemented piece of legislation that allows public assistance recipients to count work-study and internship hours toward WEP. Because Michelle knew about this bill, she was able to make a case for herself to remain in school and avoid a workfare assignment cleaning the ferry terminal.

And yet, the story of Michelle is not a perfect success story. She did not sail through school, free and unfettered, and her days at the College of Staten Island were marked by compromise. Michelle struggled. The stress of constant welfare appointments wore her down, as did the need to fight for every step of her education. Her schoolwork suffered. As with so many women in her position, her grades slipped and she had to repeat classes. A program that might have taken her two years took her much longer.

Moreover, Michelle dreamed above all of a bachelor's degree in history or political science. However, the welfare system would not give her any kind of credit for a four-year, nonvocational program; even the twelve-month education waiver would be off limits if she wanted to pursue a liberal arts degree. So Michelle settled instead for an associate's degree in medical lab technology, a profession that she feared did not offer long-term security. She downsized her dreams—and her opportunities—to fit within the box of the welfare system.

This is not to say that Michelle was defeated. Her survivor's spirit remained intact, bolstered by a profound sense of right and justice. No doubt it was this spirit that kept her fighting sanction after sanction, fair hearing after fair hearing.

....

REBECCA

TO BE STABLED

My personal responsibility is my children, 'cause I can't just think about myself, I have to think about them. I want them to see me as a role model, you know? I want them to be like, "Wow, my mother's got a great job and she's got a career, and we have a house or we have a nice apartment and we go here and we travel there and, I've been to Disneyland!" You know, things like that. I've never been to Disneyland, and that's something that I wanna give my kids. I wanna at least one time in their lives, you know, "I went there!"

"Welcome to my humble abode," says Rebecca, swinging open the door to her two-room Bronx apartment. "I had to take it, because if you live in the shelter, whatever comes, you can't deny it."

Rebecca is a voluble woman, thirty-one years old but with the face of someone younger. Sitting on a stool in her kitchen, she speaks for almost two hours, her words rushing out with a blurry intensity. Within minutes of sitting down to talk, she is describing her childhood in the Bronx, her dreams of becoming a licensed practical nurse (LPN), her six-month stay in the New York City shelter system. After losing her mother's apartment "over a piece of paper"—a Housing Authority snafu that left her without a lease—Rebecca, her two children, and the children's father spent nearly half a year negotiating their way through the Department of Homeless Services. "It was very hard," she recalls. "It's like another welfare." Now that she is settled in her own apartment, she is eager to move forward with her life.

Okay. I have two children, a three-year old and a one-year old, and I live with the father of the children—we're not married. And, um, I was on welfare up until I was eighteen years old—you know, with my mother and my sister. I went ahead, I got married then, when I was eighteen. I got off the public assistance, and I worked, like cashier, petty jobs until I was like twenty-four years old, and I started feeling it. I said to myself, "Wait a minute. I can't keep working for minimum wage. This is not for me." Seven dollars and that's it, you know. So I went and I got my GED. I felt that that opened doors for me, that I was able to do for me and help myself, you know.

When I got the GED I worked part time for an ophthalmologist. I worked there twenty hours; I got $200 a week. That was my first $10-an-hour job. And then, then after I was married for ten years, I got divorced. I [moved] in with my mother. I had my own room. I was working. I was making $400 a week, bringing home like $325, something around there. I was *fine*. And, I got pregnant with my first child.

When I got pregnant, I had no choice but to get on welfare. I was working for Print Zone, I was doing customer service, and I got—something happened there—so I got laid off and the point was that I wasn't able to collect unemployment benefits, and so I had no choice [but] to go ahead and file for public assistance. And ever since then, since '97, I've been on public assistance.

Since I got on public assistance and I had the children, it's not sufficient for me. There's no way. It's not enough what a person gets, especially when you have children. So I said to myself, you know, in order for me to give my children more than what I have now, I know that a GED's not gonna cut it, you know what I'm saying?

That's why I said right now I think it's time that I continue my education. I wanna do my LPN and see how far I can go. I want to be grounded. In order to get grounded, it takes a step at a time. I mean, there's no job that's gonna hire you with complete full benefits and tell you you're gonna make $35,000, unless you have a good degree or something like that. You know?

The reason why I chose more the medical field than any other is because of the history in my family. A lot of the family has passed away because of, like, tumors in the head and, you know, cancer in the vaginal area, the uterus. The family suffers from diabetic [diabetes] and stuff like that and depression, a lot of depression. And, my grandmother has Alzheimer's, you know? So I said to myself, "This is it. I'm going into the field." It was the family. The family, you know?

Supposedly I'm supposed to be graduating from my LPN in the fall of '02. That was the original plan. That's how it's supposed to be.

But the thing is, they only accept an educational and training program for twelve months, that's it. I did a semester in Bronx Community College, and I did another semester at Hostos Community College, and my twelve months is up now, this semester. So now I don't know. I don't know what's gonna happen. I don't know if maybe I'll attend in September, I don't know if I'm just gonna work full time and see. 'Cause when you're juggling a full-time job and you're juggling with two children, and your spouse is also working, I don't know how that's gonna fit in.

This all started this semester, at the very beginning of this semester. I went for an appointment [at the welfare center] and this lady, the first thing she said to me was, "Are you ready to accept an assignment?" She didn't ask me for my credentials, she didn't say, "Do you at least have a GED? Let's see if we could put you somewhere so you could get yourself a little on your feet." None of that. Nothing. I looked at her; I was like, "What assignment? I'm going to school."

So she told me, "Well you know this is your last semester, blahsie-blahsie. After this semester, we're gonna put you to work for the money, and if you don't comply, we'll sanction you." And then she said, "In five weeks your whole family will be cut off."[9] She said that. So me, as a mother, I'm like, "No way!" You know? No way!

So to them, this semester, this is it. They don't expect me to go back to college in September. So this is a whole big debate thing, and that's why I said to myself, "I'm not gonna let this happen." I'm not gonna let them interfere with schooling and stuff. But then I was goin' to school, and I was just, I don't know, kept thinkin' about what she kept telling me and stuff like that, and—you know, she put me in a spot where I had to think ahead. I have to plan ahead, because if I don't do that then my kids are gonna get screwed. 'Cause right now the law's not passed that a two-year college is accepted or a four-year college is accepted.

If they were to say, "Yeah, we're gonna go ahead and accept the two- and four-year college," oh, my God, I'll be grateful. Because then you know that they're not gonna go ahead and keep threatening you. You know that they're not gonna be on your ass. You know that you'll be able to study peacefully and not have to worry and think about, "Well, what's gonna happen at the end of the semester?" And you know that you'll be ready to finish and accomplish and have your career and move on.

For example, my cousin, Marlene, she went to the College of New Rochelle. It's a four-year private college. She was on public assistance. She got sanctioned the semester before she was about to graduate. They wanted to pull her out. Picture this: after you doing three years, three-and-a-half, you're right there, they wanna pull you out! Come on, you know? So she went and did a fair hearing and she won, so they let her finish. She got money for her kids, she got money for the rent, she got food stamps, and when she graduated she started working. When she started working—she was working for a public elementary school—she gave them [HRA] the pay stubs and then she was completely off. She was set. And what helped her out was the public assistance *up until* she was able to do what she have to do, you know? But that doesn't work for everybody.

It's hard. You know, people tell you this is it, and it's like you have no other ways of going around it, you just have to give in. They put you in a spot where you have to just give in and say, "My kids are first." And that's always my saying, "My kids, my kids, my kids." But it's hard. I mean, I gotta do what I gotta do, but I wish that a person didn't have to go through so much.

At the moment, this is what I'm gonna do: I'm gonna comply with them. I don't know what the WEP assignment's gonna be, but hopefully, they said they're gonna send me out on interviews, hopefully I'm gonna land a job, you know? I'm gonna settle for whatever they give me. I mean, I went on an interview on Wednesday, and because I'm trying to get back on my feet, I'm gonna settle for $7-$8 an hour. Even though I have so much experience, I just wanna get my feet wet.

My thing is just to get off, you know? To be stabled, and never go back. That's my thing. Because there's times, let me tell you, I'll be so stressed out. If I was another person, I will be right now on SSI,[10] because of so much shit, with this and with that and then I got the little kids and, you know, juggling here and juggling there. If it wasn't that I just sometimes close my eyes, and just like, "God, please, give me a little bit of strength, help me *cope* through things," I wouldn't know what I would do. Because there's a history in my family, with my sister and my mother. I'm the strongest one, and I have to be. Because I'm juggling me and I'm juggling [my mother] and then my sister's also very depressed. She's also on disability. So what can she do?

I'm tired, I really am. I'm just worried about the job, worried about the benefits, worried about, yes, if they're gonna help me out with transitional benefits. . . . You know, these are just questions that pop up. I wanna feel *secure* for my kids. And I want him [my boyfriend] to do what he's gotta do to help me feel secure also as far as the family's concerned. I know that if he helps me out, then we could do something better and do something more. And he's got plans. Once he gets his GED, he's enlisting into the Service. And I know that he's gonna do it. You just gotta give the person the benefit of the doubt, you know? And maybe that's the thing.

Postscript: Member of the WEP-Force

Several months after this interview, Rebecca left her nursing program and joined the WEP force. Her assignment was with the Manhattan Transit Authority, cleaning subway stations in exchange for her welfare check. She was not happy with the work, but she remained somewhat hopeful, because she had found a medical billing course sponsored by HRA and asked if she could enroll in it. The answer, miraculously, had been yes. The course was set to begin in a few more weeks, and she was hopeful that it would lead her to a job.

The story of Rebecca is a classic of welfare "reform" in New York City: the flattened expectations, the sense of desperation, the ultimate sacrifice of future dreams for present survival. Like so many women in her position, Rebecca wanted to go to school, and wanted to go desperately, not only because she wanted the knowledge and experience, but also because she knew that a secondary degree was the surest route to a living wage: to a job that would allow her to feed her kids, take them to the doctor, keep them sheltered, and occasionally, just occasionally, buy them something special.

But, as Rebecca said, "it's hard" in this age of "reform" to get a degree and make the plan work. There are few degrees that can be earned in a year, and a year is all the time that the welfare system gives. One wonders how the architects of "reform" managed to arrive at this number, how a year became the magic figure deciding so many students' fates. Was it arbitrary? Was it the result of research? Whatever their calculations, it may be time for them to reevaluate. There have been too many women like Rebecca, too many people forced to leave school in mid-program because the alternative was losing part of their welfare benefits. Of course, in Rebecca's case, she actually thought she would lose all her benefits if she did not participate in WEP; that, after all, is what her caseworker told her. In the age of welfare "reform," it is hardly unusual for a caseworker to stretch the truth in the direction of severity as a means of forcing compliance. But even if Rebecca had known all the facts, her decision might have been the same: to comply, look for any job, and leave the threats and harassment behind her.

....

D. F.

That Education

I've been through a lot. I want everybody to know that I really had it up rough but now I'm making a smooth transition and that was my biggest fear, making that transition.

A Thursday evening after work: D. F. sweeps in from the rain, a charismatic, middle-aged woman with a gold and black scarf tied elegantly around her head. Her voice is low and husky, her words fast and free. She is giddy with a sense of optimism. For nearly twenty-five years, she got by on the money she received from public assistance. "It wasn't much," she reflects, "but it was something." In July 1999, after completing her associate's degree at LaGuardia Community College, she was hired to work in her school's dean's office. Since then, she has not received assistance.

Okay. I was born and raised in Brooklyn, in the Marcy Projects. I had three sisters and two brothers, and it was pretty good, you know?

As I was growing up we had a few problems in the family. My older sister got pregnant at the age of thirteen and had a baby when she was fourteen. My mother sent her away to some home, some foster home, to live and have her baby. The next sister under her was heavily into drugs. Then it was me and my younger sister. Me and my younger sister we hung out together a lot and we got in trouble, not that bad, but you know, a few times my mother, she didn't actually kick us out, but she said "get out" or whatever. My younger sister ended up going to a group home in the Bronx. She was there and I was left at home. I wasn't as bad as my sisters, just a little.

Actually what it was that really kind of made me leave home was because of my mother's new husband. He didn't like girls. He told us he didn't like girls and he used to give us fever: "Do this, do that; do this, do that." So my mother used to say the same thing to keep him happy. And we would do it, but when he came in if he said that it wasn't done good enough or if it wasn't done, she would make us do it all over again. I used to get so mad at them; I wanted to beat him up. And that's why I left the home. I asked my mother if I could go where my sister is—my younger sister—because I had went to visit her a few times and it was very, very nice. It was 250 girls and 250 boys, and it was like a dorm. It was like a college dorm, and I loved it.

I only stayed there till I turned about seventeen years old and then I ended up pregnant by my first love. While I was pregnant I got transferred to another group home. Then I ended up getting my own apartment. I had my own apartment, and I was on public assistance. I'll never forget, I was about four months pregnant with my son when I first got on public assistance. I knew I needed some kind of help, some kind of assistance because the baby's father—you know, things didn't work out that well. So that was it.

I didn't ever consider working—I don't think there was that many things out there I could do. Because I don't think anybody really puts a lot of emphasis on "Oh, you really need that education." The only person I really heard that from was my mother. Everybody else, they didn't say anything about you need that education. They might have said something about work, but the only work that I knew I could only get was factory, and I didn't want that, a factory job, which I have done. And the sad part about those factory jobs that I've had is that I've never collected a paycheck from them because I didn't stay with them. I think the most I've stayed with any factory job was maybe a week, maybe two weeks, because I couldn't take it. I just couldn't take it. I remember I worked for a company making costumes, masks, Halloween stuff, standing up on my feet all day. I just couldn't take that. So I stayed there maybe a week, the most probably two weeks.

I always knew in my head that you need that education. I always knew that, you know? But I don't know why I kept thinking that I could avoid it and still get something better. I imagine some people probably have done it like that, you know, avoided it and still ended up getting something better but I don't know. My mother always instilled in me that you need your education: "You should never have to pay for education. You need that education." So that always stuck in my brain. I knew I had to do something.

I decided that the way to get started was to get my GED. It had to have been around '95. I went to this place called TAP[11] Center #5 that was in my neighborhood. I started taking classes, maybe every night of the week or a couple nights a week. I'd go there for a few hours. The teachers would teach me a little math, a little English, a little of every one of the subjects in preparation for this GED. I worked really, really hard in getting ready for the test.

I went to take the test and I was extremely nervous. Now prior to me taking the test, I'm saying, "Yeah, I'm going to get my GED because I'm going to college. I'm going to college! That's the first thing I'm going to do. As soon as I get my GED I'm going to college." So after I take the test, I'm home waiting for the results. When I get the results, I failed by one point. I was so heated! I'm like, "They could've gave me one point from somewhere!" I was so upset.

So I asked my counselor when was the next test coming up, and he said it was a month later, something like that. And I'm like, "No, no, no, no, no!" I wasn't waiting that long. So he said well, some places do have walk-ins. Now, mind you, they take about ten walk-ins. I remember getting up about maybe five or six o'clock in the morning because I was on a mission. The sun was just coming up and everything. I said, "I'm going to be one of those walk-ins." So I stood outside on that line and I'm telling you I was saying, "If *anybody* act like they're not going to let me take this test, I'm gonna whip ass." Excuse the expression, but that's exactly the way I said it: "I'm gonna whip ass."

I wasn't actually too sure which areas I failed the test in, so I took all five parts all over again just to make sure. I knew I was going to get that one point from somewhere! So I knew I had it. I said, "As soon as I get my GED I'm going to college." Didn't know I had to apply for college first, you know? I'm thinking, I've got my little GED in hand, I could just walk in there and get in school. Un-unh, had to apply. I researched quite a few CUNY colleges, but none appealed to me except LaGuardia Community College, so I applied and they accepted me. I was just so excited. I'm like, "Yeah-h!" I couldn't wait to get started.

I guess the reason why I wanted to go to college is because—I don't know, I just felt maybe going to college made you feel a little more important. Because I know I did. I felt a little more important. I felt like "Oh, I'm getting ready to get this big knowledge that a lot of people don't have! Let me go for this." I'm telling you, I went every semester. I never took off no time. I enjoyed it. I enjoyed it, because the setting was just so nice: the programs, the people you could talk to—because there were special staff members there that helped you out with you being on welfare, telling you what to do, where to get this information from, where to get these letters from, how to do this, that and the other. There was just so much knowledge to absorb. I'm like, "Yes! Give me, give me!" You know? LaGuardia was very interesting for me. I thought that I would be too old to be sitting in college with the majority of its students being young teens just getting out of high school, but that was not the case.

My chosen major was Microcomputers and Applications because I had a fascination with computers. I knew computers were going to be the thing somewhere down the line. So I'm like, I'm going to try to get as much knowledge of the computer as I can. And that's what I did. I learned the four basic programs—Excel, Access, Word, and PowerPoint—as well as the basics: math, English, et cetera.

They were trying at one time to have me do WEP. They wanted me to come to one of the IM Centers[12] to see where they could place me. But see our school, they're a stickler on you getting your education, so they're not all up for that WEP business. So I went to our COPE[13] office to see if they could help because I did not want anything to affect me being in school, and they did, just because they know that education was so important. They were already aware of changes of PA [public assistance] so they had already created various WEP assignments within the school system. That helped a lot.

I think if I was forced to go and clean the parks, I would have tried to find out what would happen if I didn't. I might have opted for me being off as opposed to getting out there cleaning the park, because I was just so into education. I would have talked to someone, I would have went somewhere. *Someone* would have had to tell me *something*, because I wouldn't have stopped. I wouldn't have wanted to get out there. What's the sense in you getting out there cleaning? I don't understand why anyone wouldn't want somebody to get education. I mean, if you want productive citizens out here, they *need* education. If they don't have no education, how do you expect them to be productive? How do you expect them to even get anywhere? Because to clean the park—hell, if you got your house you got to clean your house. So that's not learning nothing new.

Education to me is just always the key. It's given me energy. It's given me a whole new outlook on a lot of things. I feel so good with the knowledge that I've absorbed. And I'm trying to absorb as much as I can still and—I don't know, I think I've changed tremendously. Not to say that I was that bad of a person before I went to school because I was pretty knowledgeable before I went to school, but now I am just truly more knowledgeable, you know? It has changed me a whole lot and I'm really, really glad. Because I know there was a lot of talk about they didn't want you to go to school, [but] they would have just had to cut me off welfare. Because there's no way in the world I was going to stop going to school.

I prayed a lot. I'm telling you, I prayed for me to just keep going on. I said, "I am not going to stop. I'm going to graduate." I just kept going and going like the Energizer Bunny!

I graduated September 21, 1999, at Madison Square Garden. Oh, God! I was so excited. It was mind blowing. When I took the pictures with my cap and gown before the graduation I felt like the president of the United States. I looked at myself and said, "Oh God! I've done it!"

I was just so happy. It was raining, but it was just awesome! My mother was coming, I knew my children were coming, my daughter's dad was supposed to have been coming, and a couple of my friends were supposed to be coming. I know my older sister would have been there because that's all she talked about when she was alive. She was really proud of me going to school and she couldn't wait to go to my graduation. She was telling everybody, "Yeah, my sister's graduating. My sister's in college" and all that good stuff. So when she passed away and I went to her funeral, I whispered in her ear and told her, "I'm getting that degree. I'm doing it for you."

I know my family was extremely proud, because I guess they thought maybe I was going to drop out sooner or later or something like that. My daughter was *so* happy: as I walked down the aisle she kept saying, "There goes my mommy! There goes my mommy!" My son had to tell her to keep quiet. I'm coming down the aisle and I'm like, "Shush! You're going to make me fall." I felt so nervous, but I felt so good coming down that aisle. She was, "There goes my mommy! Mommy, smile!" And she's snapping pictures.

I try to drum into my daughter's head all the time: "You've got to get that education because you can't get nowhere." I try to tell her about the struggles that I had with these factory jobs, and that that wasn't the move because you don't make much money. And you work hard as hell, you know? You don't need that. You need to stay in school so you can get an education so you can decide what you want to do, you can have a choice. But if you don't go to school you have no choice. You have to accept whatever it is that they give you. You don't want that. You want to be able to say, "I got this education. I know I can do this, I know I can do that."

How did your education change things for you?

For starters it helped me get the job that I now hold at LaGuardia Community College. The references I used were the supervisor from my internship at Pfizer—the internship was part of my curriculum— and my grade adviser from the college.

I believe at the time that my boss, Linda, was looking to hire someone. She didn't actually post the job. She was more or less word of mouth telling everybody, "If you know anybody who has these type of skills . . ." She actually interviewed quite a few people.

The day of the interview, I was so nervous. This was all very new to me. I kept telling my boss, over and over again, "I am so nervous. I am so nervous." She said, "Calm down. You'll be all right." Then she talked to me a little while. She asked me all sorts of questions, and I was saying that I love LaGuardia. I said, "I love the school. I haven't worked in so many years. I've been on public assistance for a long time, and I know I'm going to go off sooner or later, this, that, and the other." After the interview, she said that she would get in touch with me, and that was it, the interview was over.

When I left I stopped back by to see [the woman who referred me for the job] and thanked her for thinking of me for the position. She said, "I have a feeling you got this position. So you know what you do, e-mail Linda and thank her for giving you the opportunity to be interviewed."

Oh, I hooked that letter up. I told her, "Thank you so much for giving me an opportunity to go for this very—I forgot the word I used, 'prestigious' or something—job. If I don't get chosen for this thing it was still a pleasure. I was very nervous and you helped calm me down, and I really appreciate that. If you want, you could call me, but if not, whatever." In other words, I was trying to tell her I don't hold nothing against you if I'm not chosen and it was all good.

So I guess that cinched it, because she called me and said, "Hello, this is Linda. I just called to tell you that you have a job!" I said, "What! Are you sure? You're not joking with me, are you?" My heart was about to come out of my clothes. I wanted to cry and smoke cigarettes right there. I was so nervous I didn't know who to call first. I was trying to call my mother—I couldn't get in touch with her. I wanted to call my sister that's passed away—and I'm like, "God, I can't even tell her!" I wanted to shout, "I got a job! I got a job!" I wanted to tell the world. I mean I was thanking everybody, you can't imagine.

I left my internship on a Friday, June 26, 1999. I started work June 28. I've been working ever since.

POSTSCRIPT: "OUT OF THE DANGER ZONE"

It has been more than two years since D. F. landed her job at LaGuardia Community College, and she is still working. By almost all measures, her story is a success. After twenty-five years of public assistance, she put herself through community college, earned an associate's degree, and found herself a job with a union, benefits, and living wage salary. As she herself said, she is "out of the danger zone." But she does not want to stop there. In a few years she would like to go back to school and complete her bachelor's degree. She is simply waiting until she has saved enough money.

The story of D. F. is in many ways the bookend opposite of Latesha's. At forty-two, she feels young and alive, while at twenty-four, Latesha feels old and tired. Not that D. F.'s success came easily or quickly. It was built on lots of hard work and a good dose of luck and circumstance. Unlike Latesha, Michelle, or Rebecca, D. F. does not have young children to raise and look after; her son is grown and out of the house, and her daughter is a teenager who spends most of the day in school. As a result, she had no babysitter to pay, no child care forms to complete, and no payments to lose for "failure to comply" with the welfare system. D. F. was immune to one of the biggest pressure points the system can apply. She was free—or freer—to pursue her own dreams without fear of harming others.

Moreover, D. F. also had the good fortune of beginning her degree program well before the fall of 1998, when Jason Turner became commissioner of HRA and welfare "reform" took its full and tragic hold on New York City. Fewer people were required to do WEP, and when they were, they were required to perform fewer hours. For the determined student, the loopholes were a bit bigger, and the obstacles a mite smaller.

D. F. also was in a supportive environment, a school that was a "stickler for education." Not only did it have counselors in place to help guide students through the thickets of the welfare system, but it also helped D. F. negotiate a WEP assignment on campus. The assignment was convenient and closely tied to her curriculum. There was no shoveling in parks, no sweeping on subway platforms, no lengthy commute to a distant WEP site. D. F. could study and learn even as she logged time with WEP.

Because HRA did not use all its force to thwart or demean her, D. F. was able to go to school, graduate, and accomplish tremendous things. Perhaps it is time for the architects of welfare "reform" to begin doing *their* homework. For D. F., the story ends, or at least pauses, on a happy frame: with her associate's degree in hand, her hope intact, she marches into the sunset of career and self-sufficiency. But for many recipients—for Latesha, Michelle, and Rebecca—the story, if not the struggle, still continues. Until today, none has been able to earn her degree, although Michelle is certainly trying; and none has found a job to take her off the rolls, although Latesha and Rebecca have not stopped applying. Certainly family pressure, personal crisis, and raw, cruel life have all chipped away at these women's opportunities; but the role of the welfare system—its pressures and restrictions—cannot be denied. Amidst the tangle of work-first reforms, one cannot help but wonder: If these women hadn't been thwarted at each and every turn, how might they lead easier lives today? If they *had* been allowed to pursue their education, where might they be?

Admittedly, education is not a panacea. Neither an associate's nor a bachelor's degree can guarantee a job or a lifetime of security. Nor, for that matter, can they "make you free." Job discrimination, wage deflation, and lack of child care are just some of the barriers to meaningful employment, and they can deflate the worth of the most advanced degree. Moreover, for some people, the barriers to work—real, paid work—may never disappear, and for them a reliable safety net must always be in place. Life is too varied and complex to be pinned on a single solution, even one as appealing as college.

But without education, without at least the choice or the opportunity, the prospects for many welfare recipients are shaky at best. In the past quarter-century, the requirements for entry-level jobseekers have increased dramatically. Whereas a robust and high-paying manufacturing industry might once have absorbed the least-educated workers, today's economy is not so forgiving. According to the New York State Department of Labor, as many as 75 percent of major New York City employers require either a college degree or post-secondary training for entry-level positions—a disturbing trend, particularly for the roughly 90 percent of the welfare population that lacks post-secondary training (Task Force for Sensible Welfare Reform 1997). For these men and women, finding a job can be extremely difficult, and when they do find work, they tend to earn less than their credentialed colleagues. With wages that run a good 28 percent lower than for individuals with associate's degrees (Grubb 1999), and a solid 39 percent lower than for individuals with their bachelor's

(Kane and Rouse 1995), it is little surprise that they rarely make enough money to outrun poverty.

In this context, the policy of denying education to would-be students seems both misguided and cruel. It flies bluntly in the face of decades of research, and it all but condemns those on welfare to a sub-poverty oblivion. Not only does it rob people of the chance to make a living wage, but it can also crush their hopes and fracture their dreams in a way that is so damaging, so disempowering, it unravels any prospects of self-sufficiency.

So why has the federal government blocked the path to education? And why has New York City? Surely it cannot be the success of WEP, which has a job placement rate of just 6 percent. Nor can it be the effectiveness of job-search requirements, which rarely lead to a living income. So why does New York continue to push this model? It certainly does not have to.

In Maine and Illinois, Vermont and Hawaii, state governments have developed creative ways to make education count, with the result that there have been fewer losses for the schools and more diplomas for the recipients. If New York truly wants to be a leader, it can easily do the same. It can pass a bill in its city council redefining education as an allowable work activity; it can use funds from the state TANF surplus to create a parallel, unrestricted welfare program for would-be students; and it can honor existing laws, such as the Work Study and Internship Bill, that were passed to help low income students stay in school. Although some conservatives may fight these moves, arguing as they have in the past that education in the absence of WEP is a "disservice" (Diamond 1998) to welfare recipients, there are valuable arguments to do the reverse.

Throughout the nation's history, educational policy—or, more accurately, education's denial—has been used as a means of maintaining inequalities and ensuring exclusion. From the days of the Old South, when it was illegal for slaves to learn to read, to the Victorian prohibition against women's higher education, to today's underfunding of inner-city schools, the country's record is filled with examples of institutional discrimination. Although the PRWORA does not explicitly forbid welfare recipients to go to school or receive training, it effectively bars many from pursuing these options. It undermines and restricts to the point of impossibility.

All of this should make people suspicious. Any time a group, particularly one defined largely by women and people of color, is blocked from receiving an adequate education, sirens, loud and wailing, should sound in our minds. These sirens should remind us that the history of education is a history of exclusion, and that it is no small accident that so many poor women have been forced from school by the PRWORA. As Latesha said: "It's like they're trying to keep us on a certain level. They're controlling our lives. . . . I think they don't want us to move forward."

And she is probably right. The American welfare system has always served as a tool of control, a means of regulating women's lives and policing poor people's bodies. As scholars Mimi Abramovitz, Frances Fox Piven, and Richard Cloward have argued in their books, *Regulating the Lives of Women* (1988) and *Regulating the Poor* (1971), welfare policy has historically functioned to enforce low-wage work, prevent social unrest, and preserve gender inequities. The PRWORA's restrictions on education build on that cruel legacy. They keep low income women unskilled and willing to take poorly paid jobs that have neither benefits nor security. They fasten low income women to gendered jobs, like housekeeper, babysitter, and home-health aide. They keep low income women obedient, holding them in a state of fear by threatening to yank their benefits for the smallest infraction. And they teach them they should not aspire and dare not fight, because aspirations will be met with defeat and fighting with punishment. With such an agenda, it is little wonder so many poor women have compared the welfare system to a brutal cop or abusive husband.

In March 2004, the PRWORA is expected at last to come up for reauthorization. After several false starts and delays, the law will finally be evaluated, amended, and resubmitted for a vote in Congress (the original reauthorization date was set for September 2002, but Congress has stalled and rescheduled several times). For years, welfare rights activists anticipated this date as an opportunity, a chance to right the wrongs of the original welfare "reform" law. They organized and protested, wrote reports and gathered testimonies, appealed to the media and lobbied Congress. They called on the country's leaders to reduce the work requirement and urged them to allow more schooling.

But rather than heed their call, the president, his advisors, and a dispiritingly large number of congressmen have endorsed even harsher welfare laws. In February 2002, Bush unveiled a plan that not only increases the number of hours recipients are required to work but also reduces the education credit from twelve to three months every two years. The House passed a carbon copy version of this plan in February 2003, and the Senate is debating a similar, if slightly more modest, proposal. Both plans effectively eliminate post-secondary schooling from the map of possibility, and both confirm that for the president and all too many Republican and Democratic legislators, poor women do not need education. They do not need genuine economic opportunity. They just need a wedding ring. "We will work to strengthen marriage," Bush declared on February 26, 2002, the day he introduced his welfare "reform" agenda in a Washington, D.C., church. "As we reduce welfare caseloads, we must improve the lives of children. And the most effective, direct way to improve the lives of children is to encourage the stability of American families" (Bush 2002). The plan calls for $300 million a year to "promote marriage" among low income couples: $200 million from the federal government and $100 million in matching funds from each state government. It is a plan that smacks of paternalism and outdated theories of social control. It is a plan that would have made George Orwell shiver.

Yet outrage is muffled. A whole class of people has been failed, told they have no right to strive for equality, opportunity, or a just and decent life, but the country is silent. The principles of democracy have been slashed and freedoms crushed, but the mainstream says nothing. And this, perhaps, is the greatest failure of all.

NOTES

1. On July 20, 1998, Mayor Rudolph Giuliani announced that he would end welfare dependency by the year 2000 by placing all able-bodied welfare recipients in a thirty-five-hours-per-week work activity. It was at this point that the New York City welfare "reform" project became significantly tougher than state and federal laws demanded.

2. As of June 2002, the number of welfare recipients engaged in WEP and HRA-sponsored education, training, and job-search activities came to 21,770 (http://www.nyc.gov/html/hra/pdf/citywide.pdf). At the height of the welfare-to-work push in 1998 and 1999, this number jumped above 40,000 (New York City Independent Budget Office, "Inside the Budget," no. 72, 1 November 2000, p. 4).

3. The Human Resources Administration's Office of Policy and Program Analysis reports that the number of individuals receiving public assistance in March 1995, on the eve of welfare reform, was 1,160,593; its figures for March 2001 place the number of public assistance recipients at 518, 823.

4. In the fall of 1998, shortly after Jason Turner took over as commissioner of HRA, the agency announced a fifteen-hour increase in the number of hours that all WEP participants were required to be engaged in work activities. Although the PRWORA itself mandated only twenty hours of workfare a week at this point, to be increased to twenty-five hours in 1999, New York City initiated the "simulated work week" and accelerated its own program to thirty-five hours.

5. In the fall of 2000, a statewide coalition of advocates and welfare recipients succeeded in convincing the state legislature to pass the Work Study/Internship Bill, which allows hours devoted to work-study and/or school-related internships to count toward the work requirement.

6. Center 99, also known as the Richmond Job Center, is the name commonly used for Staten Island's only welfare center.

7. "Face-to-face" is the term for the regularly scheduled appointments between a recipient and her welfare center caseworker. They take place two to four times a year and are used primarily to review eligibility and budgeting. The penalty for missing a face-to-face—and most other welfare center appointments—is a case closing.

8. Jason Turner was the Commissioner of the Human Resources Administration. After overseeing the Wisconsin Works (W-2) program for former Governor Tommy Thompson, he was brought east in 1998 to implement similar reforms in New York City.

9. In fact, unbeknownst to Rebecca, the rest her family would not have been cut off from public assistance if she refused to participate in WEP or BEGIN. Only she herself would have been removed (sanctioned) from the budget. It is not uncommon, however, for workers to convey inaccurate information to their clients.

10. Supplemental Security Income (SSI) is a means-tested public benefits program that provides cash assistance to low income individuals with physical and/or mental disabilities.

11. TAP stands for Testing Assessment Placement. D. F. described it as "a school that helped prepare people for their GED as well as a place to help people find jobs."

12. An IM Center, or Income Maintenance Center, was the formal name for the welfare center in New York City before it was changed to "Job Center" in 1998. Many people still refer to these centers by the old shorthand.

13. The College Opportunity to Prepare for Employment (COPE) program is located throughout the CUNY college system and was initially designed to provide additional support to students who receive welfare.

REFERENCES

Abramovitz, M. 1988. *Regulating the lives of women: Social welfare policy from colonial times to the present.* Boston: South End Press.

Bush, G.W. 2001, 27 February. The Bush education initiative: Address to joint session of Congress. Available at http://www.usinfo.state.gov/usa/edu/bush0227.htm.

———. 2002, 26 February. President announces welfare reform agenda. Available at http://whitehouse.gov/news/releases/2002/02/20020226-11.html.

Casey, T. 1998, August. *Welfare reform and its impact in the nation and in New York.* New York: Federation for Protestant Welfare Agencies.

Cohan, M. 2002, November. Interview with Marc Cohan, Director of Litigation, Welfare Law Center.

Diamond, S. 1998, October 14. Testimony before the Committee on Higher Education jointly with the Committee on General Welfare on the Work Experience Program at the City University of New York (CUNY).

Gittell, M., M. Schehl, and C. Fareri. 1990. *From welfare to independence: The college option.* A report to the Ford Foundation. New York: Ford Foundation.

Grubb, W. N. 1999, April. Learning and earning in the middle: The economic benefits of sub-baccalaureate education, 14–15. New York: Community College Research Center.

Human Resources Administration (HRA). 1995, March. HRA facts. Data Analysis and Research, Office of Policy and Program Analysis. Available at http://www.nyc.gov/html/hra/pdf/facts0301.pdf.

———. 1998–2001. Our mission statement. Formerly available at http://www.ci.nyc.ny.us/html/hra/out_mission.html.

———. 2001, March. HRA facts. Data Analysis and Research, Office of Policy and Program Analysis.

———. 2002. PA: Monthly report, June. Available at http://www.nyc.gov/html/hra/pdf/citywide.pdf.

Kane, T., and C. Rouse. 1995. Labor-market returns to two- and four-year college. *American Economic Review* 85(3):600–614.

Lane, M. 2003, October. Interview with Maureen Lane, Welfare Rights Initiative.

New York City Coalition Against Hunger. 2001, November. Annual New York City Hunger Survey. Available at http://www.nyccah.org.

Piven, F. F., and R. Cloward. 1971. *Regulating the poor: The functions of public welfare.* New York: Vintage Books.

Task Force for Sensible Welfare Reform, Herbert J. Milano Graduate School for Management and Urban Policy, New School for Social Research. 1997. Welfare policies for New York State. June: 21.

Turner, J. 1998. Speaking on WNET-TV's call-in show *Thirteen on the Line with Brian Lehrer*, 25 June.

Welfare Law Center claims that NYC job centers deter food stamps, medicaid and cash assistance applicants: Court grants TRO. 1998. *Welfare News*, December. Available at http://www.welfarelaw.org/jobctr.htm.

Chapter 3

"That's Not How I Want to Live"

Student Mothers Fight to Stay in School under Michigan's Welfare-to-Work Regime

Peggy Kahn and Valerie Polakow

[My caseworker] actually told me, "We don't care about you going to school, that is not what we want, Governor Engler wants ladies to work." . . . I was like, "Well, where is Governor Engler at, because he is obviously not trying to help me if he doesn't want me to further my education to get a stable job. I mean this $6-an-hour job, I don't want that for the rest of my life. That's why I'm in school, so I can have a better life for me and my child."

—Sandra, a university student and single mother of one child

INTRODUCTION

Throughout the 1990s, the state of Michigan was determined to slash expenditures on poor families by reducing the welfare rolls, cloaking its brutal cuts in the language of "personal responsibility" and "family independence." With both the executive office and legislature dominated by the Republican party, led by Governor John Engler, state policy makers ascribed poverty to welfare programs that indulged the work aversion and personal and family disorganization of the poor. State officeholders prescribed "Work First"—an uncompromising regime of required job searches, low-wage jobs, and welfare exits—as the remedy for deficient poor women.

In his January 1991 inaugural address, Engler called for "personal responsibility." Ten months later, in October 1991, the state summarily ended General Assistance, Michigan's program for unemployed childless adults, many with disabilities, little education, or seasonal jobs, announcing that these "hit the road, Jack, cuts" would force able-bodied scroungers to work and save taxpayers hundreds of millions of dollars (Henly and Danziger 1996; Thompson 1995).

Following this ideological and political "victory" and with legislative majorities shifting to the right, in 1994 the Republican-controlled legislature required clients to seek and retain low-wage work when applying for Aid to Families with Dependent Children (AFDC) cash assistance. Engler touted Michigan as a model for national reform and state policy because it had the "toughest work rules in the nation."

In early 1996, the legislature enacted a strong work-first policy that set the framework for implementation of Michigan's Temporary Assistance for Needy Families (TANF) block grant, administered by Michigan's renamed Family Independence Agency (FIA) and the state's Department of Career Development Work First subcontractors. The policy makes cash benefits contingent on immediate attendance and enrollment in job-search and placement programs; lack of compliance with job-search and work requirements brings rapid sanctions and terminations; and work requirements mandate clients to accept job offers of up to forty hours per week. Only a very restricted set of clients (those with severe, certified disabilities, for example) is exempted from attendance at job-search programs, and Michigan is one of only a few states that require mothers of infants to meet work requirements when their infant is twelve weeks old. Benefits are extremely low, 39 percent of the official poverty threshold in 2001, making it nearly impossible to subsist on these payments even for a short period of time (Michigan League for Human Services [MLHS] 2002b, 2001c).

During Engler's governorship from 1992 to 2000, the Family Independence Program (FIP) caseload dropped from 225,349 to 68,200, a decline of almost 70 percent, although in the year 2001 the caseload increased 16 percent, as the economy faltered (MLHS 2002a). Despite the economic expansion of the 1990s, those whose welfare cases were closed—due to the earnings cap—held dead-end jobs paying an average hourly wage of $8.50. They were unable to find full-time, steady work, and faced continuing serious hardships such as housing insecurity and hunger. During this same period, the number of people in the state with incomes below 200 percent of the official poverty threshold increased (Institute for Human Services Research 2001; MLHS 2001a; Bernstein et al. 2000; Danziger et al. 2000). Thirty-four percent of children continue to live in households with incomes below 200 percent of the poverty threshold (MLHS 2001b).

Single mothers struggling to stay in school in Michigan, therefore, face a rigid work-first welfare regime, which aims to reduce the welfare rolls by forcing recipients into any low-wage job. Policy that supports education risks reducing the rapid short-term decline in the welfare rolls that politicians and policy makers view as the primary indicator of success; and allowing clients to enroll in college is seen as unwarranted tax expenditure on welfare, even though in the long run such support would more than pay for itself (Coalition for Independence

Through Education [CFITE] 2002, 39–50). Not only policy makers but also front-line caseworkers treat enrollment in post-secondary education as an undeserved benefit, as work avoidance, and as beyond the capacity of most low income mothers.

Yet despite the nearly insurmountable obstacles deliberately put in their path, single mothers in Michigan have continued to aspire to, initiate, and progress in post-secondary educational programs, convinced that only post-secondary education will position them to achieve meaningful self-sufficiency and improve the lives of their children. After briefly discussing the specific policy framework that makes post-secondary education extremely difficult to access, this chapter focuses on the stories of four mothers who struggled to complete their degrees in Michigan after 1996. Their stories of life and education under Michigan's welfare-to-work regime reveal onerous and problematic work requirements, continuing crises of child care and parenting, withheld and incorrect information about a variety of policy requirements and opportunities, and bureaucratic harassment and subversion of mothers trying to go to college. Despite repeated pressure to accept low-wage work and withheld resources, these student mothers cultivate their internal emotional strength; approach the state bureaucracy strategically; use the resources of family and friends where available; and make very difficult compromises as they adhere to their educational goals.

The Policy Framework: A Brief Overview

In its plan for implementing the TANF block grant under the 1996 Personal Responsibility and Work Opportunity Reconciliation Act (PRWORA), Michigan made no effort to provide educational resources to single mothers. Instead it adopted a strict welfare-to-work approach that did not count education as an allowable employment-related activity for recipients of the cash assistance program (the Family Independence Program). Michigan failed to take advantage of a provision in federal legislation that allowed states to count up to one year of vocational training as meeting work requirements for up to 20 percent of the caseload. It has declined to use a federal caseload-reduction credit to expand education and training opportunities.[1]

In summer 1999, state legislators and the Family Independence Agency and Work First agencies modified the no-education rule but in a manner that failed to provide the flexibility and support post-secondary students require. These new rules were a response to advocacy by state nonprofits, more available TANF money per case than expected, and rapidly falling welfare rolls. They also reflected a new state workforce development effort to encourage short-term technical training as a solution to labor shortages in certain sectors of the economy. The new policy, administered primarily by Work First agencies rather than by the FIA, allowed clients to use hours spent in certain types of education and training programs to meet some or all of their work requirements, as follows:

Full-Time Vocational Programs. Single parents could use an approved, full-time (thirty hours a week) vocational program of less than six months to meet work requirements in full.

Internships. Policy makers reaffirmed that a full-time internship, practicum or clinical assignment required by a school to complete a degree or for professional certification could also meet the thirty-hour requirement, a policy originally passed in 1999 in response to emerging problems noted by legislators.

10/10/10. Single parents were permitted to count either a program of twelve months or less or the last year of a 2-year or 4-year program towards work requirements. If a client was working ten hours a week, she could count up to ten hours per week of classroom time, and up to one hour of study for each hour of class time (up to ten hours), toward meeting her thirty-hour requirement (thus, this program is referred to as 10/10/10). Approved educational programs qualified clients for tuition assistance, child care subsidies for class but not study time, and transportation assistance.

In spite of legislatively mandated policies to allow some education to count toward work requirements, very few parents participating in the Family Independence Program have been approved by Work First contractors to participate in education and training. Less than 2 percent of parents were enrolled in approved education of all kinds in 2000–2001. A telephone survey done by FIA indicates that 5 percent of parents receiving cash assistance are enrolled in a college or university. Although this percentage is very small, it is greater than the percentage approved by Work First agencies and suggests that many poor, single parents are struggling through school despite the disapproval and without the supportive services of Work First and FIA. Survey and ethnographic data suggest why only such small percentages of recipients are able to stay in school: FIA caseworkers and Work First managers express hostility to clients pursuing education, information about education is not available to clients, work requirements preempt educational commitments, and good-quality child care is unavailable (CFITE 2002; Kahn and Polakow 2000).

Very recent policy changes make pursuit of education even more difficult. Whereas Michigan had a de facto work requirement of forty hours per week for all single parents in place by 1998, changes implemented in April 2002 formalized a forty-hour requirement for each parent receiving assistance, including those with children under six whose federal work requirement was only twenty hours; including those in two-parent families who previously had either thirty-five- or fifty-five-hour combined work requirements; and including those with disabled children (receiving Supplemental Security Income [SSI]) if they did not succeed in establishing the need to be exempted on a case-by-case basis. Although parents with disabled children were never able to use child care subsidies for educational hours because they were not meeting work requirements, they could try to use the time during which they were not caring for their children to pursue education. In April 2002, the general exemption from work requirements was revoked for parents of disabled children, destroying their predictable time availability, but opening up their option of using the 10/10/10 program. However, a new, formal forty-hour requirement raises questions about whether the 10/10/10 program will now be eviscerated by requiring twenty hours of work during the last year of a 2-year or 4-year program. Those parents struggling to go to college outside the 10/10/10 program will likely be forced to drop out entirely if their state work requirement rises from thirty to forty hours per week, and many prospective students will not be able to begin college programs even part time. Once again, Michigan's harsh work-first policy seems to have preempted and prefigured more demanding national work-first legislation. The Bush administration's recent reauthorization proposal increases the work requirements to forty hours, with at least twenty-four in direct employment, and permits only a three-month-long waiver from work requirements every two years, endangering even Michigan's small concessions to post-secondary programs.

In addition to work requirements, child care policy remains an immense obstacle to pursuit of post-secondary education. In Michigan, child care policy is operated merely as an adjunct to work-first policy. With few exceptions, policy does not support child care for hours parents are in post-secondary programs. In addition, the general administration of child care subsidies has been problematic for all welfare recipients, including those in education. Although very few parents are able to access FIA child day care subsidies for time spent in education, those who are able to obtain Work First approval and receive such subsidies are often unable to access safe, appropriate child care as FIA child care subsidies are low. Even the maximum payments available often cover only 50 percent of the full cost of care, and parents report numerous problems including arbitrary denials, reductions, and cut offs, slow start-ups and late payments, and inaccurate under-calculation of subsidies. A mere 19 percent of income-eligible children, 120,100 out of a total eligible population of approximately 600,000 children, receive a child care subsidy. Fully two-thirds of all children receiving subsidies are in unregulated, informal care settings, and an even higher percentage of children of cash recipients are in such legally exempt care. Despite an acute shortage of infant care facilities, Michigan requires mothers to work when their infants are twelve weeks old (Michigan Kids Count 2001; Kahn and Polakow 2000). High-quality child care is never discussed as an important service to working mothers, as an essential support for parents pursuing education, or as a vital factor promoting the healthy development of children.

These policies structure the difficulties of student mothers trying to juggle work, child care, and education. They create temporal and financial burdens and impose intense psychological and physical stress. They compromise student mothers' parenting, educational progress, and work histories. Independently minded low income parents engaged in strategic planning for self-sufficiency are forced to make painful short-term sacrifices in the hope they will achieve long-term gains. The result has been a steep decline in the numbers of poor, single mothers enrolled in post-secondary institutions and almost insurmountable problems for those struggling to complete degrees.

Narratives of Resistance and Struggle

The stories of mothers who have persistently and actively challenged a welfare regime that restricts and regulates their post-secondary aspirations and opportunities open a window on the world of Work-First, Education-Last policies in Michigan. From 1997 to 2000, we followed ten single mothers on public assistance attending Michigan universities, documenting their experiences through cumulative open-ended interviews.[2] The following stories of Lisa, Lakeisha, Tina, and Susan dramatically illustrate the obstacles confronting low income single mothers struggling to succeed in post-secondary education, achieve economic self-sufficiency, and shape a different future for themselves and their young children.

Lisa

Twenty-three-year-old Lisa has been living alone since she was sixteen years old. She became pregnant with her daughter when she was nineteen; Gabrielle, who is biracial, is now four years old. Lisa is a survivor of domestic violence, and from a young age has encountered multiple roadblocks from a welfare bureaucracy that she has challenged at every turn. Despite the seemingly insurmountable obstacles she has frequently confronted, Lisa has resisted, fighting against a work-first future and refusing to "drop out of school and never go anywhere." She is determined to complete her four-year degree and graduate as a teacher.

Lisa describes leaving her drug-abusing boyfriend after he assaulted her during her pregnancy. When she applies for assistance, she refuses to divulge paternity because she wants to sever all ties with him:

> So I said all this to the intake worker, and she said, "Well you're going to have to tell me who he is . . . [or] we're not going to help you." So I left and figured I'd try my hand at it again—so a month later I reapplied, hoping I'd get a new intake worker. It's kind of like playing cards and I did, and I told her, "Well I don't want to give his name" and I explained the situation and she said, "That's fine, don't worry about it," and she told me she knew I must really need it, and that basically when a White person comes in, it's obvious they really need it, and I was really uncomfortable because I'm pregnant, and I'm carrying a Black child, and she's telling me "Well, because you're White basically I understand you need it" . . .

Lisa receives preferential and racialized treatment because she is White, but she is never informed of the state domestic-violence waiver in terms of work requirements.

Lisa enrolls in school and in 1996 receives a notice that she has to meet mandatory work requirements. Her caseworker tells her that under Work First policies school "is not a priority" unless she considers vocational training or a two-year program. Lisa attends a mandatory Work First orientation and is appalled by what she is told:

> I talk with this gentleman doing the orientation, and I tell him I'm majoring in education; I'm going to be able to give back and I'll be out in four years. . . . And he says, "Here is the paper, this is what you can do. You can do voc-tech—there's not a lot of female electricians or construction workers—or you can go to a two-year college. . . . You can't do the four-year. . . . If you do voc-tech, you don't have to work. If you do the two-year you only have to work ten hours. If you want to do the four-year, you have to work like forty hours!" . . . I say, "Well how do you go to school and work all the time?" He says, "Well you have to; if you are going to go four years, you must also work forty hours a week!" He told me it's because of Work First, and somehow I kept talking to him, and I told him that this is ridiculous and that I'd just be on welfare forever. . . . "I'm just going to be part of the working poor who isn't poor enough to be on welfare but not rich enough to own their own charge card, you know." So he just waived it and let me

through. He said he waived it for two years and then after two years "there's no telling what's gonna happen but at least you got two years into it and maybe you can make your argument then."

Lisa succeeds in persuading the Work First counselor to waive the forty-hour work requirement (despite the fact that under the 1996 federal law she should only be required to work twenty hours) by challenging the policy and making an articulate case for an exception, just as she succeeded in arousing the racist sympathies of a second caseworker regarding nondisclosure of the paternity of her child.

As she becomes more and more aware of policy loopholes and her own rights, Lisa seeks out information and confronts a new battle for child care subsidies after she enrolls her daughter, now twenty months old, at the campus child care center and finds herself facing mounting child care debts:

> The caseworker failed to mention that they will pay for day care. . . . They just don't tell you. . . . You have to ask for it to get it! I didn't know. . . . This is the first time I've had my daughter in day care and the director said to me, "This is what you have to do—you've got to call them and tell them you want day care assistance."

After Lisa discovers that she is entitled to receive child care subsidies and that she has been unknowingly a victim of the FIA's "don't ask, don't tell" policies, she angrily confronts her caseworker to claim her child care subsidy and receive retroactive payments: "And after that they back-billed and I mean it came to like a $900 check for all this day care I didn't know I had—I mean it was just ridiculous!"

As Lisa enters her junior year in college, maintaining a 3.8 grade-point average and working twenty hours a week on campus, she continues to struggle to stay afloat financially. She finds out from another student mother that she could use work-study earnings without having that money count against her FIA grant, which would increase her monthly income and considerably ease her precarious financial situation:

> So I called my caseworker, and he said "No, absolutely not!" And I said, "Well it makes sense because it's financial aid, and financial aid is Title IV and Title IV can't be counted," and I'm explaining this all to the gentleman! And he says "Well I'd have to see some paperwork or something on that" and I said, "Well where would I find this paperwork," and he tells me go to the library and get the PEM [FIA's Program Eligibility Manual]! . . . It took me about a week and a half to find all this—my girlfriend and I, we were tag teaming on this—I mean it's stacks and stacks of stuff—so basically we found it. We found this page which said work-study counts for hours, but that does not reduce your cash assis-

tance, and we screamed in the library, and the librarian had to turn around and look at us, and we made a copy for the day care because there are lots of parents who could use that. . . . So it became my responsibility to prove to my worker what my rights were! I knew I could prove it because it made no sense; I knew I could argue my way through it, and I threatened a hearing, because I knew I was right!

Either through ignorance, indifference, or deliberate concealment, Lisa's caseworker does not provide her with accurate information; nor, apparently, have many other caseworkers in several counties in southeast Michigan given their clients accurate information, because Lisa's discovery has ripple effects for many student mothers at her college as she begins to disseminate the information.

During this same period in summer 1998, Lisa receives notice that her work hours will increase to twenty-five hours:

I receive the notice with the second check of the month—so basically I'm given four days' notice that I need to get another five hours worth of work by July 1. . . . So I contacted my caseworker with "What the hell is this. You can't work twenty-five hours on campus fall and winter!" I mean basically that meant I would have to find another job but nobody is going to employ me for five hours—so do I quit my work study job here just to get an extra five hours? . . . And now I come to find out because she [Gabrielle] is under six, she's not even five yet, I don't have to!

Once again, FIA violates Lisa's rights although she is meeting federal work requirements of twenty hours a week for a single parent with a child under six, and once again Lisa, after being informed of her rights by a local advocate, must challenge the policy and threaten a hearing before her hours are reduced to twenty. She describes the treatment she receives from FIA as "degrading" and "humiliating" as every aspect of her life is placed under surveillance and she must constantly fight to claim her limited rights. As Lisa approaches her final semester of college, well informed about recent 1999 state legislation that permits an unpaid internship to count as meeting the mandatory work requirement in the terminal year of a degree program, she prepares to do her semester-long student teaching. However, Lisa has to inform her caseworker, day care worker, and Work First worker about her right to use the internship; she is never informed about this by any agency official despite the passage of the legislation in July 1999 and its implementation in October 1999.

As Lisa approaches her graduation, she looks back on her four-year struggle to survive the unremitting obstacles of a welfare regime that actively discourages post-secondary education and withholds information about such options from its clients:

It's like pulling teeth. . . . I feel really bad for women who either don't
have the time to do this, or don't have the ability to do this, or have
never been taught they have the power to do this and in a lot of cases,
there are a lot of people who have caseworkers who you really don't
want to mess with. . . . They keep changing [rules] and nobody knows
what's going on, and the only people who get what they really need
are the people who fight for it!

....

LAKEISHA

Lakeisha, a twenty-six-year-old African American mother of an eight-year-old
girl and five-year-old boy, was identified in high school in Oakland, California,
as a promising inner-city student in math and science, recruited into an off-
campus enrichment and college-bound program, and later admitted to two top
public universities, including the University of Michigan. After moving to
Michigan with her father, Lakeisha became entangled in a dangerously abusive
relationship and then endured homelessness. Despite new parenting responsibilities and recent traumas, she successfully completed a two-year degree program in math and science at a community college and transferred to a four-year
degree program in computer science. Now, however, rather than a promising
student, she was a "welfare mother," positioned by policy as undeserving of
post-secondary education and thrown back on limited resources as she recon-
ciled the intensive needs of her children, work requirements, and a demanding
program of study.

In 1997, FIA informed Lakeisha, about two years away from finishing her
bachelor's degree, that she must work twenty hours a week. She located a
work-study job on campus paying minimum wage to satisfy the requirement.

Well, the twenty-hour mandatory work requirement, it has caused me
to leave my children in the care of day-care providers for the majority
of the day. Like I go to school full time and I have to work an additional twenty hours during the week, so my day here will begin at 9:00
in the morning and end at 6:00 P.M. Between here and going to get the
kids from day care and getting back home, that takes about forty-five
minutes. The kids have to be fed, so I'm not spending any quality time
with them. They have to be prepped for the next day, so they have to
get their baths, the clothes out, we have to go over homework, and it's
time to go to bed. There's no time for quality time with my children,
and on the weekend I'm trying to play catch-up with homework, my
homework that I couldn't complete throughout the week because I
was so tired when they got off to bed. It's really taken a toll on me, and

> I think the requirement is ridiculous for students who are taking full-time loads. . . . I actually withdrew from the university because my grades were falling. I took two weeks off work to try to bring up my grades, but when I went back to work my grades started falling again. And my kids . . . I don't know what kind of damage I'm doing in the long run, whether it can be repaired or not.

Because of her long school and work hours, her summer cut-offs from a child care subsidy due to higher earnings, and her preference for developmentally enriching child care, Lakeisha uses a combination of licensed formal care and informal care for her children, sequencing as well as combining them. Studying in an applied field in high demand in the locality, Lakeisha moves between lucrative summer internships, which result in benefit termination, and impoverished academic semesters when she needs all her benefits to make ends meet. The transition creates immense financial and psychological stress. Although she regularly tries to coach her caseworker in advance of the transition, her luck runs out the second year she tries to ensure a quick and timely restart of her child care subsidy. Her caseworker certainly never informs her of Quick-Start, a program that is supposed to expedite approval of subsidies. On the contrary, approval and payment of the subsidy takes so long that her son loses his place in his child care center, a center with a good reputation that her daughter has also attended and at which she has priority because of its connection with the homeless shelter in which she lived previously. At the same time, also at the beginning of the semester, Lakeisha's best friend and informal caregiver dies prematurely of asthma at age twenty-seven. Hardly able to grieve, Lakeisha is concerned about the reaction of her six-year-old daughter, to whom the friend was an important caring adult, and her daughter speculates anxiously that the death resulted from her godmother's devastating workload, similar to that of her own mother.

During the summers when Lakeisha works a long-hours internship and tries to pick up additional classes at another university, she sends her children south to her mother for long periods of time. In fall 1998, she looks back over the past summer.

> I would prefer to put my children in day care here, but my mom takes over. My son is starting pre-K . . . and I had felt that he needed someone to work with him, and because I was always at school or work I didn't have the time and didn't think my mother really had the time in the summer. So I would have liked him to be enrolled in a day camp at the school or something. My son had just started talking, and that bothered me that I couldn't tell how he was feeling. But my daughter, she wanted to come home; it was "Ma, when you comin' to get me?" every other day. She wanted to play with her friends.

In early 1999, the longstanding behavioral problems of Lakeisha's daughter escalate. Lakeisha has noticed her daughter's destructive attention-seeking behavior before, but because of her heavy work requirements was unable to spend more time with her. Lakeisha now enrolls them both in therapy. When her daughter begins seriously disrupting her classroom, however, Lakeisha is compelled to spend more time at the school and at home with her. Her son also is diagnosed as developmentally delayed, after an assessment appointment that she is not able to attend. She feels she needs to redouble her efforts to ensure that teachers do not treat him as a hopelessly impaired and unteachable child. These developments with her children never reach her caseworker nor make an impact on her work requirements or benefits.

Toward the end of her degree program, Lakeisha describes her university experience as one of constant stress. In her demanding program, she has encountered race and gender discrimination, and her parenting responsibilities have been invisible and unaccommodated.

> Coming over here the road got real bumpy. . . . There's not many females in my classes . . . and if there was another female, I was the only Black. And that was really hard because . . . no one would answer my questions. One of [my instructors], you couldn't get around her courses. . . . Her hours were unbelievable. If you wanted to get to school at 6:30 in the morning, she would be glad to sit and talk to you. Well I got two kids and I can't get here between 6 and 8. I've had to withdraw from classes so many times it didn't make sense. I got Ws on my transcript where I'd gone all the way to December, thinking I'm gonna pass this class, I'm gonna do it, I'm gonna do it, beating my head against the wall. And I had to withdraw.

In fall 1999, never informed that Michigan has modified its work requirements for students in the last year of an undergraduate program and convinced that cash assistance and child care subsidies are unreliable and inadequate, she leaves cash assistance, works during the day, and goes to school at night to finish a modified degree. She tries to see her children in the early morning and before classes at night; she uses informal child care at night.

With relief and in triumph Lakeisha graduates in December 1999. But she is indelibly marked by years of anxiety, depression, and stress and haunted by the unknowable costs of these years on her children.

> I don't know if my struggle is gonna help us financially. As far as with my son, I don't think everything I went through will affect him. He's still too young. . . . But for my daughter, we've gone from counselors to psychiatrists, and a lot of different things. I really feel like she hates me. So I think that the only positive thing that probably will come out

of that is that she saw me go to school and work. Now hopefully as she gets older and we try to mend things back together, you know, hopefully after she has her own family she can look back like I did with my mom and say now I understand.

....

TINA

Twenty-five-year-old Tina is the African American mother of an eight-year-old son and a four-year-old daughter. She recently transferred from a local community college in a poor neighborhood to a four-year university to pursue a career in criminal justice.

Moving from a large urban area where she had family supports and ready access to child care from her mother and siblings, Tina has encountered harassment from her caseworker and severe child care obstacles since she relocated to the university campus. For many months, she was repeatedly refused child care subsidies by her FIA worker, which jeopardized her educational plans and almost caused her to drop out of school. Tina relates how she lost her first job at a large department store earning $7.85 an hour because the FIA worker did not approve her application for child care subsidies:

> I lost my first job because the worker would not give me child care. . . . I had brought my daughter to work with me. I know I shouldn't had done it . . . but I missed so many days that they told me the next time I missed a day they were going to fire me. I was a cashier. . . . I set my daughter on the bench, and you know at the time she was four years old. . . . The manager she told me you can't bring your child to work and stuff . . . so I got terminated from my job. . . . So then I went to the Work First Program and the Work First counselor called my worker and she said, "Well we can't give her day care until they verify employment and she gets a receipt for a first check"!

Terminated from a job because she has been refused child care subsidies, Tina finds herself caught in a bizarre Catch-22 as she is now told she has to have her employment verified before she can receive any child care subsidies! After being informed of her rights by other student mothers on campus, and with help from a local advocacy group, she enrolls her child in a campus child care center and takes a campus job. While the pay is low, $6.00 an hour, there are many benefits: she is close to her daughter's child care center, her older son's school bus drops him off on campus near her work site, there are flexible hours, and her supervisor is very supportive.

However, she still does not receive her child care subsidy and the child care center tuition bill mounts to $800:

> I mean it's just like such a struggle to deal with them. . . . I told her (the FIA worker) I want a hearing because I called the lawyer and he said I'm entitled to it (the child care subsidy) as long as I'm working . . . and then the next week the FIA paid some of it—but the lawyer said even if it goes back I'm still entitled to it because it's their fault and stuff and I asked—did she want to talk to the lawyer about it? And then they added more units to my child care. You know there are so many things, so many obstacles you gotta go through just to get $2.50 an hour which don't cover near the whole day-care cost!

Only after Tina seeks advice from local advocates and demands a hearing does her child care subsidy get approved, almost four months after her initial application. Because the subsidy was delayed, she has had to take out extra loans to pay for child care. When her daughter's child care subsidy is finally paid, it is already summer and her son is out of school and also needs child care. One of Tina's relatives offers to provide summer care in Tina's home and once again she applies for a child care subsidy—$1.60 per hour allowed by FIA for her son—and the same cycle repeats itself:

> I asked them for day care for my son and she was like, "Well you need to fill out these forms . . . and I need verification that you're in school." So I sent them my confirmation course and I sent them a schedule and I do everything they asked me to do. Then she says I have to send verification of my report card to show that I completed the semester. I send it and then she said they need more information . . . and then she sends me another form out . . . and it's the same form I filled out before, and she says that she needs a copy of it. . . . I mean I don't know how many times they need me to fill out the same forms, it's just ridiculous! I had to tell her again that I want a hearing, and I talked to the lawyer and then she went on ahead, and approved the day-care money for my son.

As the fall semester approaches, Tina relates how her FIA worker actively discourages her from working on campus:

> I tried to explain to the worker everything is centered around here. If you get a job outside you have to have transportation . . . but I keep telling her it's the convenience . . . but she keeps saying I should be looking for a better job . . . but to my mind this job is doing what it's supposed to do. It's helping me out a whole lot. . . . It's on campus and I have really good employers—like if my child gets sick, they will

come to my class and tell me, and they picked up my daughter for me—I mean they are real good . . . and they really support me being in school, and my employer, she said to me when I was really down, "Hang in there . . . it will be so much better for you and your kids when you graduate . . ."

Not only has Tina experienced constant harassment about her on-campus job, but her worker has also disregarded both her work and school schedules when setting up bi-monthly home visits, creating another source of ongoing stress for Tina. On numerous occasions, the FIA worker has sent a notice to Tina informing her of a mandatory home visit during the time that Tina attends class or is working.

As Tina struggles to balance the demands of work, school, and parenting, she expresses concerns about her falling grade-point average:

I made the dean's list at the community college but here I'm just struggling to maintain my grades. . . . I'm doing fifteen credits and my GPA it's gone down now from 2.8 to 2.6, and I'm so uncomfortable when that happens. . . . I want to be in school and I want to graduate and get a real job so I can support my family.

Tina's time demands are enormous and she describes herself as chronically tired: some days they come home at six and she "just falls asleep" and the kids eat cereal or microwave their own dinners and "I wake up at 10 o'clock, and they're on the floor sleeping. . . ." But despite the exhaustion, she struggles to maintain an active parental involvement in their lives:

There are days when I am so tired but usually if I have enough energy I'll fix them something to eat, and then I'll send them to bed at about 8:30 and then I'll go to sleep, and I'll wake up in the middle of the night to study. I study at work, I study right between classes, I study while in class. . . . Tuesday I've got Girl Scouts for my daughter until 7 and on Wednesday my son's got Boy Scouts. . . . I like to do activities with them to make up for the fact I'm not with them, so I try and spend time with each one of them individually. . . . On weekends we go to the library or stuff . . . that's our family trip—to the library so they think it's cool because there's computers there, and I study while they're on the computer. . . .

It is apparent that, despite scarce financial and time resources, Tina's children are doing well in school. Both children have already developed an early awareness of the importance of education in their mother's own life, and Tina describes her sense of pride in her children and in their images of her:

They are both really good kids and they talk about going to college now—they're like, "when I go to college," and I think my whole life has had an impact on them—they see me struggling, and it's like I'm leading a pathway down so they can follow because they are always talking about college. . . . My daughter, she always asks me when is she going to college, and I'm like, "Well, after kindergarten you got to go through the first through twelfth grade and then you can go to college.". . . And my son, he is at school with kids whose parents are professors, you know, and they have real good jobs, and I want him to be around that environment.

Tina also relates the impact studying has on her children's literacy development; she describes how they all read when she is studying, and her daughter, who just started kindergarten in the fall, is already reading:

I think they see me, and they do it. Because I read all the time. I love to read. And so both my children read, my daughter especially. She loves books, you know. And we turn off the TV, and we'll all just sit there and read.

Tina is the first in her family to go to college; she grew up on welfare and she determinedly pursues a different future for her children, even as she constantly worries about her grades, mounting debts, precarious child care subsidies, and constant threats of termination from her worker. Yet for Tina, escaping her life of poverty by completing her education and bringing her children up with a vision of a different world is a compelling passion:

I've seen people that I was like, and I cannot believe I used to live like that. . . . I want to be able to provide for my kids and give them things my mom couldn't give to me. . . . I refuse to let my kids see a food stamp. . . . I refuse because when we were little it was all right to go to the corner store with food stamps but now I don't let them see them or touch them. . . . That is not how I want to live. Every time I just want to stop and not go to school—it's like, OK, I came all this way and I gotta do this . . . my kids need a chance to grow up different!

....

SUSAN

Susan, a White woman in her early thirties, is the mother of two girls, aged six and five. She was forced onto welfare by lack of child-support payments, lack of a college degree, and an inability to work steadily because of the needs of her six year old, who suffers from a rare and dangerous skin disorder. Susan, under Michigan's 1996 welfare plan, receives benefits but is exempted from work requirements because her six-year-old daughter receives Supplemental Security Income (SSI) and needs parental care. Because her disabled daughter's care needs are only intermittently intensive and college schedules afford considerable flexibility, Susan begins to train to be an early-childhood and elementary school teacher, receiving honors in a community college program. She then transfers to a four-year degree program where she is an excellent student. Her caseworker nevertheless harasses her because of her educational objectives and pressures her to go through Work First and meet work requirements despite her official exemption. In April 2002, following changes in Michigan's Social Welfare Act, she faces withdrawal of her exemption from the work requirement.

Susan explains her attempts to provide for her family's basic needs through the FIA and other public agencies after her divorce:

> When I applied for assistance, I checked off every box available. My worker was very annoyed, because she said she would have so much more work to do to assess my eligibility. I was able to receive Medicaid for myself and the two children. My oldest daughter was also eligible medically and financially for SSI but was delayed in receiving it seven months because of false information my ex-husband supplied to my SSI worker. My ex-husband is $14,000 behind in child support, and with his sporadic payment history, I have to sign my child support checks over to FIA to receive cash assistance on a regular basis. Since my oldest daughter receives SSI, she cannot also receive FIA, so the child support check is cut in half. . . . My ex-husband has an income-deduction order against him to collect the child support from his employer, but since it's he and his wife who own the business, they just don't abide by the order, and nothing is done to them. . . . But if my ex-husband does make a payment, my support is decreased in all areas. If he doesn't make any payments after my support has been decreased, I will not receive enough assistance to make ends meet for the month, since my income test is from two months before. . . . My experience has been one of anxiety, humiliation, and a never-ending uphill struggle. It's a constant battle to receive enough assistance to survive on. If I didn't constantly keep on top of my workers, overcome the anxiety of talking with them on the phone, and keep up with mountains of paperwork that need to be submitted, I would definitely fall between the cracks.

Despite her exemption from the Work First program and work requirements, Susan is ordered to Work First several times, and Work First discourages her education:

[Work First] didn't know what to do with me or where to send me. When I told them I was attending college, I received a negative reaction. They told me they supported their work training but had no room for college. When I said that didn't make sense, I only received blank stares. I couldn't understand why college was not supported. If people were allowed to receive a good education, they would leave the welfare system. Work First and FIA personally resent that I am going to school and see themselves as not having the same chance. They want me to go to their skills classes and take a job at McDonald's or K-Mart. Work First told me they never approve college to count towards the work requirement. Now Work First tells me I should never have had an exemption from the work requirements. FIA used to do the exemption themselves, but my worker says she no longer has the power to exempt me based on my daughter's disability.

Thus, the April 2002 welfare changes are not only being aggressively implemented, but also lead workers, through their retrospective misconstruction of the policy, to imply that Susan had received something she neither deserved nor was entitled to, thereby delegitimating her previous use of her time for education.

Securing child care for her two daughters has been especially difficult, and in the last years of her education program, Susan is approaching the coming semesters with very heavy time commitments and increased child care needs. This is precisely the sort of situation for which the 10/10/10 program, the acceptance of internships as meeting work requirements in full, and the availability of child care subsidies for hours in class might alleviate stress, but with a (somewhat tenuous) exemption from work requirements and the implementation of 10/10/10 in disarray, Susan is told she cannot receive child care subsidies as she approaches the last calendar year of her program.

Workers have told me my applications weren't complete when they were. This past semester I have been told that I don't qualify for child care because I'm not working, so I have had to schedule my classes back to back while the girls are in school. But I can't continue to take all my classes and do all my work when they're in school. I need child care to continue school during the spring term (my classes go to June 25 and their school ends June 6) and summer, so I can finish, and I need child care during their school holidays, like the Easter break. In spring, I have to take a daytime class, do 120 hours of education-related community service, and take a night course. I'll be ready to do my full-time student teaching in winter 2003. I don't see how I can do this without child care.

Susan is acutely aware not only of how important her education is, but also how difficult it would be for her to maintain regular attendance at a low-wage, inflexible job especially in view of her daughter's disability. Her six year old's skin disorder involves ongoing, costly, and disruptive medical treatment. As a result of her medical problems and physical disfigurement, the child also requires extra social and psychological support and intervention. Susan has to spend three or four weeks at a time with her daughter during and after her many surgeries, and she has frequent doctor's appointments. Her educational schedule accommodates these long periods of medical support and her shorter appointments, but low-wage jobs with limited flexibility would not. Susan is also careful about child care and school settings, sensitive to her daughter's need for acceptance and support. Her daughter has special physical needs but so far no behavioral or psychological problems, and Susan feels that her presence and engagement with her child have been important. A professional teaching job, she is sure, would allow her the temporal and financial resources to meet the needs of her two children. However, Michigan's policy requirements and implementation practices—forcing parents of disabled children to work forty-hour weeks, devaluing post-secondary education, poorly implementing the 10/10/10 program, and withholding child care subsidies—endanger her family's survival and threaten her potential public contributions.

WORK FIRST, EDUCATION LAST

These stories of student mothers fighting to survive under the welfare regime show that work—any work, no matter how unproductive or at what social cost—forms part of the coercive environment that welfare-reliant single mothers must confront as they attempt to pursue their educational aspirations. The mothers in our study, who were both highly motivated and academically successful, were consistently coerced into attending mandatory Work First orientations and harassed to find employment in the low-wage service sector, in jobs that, as one student mother put it, "guarantee I'll stay in poverty forever." The continuing pressure exerted by caseworkers on student mothers to find low-wage work for twenty hours or more frequently undermined their academic success and capacity to stay in school and threatened their family stability.

All the women in our study encountered routine violations of even their limited existing rights that would have helped them receive an education, improve the well-being of their children, and reduce their family stress and instability. They were faced with withheld information—"don't ask, don't tell" policies—and misinformation conveyed with great authority and sometimes backed by punitive sanctions. They encountered concealment and misinformation about educational options, enforcement of excessive work requirements, improper denials and slow payment of child care subsidies, concealment of information about available support services, random punitive cuts in benefits and post hoc denials of disability waivers, and continuing threats, surveillance, and harassment—so that as Gwendolyn Mink puts it, the welfare legislation of 1996 "removes poor single mothers from the welfare state to a police state" (1998, 133). They were not informed about using internship experiences to meet their work requirement, nor as of October 1999 of the 10/10/10 legislation that permitted ten hours of class time, ten hours of study time, and ten hours of work in the last year of a terminal degree. Many were told that work-study jobs would not count toward work requirements, or that their work-study earnings would decrease their benefits eligibility. Other vital information, including information about child care subsidies, was also withheld from student mothers, exacerbating their stressed family lives and contributing to family instability. Because all had children under the age of six, federal law specified their mandatory work requirement as twenty hours;[3] yet workers were either uninformed or they willfully harassed their clients and enforced excessive requirements under the ever-present threat of benefit termination, frequently sabotaging educational progress.

A critical, ongoing problem encountered by these student mothers involved access to good-quality and affordable child care. The obstacles encountered in accessing child care subsidies from the FIA included outright denials, inexplicable subsidy reductions or cut-offs, slow start-up and late payments, and inaccurate under-calculation of subsidies; and all these obstacles contributed to a tenuous and unstable family situation with frequent damaging effects on their young children. In addition, many mothers felt powerless: as parents they were denied the authority to make judgments in the best interests of their young children because they were forced to work long hours in addition to attending school. Mothers of children with intensive needs, such as Lakeisha and Susan, found little policy flexibility or sympathy among caseworkers and case managers, who insisted that they maximize work hours regardless of family circumstances. Stressed and stretched parenting, few outside resources, limited support networks, and lack of time all took a psychological toll on the student mothers in our study.

The multiple barriers to women's pursuit of post-secondary education pose a striking paradox. On the one hand, current Work First policies and practices have created escalating pressures on low income women to find jobs—jobs that are typically unstable, low-wage, and odd-hours—under severe threats of sanctions and benefit terminations. On the other hand, these Work First policies and practices threaten post-secondary educational access and opportunities that could ensure long-term economic self-sufficiency for the women and their families. Work First policy fails to see the economic and social realities of poor women's lives: the difficulties of finding family-supporting jobs; the problems of scarce, inadequate and inaccessible child care and limited time for parenting; the daily stresses of functioning with very few public or family resources; and multiple responsibilities. Current welfare policy deprives poor mothers of access to post-education, as if they are incapable students undeserving of the opportunity to transform themselves. Yet student mothers nevertheless claim their autonomy and right to education as they fight—often successfully, sometimes not—to stay in school under Michigan's welfare-to-work regime. They are making strategic decisions to ensure long-term self-sufficiency, and they are fighting for a different future. They resist and sometimes prevail, even though policies frequently ensure they will fail.

NOTES

1. Under PRWORA (1996), to receive their full TANF federal grant, states must demonstrate that a certain percentage of the welfare caseload is working. In 1999, for example, the requirement was 35 percent of the caseload. However, a caseload-reduction credit lowered a state's requirement by the amount its welfare rolls have fallen since 1995. In Michigan in 1999, the state qualified for a 39 percent reduction in its requirement. Because 39 percent was larger than the required 35 percent, Michigan essentially had no federal work-participation requirement. Michigan, therefore, could have redirected many recipients into education and training without any federal penalties.

2. This chapter is a revised and updated version of an earlier study, "Struggling to Stay in School: Obstacles to Post-secondary Education Under the Welfare-to-Work Regime in Michigan," published by the Center for the Education of Women at the University of Michigan 2000.

3. As of 1 April 2002, the work requirement increased to forty hours per week for all recipients, including those with infants twelve weeks and older.

REFERENCES

Bernstein, Jared, Elizabeth C. McNichol, Lawrence Mishel, and Robert Zahradnick. 2000. *Pulling apart: A state by state analysis of income trends*. Washington, D.C.: Center for Budget and Policy Priorities and Economic Policy Institute.

Coalition for Independence Through Education (CFITE). 2002, February. Access and barriers to post-secondary education under Michigan's welfare to work policies: Policy background and recipients' experiences. Available at http://www.umich.edu/~cew/pubs.html.

Danziger, Sandra K., Mary Corcoran, Sheldon Danziger, and Colleen Heflin. 2000. Work, income and material hardship after welfare reform. *Journal of Consumer Affairs* 34:6–30.

Henly, Julia R., and Sandra K. Danziger. 1996. Confronting welfare stereotypes: Characteristics of general assistance recipients and post-assistance employment. *Social Work Research* 20(4):217–226.

Institute for Human Services Research. 2001, 15 March. *Report on former Work First participants: Fiscal year 2001*. Report prepared for the Michigan Department of

Career Development and the Michigan Family Independence Agency. Available at http://www.mfia.state.mi.us.

Kahn, Peggy, and Valerie Polakow. 2000. *Struggling to stay in school: Obstacles to post-secondary education under the welfare to work regime in Michigan.* Ann Arbor: University of Michigan, Center for the Education of Women (CEW). Available at http://www.umich.edu/~cew/pubs.html.

Michigan Kids Count. 2001. *Data book 2001: County profiles of child well-being.* Lansing: Michigan League for Human Services.

Michigan League for Human Services (MLHS). 2001a, September. *FIP caseload trends overstate good news for Michigan's poor families.* Lansing, Mich.: MLHS.

———. 2001b, September. *A snapshot of family well-being: A focus on Michigan.* Lansing, Mich.: MLHS.

———. 2001c, October. *Economic self-sufficiency in Michigan: A benchmark for family well-being.* Lansing, Mich.: MLHS.

———. 2002a, March. *Bimonthly bulletin: Wages, work and welfare.* Lansing, Mich.: MLHS.

———. 2002b, April. *The erosion of the cash assistance safety net in Michigan.* Lansing, Mich.: MLHS.

Mink, Gwendolyn. 1998. *Welfare's end.* Ithaca, N.Y.: Cornell University Press.

Thompson, Lyke. 1995. The death of general assistance in Michigan. In *The politics of welfare reform,* ed. Lyke Thompson and Donald F. Norris, 79–108. Thousand Oaks, Calif.: Sage.

Chapter 4

Connecting and Reconnecting to Work

Low Income Mothers' Participation in Publicly Funded Training Programs

Frances J. Riemer

I talked to all the important people in my life and decided I want to become an LPN. I don't know much about schools. . . . I'm thinking of going to that LPN program in town. But I don't know how I'll do it. I'll probably have to go back on welfare to go back to school.

—Dina Haskell, nurse assistant, Church Hall

Dina Haskell, twenty-eight and a single mother from the inner city, worked as a nurse assistant at Church Hall, a for-profit nursing home nestled in a tree-lined upper-middle-class suburban neighborhood on the northern edge of a large port city in the eastern United States. Dina, Joan Ford, and twenty-one other women came to Church Hall through an often-advocated antipoverty strategy, the linking of inner-city job seekers to available jobs outside their communities. Grounded in a hypothesis sometimes called geographic mismatch, the employment strategy was based on the belief that jobs for the unemployed are available but are located in areas neither known nor accessible to inner-city dwellers. In this particular story, the Department of Public Welfare (DPW) assumed a matchmaker role for the nursing home, recruiting a total of 140 women from the welfare rolls for nurse-assistant positions over the twelve

To protect Dina, Joan, and the other women in this chapter—welfare recipients, trainers, employees, and employers alike—they all have been given pseudonyms. Many of the individuals occupied low-wage, low-status jobs, and they often reminded me of their precariousness in the workplace. To avoid any risk of their losing their jobs, I made all attempts to maintain their anonymity. In the same vein, the names of government officials and the workplaces have also been changed.

months in 1992. Of those, Dina and Joan were among the selected few offered employment by the nursing home.

Finding both work and the opportunity to become state certified as registered nurse assistants had initially been godsends to Dina and Joan. Each had been desperate to get off welfare and back into the workforce and, like most welfare recipients, each had skills and prior work experience.[1] Dina had attended a state university in the South for one year after high school and then had worked in a series of jobs, including as a receptionist in a doctor's office and as a bookkeeper at a furniture store. When her first daughter was born, she juggled two jobs, working as a part-time private-duty nurse and a claims processor for an insurance company. But after her second daughter was born, she went on welfare and soon found herself in a downward spiral of poor, single motherhood, with no income, too many children to support and, for a few months, without a place to live: "And then I end up having another baby. . . . But when I decided to go back [to work] that's when I said all right, now I need a trade." Joan Ford, on the other hand, had a long work history in nurse-care facilities that dated back to her teenage years. She had also attended classes at Private Training Corporation (PTC), a for-profit proprietary school downtown that offered training for nurse assistants, data processors, and security guards. "I have a lot of experience, all in nursing homes," Joan explained. "I went to school to be a nurse assistant. PTC. . . . for six months. I was a straight-A student, on the president's list." When Joan had completed training, however, she quickly discovered that because her studies at the proprietary school hadn't come with state certification, they didn't translate into a job. Finding herself on welfare with a $3000 tuition loan to repay, she welcomed her case manager's referral to Church Hall. "It upsets me that I found out on my own about going to PTC. I didn't know no better. The best I can do is start paying on that loan." Neither Joan nor Dina had been able to put the pieces of a job, state certification, and day care together on their own. With DPW's help, they became nurse assistants, and with the state certification Joan acquired on the job at Church Hall, she was also assured the continued possibility of work.

Yet despite their initial optimism, Dina and Joan soon found themselves in the same position as that of former welfare recipients across the country: in jobs with wages hovering around the poverty line, with bills unpaid, and with limited prospects for upward job mobility (Boushey and Gundersen 2001). In conversations about improving their workplace status, both women, as well as the other nurse assistants employed at Church Hall, talked about the desire to return to school. Over and over again I heard women offer comments like, "I'd like my RN. And I was a straight-A student"; and "I want to go back to school. I won't do LPN. I'd go for my RN"; and "Ever since I was a little girl I wanted to be a nurse. I want to go on to RN." Given the $6.50-to-$10.00 wage differential between licensed practical nurses (LPNs) and nurse assistants, and the $9.00 to $12.00 between registered nurses (RNs) and nurse assistants, these academic plans made sense. But although applying to go back to school was a constant theme in the women's conversations, like Dina, virtually no one was able to accomplish the goal.

This chapter provides a closer look at why Dina and Joan, like so many other women who have left welfare, have had such difficulty moving forward professionally, and why, despite their motivation, hard work, and best intentions, they have been unable "to escape poverty" (Tweedle, Reichert, and O'Connor 1999, 2). The argument presented here concerns the women's inability to use postsecondary education to improve their positions in the labor force, and brings to the fore questions of who has access to what kind of post-secondary education and training (Riemer 2001; Strawn and Martinson 2000; Bloom 1997; Friedlander and Burtless 1995). Historically, not all individuals, much less all welfare recipients, have had access to the same post-secondary opportunities. In fact, for men and women on welfare, access to employment-related education and training has largely been based on gatekeepers' beliefs concerning what training is needed by whom and who is most appropriate for a particular job. These gatekeepers, whether they are policy makers, DPW case workers, or training providers, ground their assumptions in shared beliefs about men and women, about skills and potential, and about needs and concerns. And for poor women like Dina and Joan, training has been positioned by official gatekeepers and local commentators not as skills upgrade but as a way of inculcating work-appropriate behaviors.

The chapter begins with the stories of Dina, Joan, and the other women who moved from the rolls of Aid to Families with Dependent Children (AFDC) to jobs as nurse assistants in a suburban long-term care facility. Their stories portray the struggles to negotiate official beliefs about what low income mothers need and deserve in educational programs and workplaces. Most of the women were African American, all were urban, all were poor, all had children but few had husbands. For case managers, teachers, trainers, and supervisors, race, economic status, and inner-city origins amplified gender and became justification for the low-level training in which the women participated and the low-wage, low-status jobs in which they found themselves. The women's stories would have been different if they had been given opportunities to participate in challenging postsecondary education and then to assume positions of respect in the workplace, or if they had been encouraged and rewarded with a work upgrade for a continued investment in accessible training. But instead, they found themselves stuck in entry-level jobs in workplaces that offered neither opportunities for internal advancement nor avenues to pursue continuing education.

Although the chapter presents the stories of particular women who found themselves off the welfare rolls and in jobs as nurse assistants, they are not their stories alone. In fact, they represent the experiences of men and women throughout the country. Many former welfare recipients have found work after the 1996 passage of the Personal Responsibility and Work Opportunity Reconciliation Act (PRWORA), but like Dina and Joan, the jobs available to them have been primarily entry-level service or retail trade, with few connections to career ladders (U.S. Department of Health and Human Services 2000; Brauner and Loprest 1999). Nearly all of these occupational sectors pay poorly; most of the jobs are bottom rung. The stories of women like Dina and Joan help us understand why workers who find themselves in these low-wage, bottom-rung jobs have been unable to advance professionally. Becoming certified as nurse assistants helped Dina and Joan move into the workplace, but was insufficient to help them negotiate subsequent rungs of the job ladder. In policy conversations, the ability to access these ensuing professional steps has been either outside the parameters of the discussion or delegated to the rhetoric of "pulling oneself up by one's bootstraps." The assumption is that after a fast, short, training-related intervention gets them in the door to a workplace, individuals should be able to access career ladders on their own. Yet Dina's and Joan's experiences illustrate that old adage is simply that: a "truism" stemming from an ideology that casts blame on those for whom the system doesn't work.

The women's experiences are also part of a century-long morality tale in which single motherhood, intensified by a combination of race and the concentration of poverty in the country's inner cities, has been equated again and again with the aberrant behavior long associated with the poor. As the sociologist Ruth Sidel (1996, 167) wrote, "Over the past several years, but particularly since the 1994 congressional election, we have witnessed the systematic stereotyping, stigmatizing, and demonizing of the poor, particularly of poor women. They have been pictured as the embodiment of the characteristics Americans abhor—laziness, willful dependence on government, wanton sexuality, and imprudent, excessive reproduction." This chapter illustrates that the blurring of gender, social identity, and ideology has shaped a social-welfare tradition that continues to prescribe psychological rather than vocational interventions for the poorest of the poor, interventions that at best support women's transition from welfare to low-wage, low-skill jobs, but keep them poor by neglecting to offer training or educational assistance toward a job upgrade.

RESEARCHING CHURCH HALL

As part of an effort to understand what happens to men and women who move from the welfare rolls into long-term, steady employment, I visited Church Hall and three other workplaces several times a week during the two-year period from 1992 to 1993. I was referred to Church Hall by administrators at the Department of Public Welfare, and over the two years of visits I watched, listened, and documented moments of everyday practice in the work lives of the men and women employed there. I interviewed 110 men and women employed at the facility, including eighty-one nurse assistants, twenty-six supervisors, and three administrators. I observed activities in various parts of the facility, assisted in a range of workplace tasks, and reviewed company newsletters, public relations brochures, applications and personnel policy manuals, in-service and training materials, handouts, and workplace activity forms. I also observed nurse-assistant certification training sessions facilitated on-site at Church Hall, met with individuals responsible for designing and facilitating the DPW and Church Hall training models, and reviewed training curricula and materials with them. This initial round of fieldwork raised additional questions; I became curious, for example, about the work of nurse assistants, the workforce practices of nursing homes, and how Church Hall's salary structure compared with similar facilities. To address these emerging concerns, I randomly selected twenty-two, or 37 percent, of the sixty nursing homes in the city, and gathered by telephone information on their wage structures, hiring practices, certification training, and turnover of nurse assistants. Through phone calls and site visits, I gathered information on three other nurse-assistant training programs in the area, two of which were government funded. Because many of the nurse assistants who had been employed at Church Hall left to do agency work, I conducted interviews with administrative staff and surveyed two hundred nurse assistants employed at a temporary agency that staffed nursing homes with nurse assistants and licensed practical nurses. To investigate and better imagine alternative work environments for nurse assistants, I also conducted formal and informal interviews with staff and trainees at a worker-owned home-health-care company and observed thirteen hours of the company's training sessions for home-health aides. And finally, because I wanted to both assess the feasibility of nurse assistants continuing their education and understand more about the demands of LPN coursework, I conducted interviews with representatives of the three LPN-training programs conducted in and around the city.

THE DEMANDS OF SINGLE MOTHERHOOD

I learned early on in this research process that Dina, Joan, and nearly all the women who had been hired as nurse assistants at Church Hall were single mothers,[2] and that the identity defined the way they were perceived and treated by both DPW caseworkers and their supervisors at the nursing home. Mothering was indeed a large part of both Dina's and Joan's lives. They woke early to drop children at friends', relatives', or day care centers before work, worried about them during the day, and conducted endless arrangements for their after-school care. Joan described the morning with her two small boys. "I have to get up at 4:30 in the morning to get the kids ready and be out the door by 5:30. That's why I took the three-to-eleven [shift on] weekends only," she explained. She relied on relatives, friends, and community agencies to negotiate the demands of being a full-time mother with a full-time job. Dina Haskell had three small girls, and the Sisters of Mercy had become part of their extended family.

When Dina found herself homeless in the 1980s, the church had helped her move into temporary housing. She explained,

> I was on welfare at the time and I met a church. Not a church, a shelter, Project Rainbow. I know a lot of the Sisters there in the shelter, and they really gave me a sense of direction. They watched my kids, I got them in their day care, and while I went to school, they would watch them and welfare would pay. The Sisters help me now too. The Sisters of Mercy. They help me with my rent and food.

But although the lives of these single mothers were full of logistical demands and challenge, DPW job trainers and the supervisory staff at Church Hall essentialized the identity of single mother, ignoring the women's work and educational experiences and, instead, equating single motherhood with a lack of workplace knowledge and decorum. Dina and Joan were poor women with children, they received AFDC benefits, and as such, they were part of a status group that has long been held suspect in the United States. This constructed image in turn shaped the way employment training for the women was tailored. When Dina and Joan talked with their caseworkers about moving off welfare, the only training they were offered led to jobs as clerks, nurse assistants, child care workers, mental health aides, home health aides, food service workers, and security guards. Both women opted to pursue jobs as nurse assistants. Joan wanted to build on her previous training and work experience. Dina, like many of the nurse assistants at Church Hall, sought out the job based on an image of herself as caregiver. She explained, "If you look at it like this was your mother or your father or even yourself, one day I might need this help myself, that's the reason I do it. I look at it like I might get old and sick and be in a nursing home, and I would want somebody to give me the best care."

The training that accompanied this professional option consisted of a five-day orientation to work facilitated by DPW at its administrative headquarters and two weeks of orientation on the job at Church Hall. Both women also completed state-mandated certification training.[3] Dina was sent to a three-month Job Training Partnership Act (JTPA)-funded program by her DPW caseworker; Joan trained in house at Church Hall. According to the women, the training focused far less on skills development than on compensating for their perceived deficiencies. Yet, at least initially, the opportunity to obtain nurse-assistant certification and a job far outweighed any complaints that they may have harbored about the training. Through DPW's link with Church Hall, they not only reconnected to the job market after a prolonged absence, but by gaining their certification, they also guarded their place in the labor force and protected what labor economist Lester Thurow (1975) called their "market share."

Too Much Work, Too Little Money

Despite the short-term, limited nature of the training classes offered at both DPW and Church Hall, the women's initial appraisals of their move to Church Hall were overwhelmingly positive. They were happy to find work that they enjoyed in a facility that was clean and where the residents were well cared for. Joan explained that she liked Church Hall, because

> [N]obody's on your back, getting you to get your work done at a certain pace. Everyone helps here. I think this is one of the best places I've worked. They're not on top of you all the time. And everybody here's just nice; everybody has a positive attitude. If you're always pressured, it makes you want to quit.
>
> There's not so many bedsores. . . . They offer different schedules. I didn't get that at the other nursing home. Here you can pick weekends only. You just have a choice of hours. I like the benefits package here—sick days, vacations, health care. If they have good people, they don't want to lose them.

But Joan's enthusiasm about the facility quickly waned as she and the other women came to realize that regardless of the trainers' attempts to inculcate a version of "official knowledge" and their own best efforts at receiving it, they would always be perceived and treated as though they were uneducated, unknowing, and lacking within the workplace itself.

After just three months at Church Hall, Joan confided, "I don't like it, but don't tell them. There's not enough people. There are never enough people. The only thing to do in this place is go on for more schooling." Although getting back into the workplace had initially seemed like a big first step, Joan soon found herself stuck on the bottom of the facility's work ladder. Despite her efforts in DPW's orientation, in Church Hall's own training, and in her work on the floor, like the other nurse assistants, she found herself overworked, underpaid, and unable to shake the identity of "inner city," of "poor African American single mother," of "less than."

It wasn't the work that reminded Joan of her lowly status at the facility. She had known that a nurse assistant's work was hard. It was the kind of job African American women have been doing for the past two hundred years. As bell hooks writes in her essay "Homeplace,"

> Their lives were not easy. Their lives were hard. They were black women who for the most part worked outside the home serving white folks, cleaning their houses, washing their clothes, tending their children, black women who worked in the fields or in the streets, whatever they could do to make ends meet, whatever was

necessary. Then they returned to their homes to make life happen there. (hooks 1990, 42)

Like all the women at Church Hall, Joan was accustomed to taking care of "white folks." She had worked as a nurse assistant in other facilities and knew the responsibilities of a nurse assistant: waking, bathing, diapering, dressing, and feeding the old and the infirm assigned to her care. It wasn't the work but the lack of support from supervisors that reminded Joan Ford of her status at Church Hall. Whereas in an ideal world each nurse assistant was assigned eight to ten residents, the reality was that the facility was always short staffed, and a caseload of fourteen residents per nurse assistant was far from unusual. LPNs, RNs, and nurse assistants alike recognized short staffing as a problem, yet the hierarchy of work at the facility remained constant. Nurse assistants may have shared work and helped one another, but their supervisors, the facility's RNs and LPNs, never pitched in to help out.

This rank ordering of nursing staff at Church Hall played out in several ways, all reminding Joan and Dina of their subordinate status at the facility. Like workplace responsibilities, knowledge was segmented hierarchically. Although certified nurse assistants were intimately involved with their residents' daily welfare, their knowledge was neither recognized nor validated at the institutional level. Nurse assistants were not included in care meetings convened to monitor residents' status nor were they afforded any other regular input on resident care. The problem was that their knowledge was local. It concerned the everyday realities of residents' lives and was composed of particulars, not medical diagnoses. This distinction, separating local from official knowledge, was important because it explained and justified the facility's rigidly defined hierarchy. LPNs and RNs, not nurse assistants, were considered the professionals at Church Hall. They were involved in care meetings, dispensed medications, and talked in medical jargon about "impacted patients," "decubitus ulcers," and "lesions." Nurse assistants, on the other hand, had intimate knowledge of their residents, but not of their medical diagnoses. The segmentation of responsibilities and officially sanctioned knowledge at Church Hall paralleled differences in formal education, cultural group membership, and wages. Each of the facility's seven RNs had at least two years' education post high school, and the thirty-two LPNs had one year post high school training. The ninety nurse assistants had earned their high school diplomas and had either participated in short-term training programs at proprietary schools or were previously employed as a nurse assistant in another facility. The result of their educational choices was a vast differential in wages. The starting salary for an RN was $18 an hour and for an LPN $12.50 an hour. An uncertified nurse assistant who often had only six months less schooling than an LPN, however, earned a starting wage of $5.25 an hour, which increased to $6.00 an hour after passing the certification test. Consensus on the floor was that the assistants' pay was low, particularly for the weight of their workload. "Too much work, too little money," was the refrain among nurse assistants. In an attempt to make ends meet, the women lived with relatives or in subsidized housing in some of the worst of the city's neighborhoods. Dina and her three daughters found housing for "low income families" with the assistance of the church. The house was "in a bad neighborhood," in Dina's words, with streets strewn with litter, walls covered with graffiti, and corners occupied by omnipresent drug dealers. Other women lived in similar circumstances. Gladys Hopkins, a nurse assistant employed at Church Hall two years prior to Dina's arrival, told me that in her neighborhood she felt forced to carry a knife in her sock.

> I have to take a bus a quarter to five. It's dark. I was mugged two times. I came in with my eye hanging out. I don't know what I'll do with it there [pointing to her ankle]. In my neighborhood you have to have something to protect yourself.

A life of poverty was even more complicated when children were involved. Phyllis Hampton, working as a nurse assistant downstairs on Joan's floor, explained that she worried about her daughter all day while at work.

> I've been callin' all day to see if my daughter went to school. They took the phone off the hook. She goes to Southern High School. After the shooting [at the school] she said she wasn't going back. It's dangerous. My sister went there. It was dangerous then.

Heavy with the worries and demands of managing families alone in bad neighborhoods, the women found themselves stretched even thinner by working overtime, one of the only ways they found to augment salaries and pay bills. The facility was always understaffed, and the women all worked double shifts, from two times a month to two times a week, at time and a half their hourly rate. "You can do it if you know you're working for something," said Charlotte, a nurse assistant on Church Hall's second floor. "My mom says I live here." But although overtime improved wage levels, the extra hours resulted in hardworking, underpaid women working even harder, in equally stressful conditions, while leaving children alone or in the care of others for long hours of the day and night.

TALK ABOUT GOING BACK TO SCHOOL

Like their co-workers, Dina and Joan initially had positive first impressions of the facility, praising it for its cleanliness, camaraderie, responsive scheduling, and benefits package. But they quickly realized that they had few options for improving the working conditions that caused them so much frustration. Management did not hold meetings at which they could discuss wages, salary increases, or supervisor relationships, and no other avenues for airing complaints were made available in-house. The union offered a ray of hope, and during my visits to the facility, the Health Care Local made several attempts to organize the facility's nurse assistants. The women talked about the union with hope, but were convinced that its chances for success were negligible. "A union's good," asserted Mary Winston, a nurse assistant on the second floor.

> But we're afraid to do anything. I know from my last job they can't fire you for trying to get the union in. But they'll find something else. I've been here a year. I want to stay here long enough to get my vacation. They give you trouble with that. And unemployment, they'll fight you on that.

The union's efforts were not successful during my two-year tenure at the facility; the women's fears and management's strength left little space for organizers to maneuver.

Believing, then, that organizational change was improbable, the women began to see an additional investment in education as their most attractive option. As Joan asserted, "The only thing to do in this place is go on for more schooling." But like the welfare recipients in Catherine Pelissier Kingfisher's study (1996, 27), *Women in the American Welfare Trap*, although "the women's talk about education represents a status quo approach," they were unable to bridge the gap between the real and the ideal. Pelissier Kingfisher wrote,

> Protagonists in a status quo narrative accept and are willing to perpetuate the dominant system of which they consider themselves to be potential, if not actual beneficiaries. In this case, the dominant system consists of mainstream models of achievement and success. In short if a minimum wage job was not the answer to welfare, a well-paid job was, and the way to get a well paid job was to get an education. . . . As striking as the ubiquity of the perception that education was crucial to "making it," however, was the frequency with which the women began but did not complete educational programs.

This incongruity between belief and reality certainly held true for Dina Haskell and her colleagues at Church Hall. Although the women all talked about going to school, they also complained that the lack of both money and time impeded their plans. Thirty of the nurse assistants (34 percent) at the facility had studied in a nurse-assistant track at a proprietary school within the area. Still paying back loans, many women were unwilling to incur more debt. Everyone talked about saving money and making plans to start school; they explored all possibilities. Dina even talked about going back on welfare to access the additional support she needed to return to school.

> You know, I defaulted on my last loan, when I went to Norfolk State for that year. I heard you can pay it off, even $5.00 a month. And you have to pay for six months before you can get another loan. Or a grant. I was thinkin' of going to John Mellisant, that LPN program in town. But I don't know how I'll do it. I'll probably have to go back on welfare to go back to school.

In addition to funding, time was also a concern. As mentioned earlier, most women at Church Hall regularly worked double shifts to earn extra income, and overtime demands, combined with familial responsibilities particularly burdensome for single parents, left them fatigued and without time for school. "I'm interested in psychology," offered Nancy Henderson, a nurse assistant on Dina's wing who supported three young children on her own. "But where am I gonna get the time or the money?" she asked. For most women, this dilemma of time and money was unsolvable, and without easier access to funding and the support of a strong kinship network, school plans remained talk. As Carol Nelson, Church Hall's physical therapist, asserted, "I hear a lot of talk about going back to school, but it rarely seems to happen."

In the absence of legitimate avenues within the workplace to air and address their concerns, the women were left with few alternatives to improve their lot. Overworked, frustrated, and increasingly angry, leaving the job began to look more and more like their only avenue for change. The women's flight was an example of what anthropologist Michael Adas calls a protest of denial (1986, 68), when individuals "quit positions that are no longer considered tenable or abandon particular social systems altogether." And quit they did. Like the industry in general, Church Hall experienced a rapid turnover of nurse-assistant staff. According to the facility's director of nursing, the average length of time a nurse assistant stayed at Church Hall was "probably six months." A more formal review of staffing over a one-year period revealed a facility-wide turnover rate of 180 percent, which translates to a turnover of the entire staff of nurse assistants nearly twice every year. Dina's colleagues from welfare were no exception. One-and-a-half years after the DPW/ Church Hall collaboration brought twenty-four former welfare recipients to Church Hall, twenty-one, or 88.5 percent, had left the facility. In fact, four months after her initial comments of, "I think this is one of the best places I've worked," Joan was gone. "Joan, she came in at 7:00," explained Church Hall's nursing director. "The nurse gave her her assignment. She said she didn't like it and left." Joan's leaving wasn't a big surprise to anyone who knew her. She was clearly unhappy at Church Hall and after just four months on the job, she just decided she had had enough.

Employees at Church Hall, whether on the nursing, food service, or environmental staff, had opinions on why women like Joan left. Most attributed at least partial responsibility to the facility's low salaries. The difference between Church Hall's starting salaries and those offered at comparable facilities meant that once certified, Dina and Joan received an average of $1,123 a year less by remaining at Church Hall, a difference equaling nearly 10 percent of their total salary. In addition, they also incurred considerable expense traveling up to two hours each way from their inner-city homes to suburban Church Hall. A transit pass cost $58 a month (that is, an additional $698 per year) and an enormous amount of time every day. Although the opportunity to reenter the job market and become certified had drawn women to Church Hall, once certified, remaining at the facility cost them money.

Lester Thurow called training like Church Hall's nurse-assistant certification "general training," because it is of value not only to the facility itself, but also to other companies within the same sector. According to Thurow (1970, 91–92), when a company provides general training, "the individual would pay for it by accepting wages below his marginal product." In other words, although the women benefited from the facility's paid training, they paid for it in lower wages and transportation costs. At the same time that low salaries, compounded by a lack of voice and respect for their work, frustrated the women, the general nature of their newly earned certification enabled them to leave Church Hall for jobs that were located closer to home. But although this oppositional behavior might be interpreted as a rational act, an expression of power in the midst of powerlessness and an affirmation of identity by women who felt minimized at work, the outcome, in terms of improved conditions, was not significant (Giroux 1983). Most women moved to other nursing homes that paid only minimally more than Church Hall. Others found work in agencies that paid a higher hourly wage but neither ensured a regular full-time schedule nor offered benefit packages. But few found a way to move up. Like poor women throughout the United States, without an investment in additional post-secondary education, Joan, Dina, and their colleagues found themselves relegated to a revolving door of low-level positions, advancing neither professionally nor economically (Gladden and Taber 1998; Edin and Lein 1997; Harris 1997; Zucchino 1997; Schein 1995).

REMAINING ECONOMICALLY PRECARIOUS

Without a lens wide enough to encompass longer-term benefits of training and other supports in the lives of real men and women, policy makers, training-program staff, participants, and the general public alike continue to be misled about the move from welfare to financial independence. Without good jobs, defined in terms of livable salaries, benefit packages, and opportunities for continued professional growth, former welfare recipients like Dina and Joan have stayed poor, and their best efforts to advance result in a revolving door of low-wage jobs, in frustration and anger, and perhaps worse, in giving up.

Like DPW's orientation to work, most of the training available to welfare recipients has focused on pre-employment, on what Strawn and Martinson (2000, 31) call "soft skills . . . commonly defined as including problem solving, interpersonal, teamwork, and communication skills . . . thought to be a prime cause of low income parents' not sustaining employment." However, the problem here is that these services have been found best suited for individuals "without sustained work experience" and as part of a "mix of pre-employment and post-employment services, case management, and skill development." But for Dina, Joan, as well as the vast majority of welfare recipients, the problem was not transitioning into work. The women had each transitioned into work at least four times in their lives. Their problem had been the inability to transition into good jobs that pay livable wages and offer opportunities for career upgrading.

According to the rhetoric about welfare and jobs, the objective of transition programs for the poor has been to move men and women from welfare to entry-level employment. The assumption is that once in the door, they will be able to access career ladders on their own. However, making a successful first move from welfare, Dina and her co-workers at Church Hall soon realized that they remained economically precarious. They began to feel undervalued at work, and without access to continued post-secondary educational opportunities, they became frustrated and angry. Career ladders that had been offered as the putative answer to low-wage jobs were inaccessible at best. At worst, they were nonexistent. At Church Hall, women who had tested the waters of health care as nurse assistants were able to gain a valuable credential, their state certification, through DPW's initiative. DPW job developers served as transition, helping women return to the workforce and obtain this now essential government requirement. Their newly earned certification, however, did not allow them to advance in the labor queue as much as it secured their current status. And whereas its possession did prod many women to search out better-paying work, they soon found themselves stuck in a revolving door of low-paying, low-level jobs in other care facilities or temporary agencies. Aware of this professional treadmill, more than half of the nurse assistants at Church Hall voiced the desire to return to school; they believed that with support they could manage the demands of both LPN training and workplace responsibilities. Yet they received no support, and school remained inaccessible. Outstanding loans to proprietary schools, a disinclination to once again become indebted to an educational institution, and lack of time, energy, and disposable income rather than interest, motivation, or ability, impeded the women's real mobility. This next step was obscured not by personal deficit, but by structural barriers.

When supported transitions to work for poor women have included skills development, the training has focused on low-level skills traditionally associated with women's work. This tailoring of training around beliefs about appropriate occupational roles for poor women can be seen in the ways Private Industry Councils (PICs) funded training after the passage of the 1988 Family Support Act. PIC, the local representative of area businesses, had been the mechanism put in place to program federal JTPA funds into local communities. Funding what was traditionally considered to be high-level training, bookkeeping training for instance, or emergency medical-technician training, or photocopier-repair training, PICs were often criticized for their "creaming" of the most academically able of unemployed applicants for its participant pool. But with the passage of the Family Support Act in 1988, local PICs merged money from the JTPA with the Family Support Act to tailor efforts to AFDC recipients, the new priority of welfare reform. To better accommodate this new target population, PICs simultaneously scaled down their training menu. In their evaluation of the PICs' new training focus, Irene Lurie and Jan Hagen (1993, 104) wrote, "Over the past three years, it [PIC] shifted the emphasis of its programs and management style away from advanced training and performance-based contracting to facilitate serving greater numbers of welfare participants, a pool of individuals who are more difficult to place in jobs than the JTPA's traditional clients." Gone were high-end JTPA training programs; low-end training was contracted in their place. Downgrading its skills training to serve this new population of single female welfare recipients with children, PIC "spent nearly three fourths of its $6.3 million on skills contracts to train clerks, nurse aides, food service workers, and security guards," all low-paying, low-end jobs, a fact reported by K. Stark in the article "Private Industry Council Job Training Draws Fire" in the *Philadelphia Inquirer* on 26 May 1994.

This refocus embodied a belief that high-level training and subsequent employment opportunities were most appropriate for unemployed and underemployed individuals with some college education. Welfare mothers like Dina and Joan, on the other hand, were more suitable, or in official terms would better benefit, from initiatives like Church Hall's nurse-assistant training. These assumptions of case managers and social workers stemmed from their own learned beliefs about poverty, merit, and deficiency. They, like many professionals in the helping disciplines, had internalized theories about the poor that have been popularized by politicians, social theorists, and media representatives and have been sanctioned by policy studies and legislative acts. As Polakow (1993, 146) wrote, "Teachers [and in this case, social workers and trainers] do not live above their culture; they too are participants in the pervasive poverty discourse that conceals economic and educational inequalities, state-induced destitution."

CONCLUSION

If the aim of welfare reform is successful transitions to work and real worker productivity, continuous post-secondary educational opportunities must be made available to all individuals, not only to those perceived to have the appropriate cultural capital or who have informal support systems on which they can draw. Dina and Joan, like women across the country, pursued dreams, struggled with overwhelming responsibilities and staggering odds, and negotiated what it means to be a low income mother in this society. But despite their best efforts, in the eyes of case managers, trainers, and employers, they never stopped being poor women, whose problem was a lack of appropriate workplace behavior, rather than a lack of technical skills. Historian Linda Gordon (1994, 304) traced this essentialization of poor women back to the Progressive Era of the 1920s, when, she wrote,

> Continuing a Progressive Era moral-reform legacy, they [social workers] never entirely shed the belief that something more than lack of money was wrong with the poor, especially poor single women. They were convinced that the poor needed casework—counseling and rehabilitation—and they designed ADC (Aid to Dependent Children) to regulate morals and housekeeping.

It was not a lack of morals or housekeeping skills that kept Dina and Joan poor, however, but their inability to access and participate in the post-secondary educational opportunities that would allow them to move from the status of nurse assistant to that of LPN or RN. Assuming that moving onto the job ladder requires not just an initial step off welfare, but second and third steps as well, we need to investigate efforts that support women over a longer term and through a combination of idiosyncratic routes from welfare to work. Efforts like Chicago's Project Match (Herr, Halpern, and Conrad 1991) warrant our attention. Nearly all on public assistance, Project Match participants were supported during idiosyncratic routes from welfare to work that stretched for periods of three to five years. Some started with an entry-level job and then returned to school full or part time; others worked through a series of jobs; others attended college classes and worked part time; and yet others volunteered, obtained a GED, worked, and then attended college. Instead of limiting individuals to short-term interventions, the project allowed for the sustained support of different career trajectories for different individuals. Project staff treated participants as adults who, like the rest of us

> [P]rogress from one educational level or career activity to the next . . . supported and facilitated by other people, as well as by the norms and expectations, in the social world [we] inhabit. . . . They get feedback from family, friends, teachers, and employers, telling them they are on track, helping them feel good about themselves, and providing motivation to take the risk of trying next steps. They meet new people who provide new role models and sources of identity, information about next steps such as job openings or interesting educational or training

programs, and assistance with transitions from one activity to the next. (Herr, Halpern, and Conrad 1991, 27)

We need to imagine possibilities; we need to reframe the debate about women in poverty from a discussion about removing welfare recipients from the welfare rolls to a conversation about a well-integrated, universal system of post-secondary education that is inclusive rather than exclusionary, provides continued rather than discrete and fragmentary access, and draws poor women into the mainstream rather than segmenting, marginalizing, and stigmatizing them. Training and education should be positioned not as an entry condition but as a continuous process, not as the movement of individuals into work, but as a transformative experience that involves the negotiation of work and life outside work. Until we are ready to engage in this kind of thoughtful examination of the relationship between education and work, women like Dina and Joan will continue to connect and reconnect to work, caught in a revolving door of low-wage jobs. Despite all their efforts and motivation, they will remain poor, with few to no possibilities for career advancement, and little to no assurance of either economic security or the financial independence they so desperately seek and their families require.

NOTES

1. Research by Jo Anne Schneider (2000, 75) also revealed that over 90 percent of the welfare recipients she surveyed had "extensive employment histories. . . . Most had held between two and five jobs."

2. The concentration of single mothers at Church Hall was an outcome of the way the state implemented the Family Support Act, the federal government's 1988 solution for reforming welfare. Grounded in the belief that the welfare system fosters dependency among poor women, the Family Support Act was designed to prevent long-term reliance on Aid to Families with Dependent Children (AFDC), the welfare category for needy individuals with one or more dependent children under the age eighteen. The act increased federal funding for job-training programs, child care, and transitional medical benefits, and its Job Opportunities and Basic Skills Training Program (JOBS) required state and local governments to offer education, training, and employment services to individuals, that is, poor women, who were most likely to become long-term AFDC recipients. As Irene Lurie and Jan Hagen (1993, 147) explained in their evaluation of the JOBS program, "To meet the targeting requirement [for JOBS services], recipients in the target groups are given priority in the queue to leave the enrollment pool."

Each state tailored JOBS funds to best meet the needs of these constituencies, with most money funding short-term academic and job-training programs. The local welfare offices in this state utilized a portion of the funds to organize units focusing specifically on job development, training and resources, literacy education, and teen parenting. The Job Development Unit (JDU) was given the responsibility of developing links with area employers; its staff both responded to employers' requests for qualified applicants and canvassed for job openings through direct mail to employers. Church Hall was one of over fifteen companies with which the JDU collaborated, and that relationship became a stage for the construction of an identity of single motherhood in both training classes and the workplace.

3. Since the passage of the Omnibus Budget Reconciliation Act (OBRA) of 1987, the state required all nurse assistants be certified to "ensure that nurse aides have the education, practical knowledge, and skills needed to care for residents of facilities participating in the Medicare and Medicaid programs" (Center for Occupational and Professional Assessment 1989). However, to become certified, the women were required to complete a 75-hour training program, at least 37.5 hours of practical training under the direct supervision of an RN or LPN, and to pass both a written or oral examination administered by Educational Testing Service and a Clinical Skills examination conducted by an examiner from Red Cross.

REFERENCES

Adas, M. 1986. From foot dragging to flight: The evasive history of peasant avoidance protest in south and southeast Asia. In *Everyday forms of peasant resistance*, ed. J. C. Scott and B. J. Tria Kerkvliet. Totowa, N.J.: Frank Cass & Co. Ltd.

Bloom, D. 1997. *After AFDC: Welfare-to-work choices and challenges for states. ReWORKing welfare: Technical assistance for states and localities.* New York: Manpower Demonstration Research Corporation.

Boushey, H., and B. Gundersen. 2001. *When work just isn't enough: Measuring hardships faced by families after moving from welfare to work.* Washington, D.C.: Economic Policy Institute.

Brauner, S., and P. Loprest. 1999. *Where are they now? What states' studies of people who left welfare tell us.* The Urban Institute, no. A-32, New federalism: Issues and options for states. Available at http://newfederalism.urban.org/html/anf_32.html.

Center for Occupational and Professional Assessment. 1989. *Nurse aide (assistant) written-oral examination.* Princeton, N.J.: Educational Testing Service.

Edin, K., and L. Lein. 1997. *Making ends meet: How single mothers survive welfare and low-wage work.* New York: Russell Sage Foundation.

Friedlander, D., and G. Burtless. 1995. *Five years after: The long-term effects of welfare-to-work programs.* New York: Russell Sage Foundation.

Giroux, H. 1983. *Theory and resistance in education: A pedagogy for the opposition.* South Hadley, Mass.: Bergin & Garvey.

Gladden, T., and C. Taber. 1998. *Wage progression among less skilled workers.* Working paper. Chicago: Joint Center for Poverty Research.

Gordon, L. 1994. *Pitied but not entitled: Single mothers and the history of welfare.* Boston: Harvard University Press.

Harris, K. M. 1997. *Teen mothers and the revolving welfare door.* Philadelphia: Temple University Press.

Herr, T., R. Halpern, and A. Conrad. 1991. *Changing what counts: Rethinking the journey out of welfare.* Evanston, Ill.: Center for Urban Affairs and Policy Research.

hooks, b. 1990. *Yearning: Race, gender, and cultural politics.* Boston: South End Press.

Lurie, I., and J. Hagen. 1993. *Implementing jobs: The initial design and structure of local programs.* Albany, N.Y.: Nelson A. Rockefeller Institute of Government.

Pelissier Kingfisher, C. 1996. *Women in the American welfare trap.* Philadelphia: University of Pennsylvania Press.

Polakow, V. 1993. *Lives on the edge: Single mothers and their children in the other America.* Chicago: University of Chicago Press.

Riemer, F. 2001. *Working at the margins: Moving off welfare in America.* Albany: State University of New York Press.

Schein, V. E. 1995. *Working from the margins: Voices of mothers in poverty.* Ithaca, N.Y.: Cornell University Press.

Schneider, J. A. 2000. Pathways to opportunity: The role of race, social networks, institutions, and neighborhood in career and educational paths for people on welfare. *Human Organization* 59(1):72–85.

Sidel, R. 1996. *Keeping women and children last: America's war on the poor.* New York: Penguin Books.

Strawn, J., and K. Martinson. 2000. *Steady work and better jobs: How to help low-income parents sustain employment and advance in the workforce. A how-to guide.* New York: Manpower Demonstration Research Corporation.

Thurow, L. 1970. *Investment in human capital.* Belmont, Calif.: Wadsworth Publishing Company.

———. 1975. *Generating inequality.* New York: Basic Books Inc.

Tweedle, J., D. Reichert, and M. O'Connor. 1999. *Tracking recipients after they leave welfare.* Denver, Colo.: National Conference of State Legislators. Available at http://www.ncsl.org/statefed/welfare/leavers.htm.

U.S. Department of Health and Human Services. 2000, August. Temporary assistance for needy families (TANF) program. *Third annual report to Congress.* http://www. acf.dhhs.gob/programs/opre/annual3.doc.

Zucchino, D. 1997. *Myth of the welfare queen.* New York: Scribner.

Chapter 5

Supporting or Blocking Educational Progress?

The Impact of College Policies, Programs, and Practices on Low Income Single Mothers

Sally Sharp

Individual and collective social, economic, and political well-being in the United States have been and continue to be predicated in large part on educational access and degree attainment (American Association of State Colleges and Universities, 1998; Education Resources Institute [TERI] 1995, 1997; Murnane 1994). Although it is generally acknowledged that all individuals benefit from college attendance, Gittell and her associates demonstrate that the potential benefits of post-secondary education may be greatest for low income single mothers, for whom a college degree is a means of escaping poverty, achieving middle-class status, and undergoing personal development (Gittell, Vandersall, Holdaway, and Newman, 1996; Gittell and Covington 1993; Gittell, Gross, and Holdaway 1993). The most important benefit of post-secondary education for poor mothers may be that it interrupts the intergenerational transmission of poverty because the educational attainment of one generation strongly predicts future generations' educational and socioeconomic success (Geske and Cohn 1998; Gittell, Schehl, and Fareri 1990).

Despite these benefits for low income families, between 1970 and 1993 students from the lowest income quartile saw their chance of earning a baccalaureate degree drop from 16 percent to 10 percent of the chance of a student from the top income quartile (Mortenson 1993). This pattern of unequal educational attainment is influenced by a variety of public policies and social relationships. Low income single mothers in particular face an array of obstacles to both initiating and completing degrees—punitive welfare policy with extensive work requirements, lack of adequate student financial aid and family resources, child care problems, discrimination and racism, internalized stigma, indifferent or negative secondary school experiences, and lack of higher educational experience and support for post-secondary education among family members.

Using three institutional case studies, I examined whether and how college and university policies, practices, and programs facilitate the successful navigation from admission to degree completion of stressed low income single mothers. Do institutions mitigate obstacles to degree completion imposed by welfare policy and the everyday stresses of poverty? I studied three baccalaureate degree–granting institutions located in a Midwestern industrialized state with strong work requirements, low levels of cash benefits, and little public child care support for single mothers in school. At Small College (all names are fictitious), I interviewed four students who were single mothers receiving cash assistance and eleven faculty and staff; at Research University, eight student mothers and thirteen faculty and staff; and at Regional University, six student mothers and thirteen staff. I also reviewed institutional documents such as college bulletins, department reports, student newspapers, and campus flyers.

The single mothers on welfare I interviewed come to school with heavy burdens. They are disadvantaged by intersections of class, gender, and, when they are African American, race. (The students interviewed were either European Americans or African Americans.) The responsibility of providing for their children, even their adult children, is of paramount concern. All the women describe how their children are a driving motivation for college aspirations, a periodic barrier to their progress, and a constant demand on their time, financial resources, and energy. They struggle to feed, clothe, and house their children, and all endure the welfare bureaucracy, experiencing new bureaucratic impositions and requirements, intensified stigmatization, and often caseworkers' condemnation of their educational commitments. The women are the first in their families to go to college, with almost no prior exposure to the expectations, responsibilities, demands, and opportunities associated with college. They experience a range of support for their educational aspirations and efforts from family living in their household and extended family and peers. Several women describe how work colleagues, friends, children, parents, and partners disparage or even sabotage their efforts to go to college, and speak of having to remove these negative voices from their lives, sometimes by divorcing husbands or leaving the fathers of their children, in order to pursue a degree. Welfare-receiving women are often admonished for being single parents, yet many of these women choose to be single mothers to improve the socioeconomic future of their children. On the other end of the continuum are women encouraged by their families, who lend whatever resources of time or money they have.

Although colleges and universities have little influence on the degree and nature of outside support individual students bring to their educational settings, they can influence what happens to students once they enroll, shaping the quality of students' experiences and their persistence in degree programs. In

particular, institutions may deliver programs and policies to integrate traditionally marginalized and socially stressed student mothers into key aspects of college and university life: the academic domain, the core of the college experience
centered around the classroom and coursework; the social domain, the area of
college life in which students relate to their peers; and the financial domain, the
sphere of planning and acting to meet the economic costs of college while also
managing other costs of living.

SMALL COLLEGE

Small College is a private, religiously affiliated, formerly all-women's college
in the largest metropolitan area of the state. It has an undergraduate enrollment of one thousand students, who are 90 percent women and 78 percent
African American, with an average age of thirty-two. There are sixty-eight
faculty offering forty associate's and baccalaureate degree programs.

The religious congregation's original vision of "scholarly excellence, service
to the professions, and commitment to social justice" has been carried forward
in Small College's current mission, which is to help students acquire compe-
tence to understand and participate effectively in the evolving world; develop
compassion to care about and respect the work and dignity of people; and contribute to making a more just and humane world. Through all aspects of its
program, Small College and its staff seek to model the capacities it tries to en-
gender in its students, and the college remains geographically located in, and
committed to, its low income African American community. Small College
"believes that talent, not money, should open the doors of the College." One
college executive officer, a member of the religious congregation, says

> [T]he best of education is the most liberating. It's meeting the students
> where they are and moving with them to where they want to be. It is
> dignity for every student. . . . [Women on welfare who get an educa-
> tion] see their lives transformed. They have had their minds opened to
> the world beyond our neighborhood, which is often practically all
> women on welfare know. It is finding community in the classroom
> with people who are highly educated treating them as peers.

The college positions itself as a place where local low income, first-
generation, single mothers can have access to a college degree. It recognizes it is
serving a unique student population, including many women on public assistance, and it recognizes that its students need support to succeed. These under-
standings pervade all aspects of the college—academic, social, and financial aid
practices all reflect them. As faculty and staff describe it, Small College has "an
ethos of hope," where the business of the college is liberating people to do their

best and welcoming them into a community where one does whatever is possible to help others. Repeatedly described by students as a calm and peaceful place that allows students to focus on studying and developing themselves, the entire campus appears open to students. They feel as though they belong anywhere and everywhere, in departmental and student services offices, lounges, the cafeteria, and library, and that Small College is a second home. The college offers services and activities to accommodate the schedules and life demands of single mothers and working students.

The academic mission of the college is both to teach the liberal arts and to prepare students for a job. In the mid-1970s, the college received a federal grant to prepare faculty to teach older, underprepared, and first-generation students; although more recently hired teachers have not had the same formal training, the legacy of this training continues. Students enroll in a first-year seminar designed to introduce students to college in general and to the particulars of Small College, or as one administrator put it, "to get students involved, get students to know each other at the beginning, get students to know themselves better, get students to know the college better." On its single, compact site, Small College also offers academic support services including academic tutoring, a writing center, computer labs, and a literary roundtable—informal discussions led by students in which students relate the themes of assigned books to their lives. Faculty are responsible for monitoring student progress through regular advising appointments. Small College also runs a preadmission bridging program, a year-long series of courses to prepare students to begin college studies. The Office of Student Services administers a federally funded program created to support low income, first-generation college students and students with disabilities who have experienced academic and/or economic setbacks. A small program that serves 155 students including many women on public assistance, it links students with campus financial and academic resources, serves as an advocate for individual students, teaches students how to advocate for themselves, and monitors and supports their academic progress.

Most students characterize their experiences with faculty in and outside the classroom as special and unique. All students mention the respectful and nonthreatening atmosphere in the classroom, with some commenting especially on the value and meaningfulness of courses that prepare them for everyday life and work or give them important opportunities for self-reflection. Faculty members appear to actively and respectfully recognize who their students are. They are often available on campus, acknowledge students in the hallways, give students their home phone numbers, and immediately return calls when messages are left. Faculty members also call students if they have been missing from class and actively engage with them over course material and personal statements for further schooling and jobs. Jane describes the relationship:

> They help you along the way until you don't need their help. . . . They talk about how important it is to help your [fellow students], because

a lot of times you better understand what your [fellow students] need and think faster than the professors. . . . It's funny, 'cause when I start thinking negative, my professors aren't anywhere around [but] they just come into my head, like "Oh my God, if she knew what I was thinking, she would kill me," so it's like I hold a lot of value of what my professors think.

Already during the admissions process, Small College begins a dialogue with prospective students about on-campus support networks, emphasizing the importance of membership in a collaborative and supportive community. Staff talk with students about the importance of building relationships with their peers and faculty advisor as quickly as possible, and students describe a variety of ways in which student mothers support each other. One student describes a group of three women whom she met in her first year who "more or less were my support system. We helped each other. We talked about personal things, as well as academic. We were very supportive of one another. We had cookouts together. We would study together." The students describe an understanding that everyone has a responsibility to make these connections and help one another, "each one help one."

The college acknowledges that women's children are central to their lives and ability to succeed and actively integrates students' children into the life of the college. Instructors discourage students' bringing children to class, because they fear it will compromise their mothers' ability to pay attention and succeed academically. However, the campus offers affordable on-site child care during the day, in the evening, and during public school breaks, in a facility in the basement of the main classroom building. The college encourages the entire family to be part of the campus by hosting student activities such as dinners where everyone brings family or other supporters, and dinner costs only $2.00. In the summer they run an educational Kids' College Program. In general, administrators take a multigenerational approach and think of themselves as educating families.

The financial aid office is aware of the unique needs of its student body, including women on public assistance, for whom financing school is not as powerful a concern as simply meeting the day-to-day financial pressures to keep their utilities turned on, their children fed and clothed, and the family securely sheltered. Throughout the repeated shifts in welfare policy over the past two decades, the director of financial aid has been a liaison between the college, students, and their caseworkers, seeing it as his job to help students succeed. For example, although the college's work-study program was designed for students to work fifteen to twenty hours a week and was unable to pay for more hours of work per student, he decided to list on students' contracts the work hours necessary for students to remain eligible for welfare benefits and deflect any concerns the students' caseworkers might raise. Nevertheless, students struggle with an understaffed financial aid office, whose staff "deals with so many students they prefer not to be bothered [with individual problems]," according to one student. Although the understaffing of financial aid offices is a regrettable, widespread reality on college campuses, it is a noticeable lapse on a campus where so much is supportively personalized.

Small College also has a unique staff position, a financial counselor who is neither part of the financial aid nor the business office, but a student services staff member. She embodies Small College's recognition that traditional financial aid services only pay for school and fail to address many financial crises—such as unpaid utility bills or being behind on rent payments—that can interfere with college. She spends her working hours meeting with current and prospective students, talking with utility and mortgage companies, getting students into federal loan-consolidation and other payment plans, and locating emergency food and shelter. For students who face daily financial concerns over how to pay for food and keep a roof over their heads, the routine availability of free food on campus is a very supportive act. "They always feed us here. Every-day they're giving something away. I never go hungry," comments one student mother on public assistance.

RESEARCH UNIVERSITY

In contrast to Small College, Research University is a fragmented and sprawling university, with its main campus of over one hundred buildings spanning more than two hundred acres in the downtown area of a major urban area. It publicly describes itself as a leading research university committed to high standards in research and teaching while serving an "urban mission." The urban mission consists of faculty framing their research around local urban problems, of the university bringing to bear research findings on the local urban community, and of faculty and staff educating students from the local community, including those from lower socioeconomic groups in the city. However, it appears that what is paramount in the minds and practices of the higher administrators and many faculty is urban research rather than service to the community through teaching low income, first-generation students.

Research University has 18,500 undergraduates composed of about 58 percent women. The average age of students in the institution as a whole is twenty-nine. Only 29 percent African American, the campus struggles with racial issues; African American staff and faculty note that racism is "alive and flourishing" in several different ways, and African American students on welfare as well as some staff are distressed by a heavy presence of mainly White police officers, a presence, however, that reassures some of their White suburban peers.

Student mothers see Small College as a small, physically easily negotiated oasis of calm and solidarity that is geographically open to its surrounding low income community. Research University, on the other hand, is experienced as threatened at its boundaries and internally by the surrounding neighborhood; overwhelmingly large in terms of geographic expanse and numbers of students; and spatially and programmatically fragmented. Many students and staff feel students need a car to get to and around campus, although parking itself is a nightmare. The decentralized and fragmented nature of the campus compounds students' sense of having to negotiate an extensive and disconnected landscape to find information and assistance. Student mothers describe themselves as "left on my own," "detached" from other students, staff and faculty, "feeling like a number," and "not really knowing where to get help."

Unlike at Small College, students at Research University express frustration with what they see as the inaccessibility of faculty, faculty impatience and arrogance, and the utter lack of understanding of their lives that faculty, even those teaching African American studies, betray. Students describe some of their most meaningful courses as making connections between classroom learning and their lives, especially in psychology and sociology.

Research University has an academic support center, staffed with several full-time professional staff, over one hundred student tutors and thirty supplemental instructors, conveniently located in the undergraduate library and focused on helping students learn how to learn. However, none of the students I interviewed knew about this center. According to staff, faculty often viewed academic support offered through student services as "lowering standards" rather than as raising the achievement of stressed and underprepared students, a view that suggests a different attitude toward less-prepared students than that which prevails at Small College. When students have positive interactions with individual faculty, it is in the context of a smaller program or academic unit such as the interdisciplinary-studies program that specifically targets adult students who graduated at least four years previously from high school. In general, students find little academic guidance through the central advising office for undeclared majors and preprofessional students in four of the university's colleges. Some students benefit from advising services in the interdisciplinary program in the College of Adult Learning and in Project Eagle, a small program for women on assistance.

Although most student mothers describe their need for peer support, they have difficulty finding and sustaining relationships with other students. Two students I interviewed came to campus from the same community college, where they felt supported by their peers; they are shocked by their isolation at Research University, and a third student says the only people she knows are the custodians in the student center. Women in Project Eagle have met other supportive students, but they have difficulty sustaining contact partly because the program has no lounge or meeting area. Although the campus has a women's commission, it is relatively marginalized and focused on issues for faculty and staff women. The women's center, which is supposed to provide information on financial aid, personal counseling and child care, is a bulletin board and a couple of staff offices from which referral services are provided if students are able to discover the center's existence and initiate a request. Students are rarely in the physical vicinity of the office, and the office's approach to working with students is simply that they respond if students seek them out.

Everything about accessing financial support is difficult on this campus, a very stressful situation for low income mothers worried both about day-to-day survival and meeting college expenses. The student handbook emphasizes the family's primary responsibility for financial aid and Research University's inability to assure students that their full financial need will be addressed. It is nearly impossible to set up an appointment with financial aid officers, much information about scholarships remains hidden, and most students have negative experiences trying to get information from the office, sometimes resorting to other student services offices.

Some report humiliating negative encounters with financial aid staff. One student describes how when she became pregnant and was forced to go on welfare, she sought the advice of the financial aid office:

> They told me I should not be in school. They wanted to see my son's birth certificate, to prove I had a child. Another staff member just said women on welfare didn't belong in the university, and I would just waste my financial aid money.

Another student, who decided to decline a loan larger than the one she was initially promised, told the financial aid officer she had been forced to purchase her books with part of her welfare check. "How can you do that? I'm not paying taxes so you can use it to pay for books," the staff member responded. Students report that the financial aid office provides no outreach or systematic education around financial issues and no assistance in connecting with caseworkers, locating affordable housing, or dealing with emergencies.

REGIONAL UNIVERSITY

The city where Regional University is located, once a bustling manufacturing center, has been in sharp decline since the early 1980s. The large company that has dominated it has both shaped and abandoned the city. The tradition of easily available, high-wage jobs obtainable with little education still leaves a mark on the city and Regional University's students. An older generation of workers in the city may not see the value of a post-secondary education, yet the children of manufacturing workers do not have access to high-wage jobs in the factory. Students who are children of factory workers see their college degree as a means not only to a decent wage, but to a fulfilling existence and a substantive role in the world of work and the larger community not afforded by assembly-line work. Yet, the university experience is not at the center of the lives of many students, who are encumbered by family and work. Formally and informally the university emphasizes teaching in its mission, and it recognizes that it teaches "working students," that is, students who spend many hours of the week in paid employment, yet at many levels of the university there is an incomplete understanding of the daily lives of students, especially those who are low income parents.

Regional University currently offers one hundred undergraduate and eight master's degree programs to an estimated 6,500 students, all of whom are commuters generally living within eighty miles of the campus. Regional University is a compact, seventy-acre campus whose primary facilities are housed in seven buildings in the urban area's downtown, adjacent to the city's relatively abandoned main business district. However, the main campus buildings are really a block away from the downtown main street and are only accessible by entrances on the inside perimeter of the cluster, reinforcing the feeling, for a group of African American single mothers, that Regional University is "in, but not of" the community. The majority of students, 82.1 percent, are White and over the age of twenty-two, and about 64 percent are women. About half the students are taking fifteen credit hours or more, a heavy full-time load, and half are taking fewer hours. Most students are employed part time or full time, and many have family responsibilities.

Although the campus has some basic practices that potentially accommodate the schedules of a diverse, working student body, and women on welfare in particular—extended daytime student services hours, limited night and Saturday classes—single mothers describe their difficulty finding enough open classes at convenient times, the remoteness of the near-site child care center that operates from 7 A.M. to only 6 P.M., the library closing at 10 P.M. on weeknights and 5 P.M. on Fridays and Saturdays (unlike the library at Research University, which has a section that remains open twenty-four hours a day), and the lack of access to the food court and student center snack bar after 5 or 6 P.M. Students try to feel at home on campus, but with few comfortable social spaces and restricted access to services, most are forced to treat it as "strictly work, school."

Students have uneven experiences with academic advisors. Some feel mistrustful of faculty advisors because of incidents in which their needs have not been accommodated, whereas others appreciate advisors who have not only helped them decide on classes but coached them about how to relate to faculty. Regional University takes pride in being a teaching university, with small classes taught by faculty rather than graduate students. Students generally describe good instructors whom they have been able to approach. One says her professor is knowledgeable about welfare and education policy and took a special interest in her after she revealed she was receiving welfare. The faculty member informed her of opportunities to continue her degree, linked her with a fellow student who wanted to be of assistance, and even encouraged her to testify about her aspirations and experience at public hearings. Another student describes being in a seventeenth-century English literature class reading about the struggles of a poor, uneducated woman who taught herself to read, passed herself off as an upper-class woman, and tricked a member of royalty into marrying her. The student explains how this text and the instructor's approach to teaching allowed her to connect her personal struggles to larger social patterns and to see historical continuities in women's experiences:

> We are all the same. For women the struggles then are the same as they are now. Women don't make as much money as men do, even if you are well educated. And if you are a mother . . . there are all those disparities, all the house things and childrearing things are yours. Her story is in a different context, but it's the same. . . . This helped me see I was not an outsider. I got to see who I am . . . that I am somebody, and I have something I belong to.

Another student talks about how a faculty member managed to see her as more than a worthless, dependent single mother, treating her instead as a whole person with intimate family ties, academic ability, and potential. She says,

> They saw something in me, they pushed me. . . . They cared about me as an individual. I would talk with them, laugh with them, got to their office, and they'd ask, "How are your children doing, what are their names?" They showed they cared about me as an individual, not a number.

As at Research University, however, low income mothers appear to be marginalized by being women on what many see as a male-defined campus, often by being African American in a predominantly White campus environment, by being older women with children amongst teenagers, by being stigmatized as single mothers, and by lack of coordination and strength among programs that might assist them. On gender-integrated campuses, well-functioning women's centers often help to integrate women's experiences into the lives of the university and advocate for individual women, but at Regional University, the women's center had recently been drained of resources and shut down, and women faculty had battled for several years to try to reconstitute it without success. One staff member in a small equal-opportunities program directed toward African American students worked hard and effectively to mentor students, getting to know them individually, providing a one-person orientation and comprehensive support service for students who encountered her, supporting them as much as first-generation students as African Americans, and running a single-parent support group.

On the whole, however, students at Regional University seem to be moving through the college experience largely as individuals with limited if any connections to social networks of their peers and limited interaction with the campus beyond attending class and working. One student explains that because she does not get opportunities to socialize or talk about her schoolwork at home, she craves social interaction. Yet, her socializing is confined to being with other people in class before class starts. "You talk to who is next to you and stuff," she says. Another student explains that the campus is geared toward White students, and that White students are uninterested in the Black students like herself. At Regional University, the orientation process does not effectively build networks, and many students do not attend the orientation sessions that occur.

Students from Regional University consistently describe how important financial aid is to their academic pursuits, and they say that the financial aid office provides helpful service: "Financial aid has made paying for college a piece of cake." The financial aid office has maintained a working relationship with the Family Independence Agency in the county to link financial aid and welfare requirements, with staff assuming the role of advocates to ensure that students are getting accurate information from caseworkers and maximizing their opportunities under existing policy. The director had worked with a faculty member to send out informational letters to students who could be identified as welfare recipients to make students aware of their rights and offer himself and the faculty member as supportive and informed contacts. Like at Small College, the director was interested in adjusting the financial aid package to increase work-study hours for those low income students with work requirements. All of the students on public assistance work on campus as part of their financial aid and as a way of complying with work requirements. Their jobs keep them focused on school, provide welcoming campus spaces for them, and extend to them more work-hours flexibility than off-campus employment; in small ways these students' jobs provide them with a strong link to the life of the university and often to supportive individuals. Financial aid and student services staff also offered workshops on scholarships. The financial aid director, however, admits to not widely publicizing emergency funds available to students for fear "that every student would say they have special needs and come in and apply for it." He describes relying instead on a network of staff who know about the funds and can make referrals, a system that means students have to encounter the right individual at the right time to access funds they need.

PATTERNS OF VARIATION AND WHAT MATTERS

The experiences of single mothers on welfare do vary from institution to institution, though each institution is pluralistic, a combination of many different programs and individuals. Students with the most positive experiences are those at Small College, where serving low income mothers is an explicit part of the mission, effectively incorporated into programs and practices across all three key domains of college experience and function—the academic, the social, and the financial. The idea of service to low income mothers pervades the institution. Research University appears to depersonalize academic life, to set students adrift in a large, confusing, and sometimes poorly or passively functioning bureaucratic institution while faculty and administrators pursue an urban mission focused on research about the city, neglecting urban mothers trying to get degrees. Nevertheless, the interdisciplinary program and some of the ethnic studies programs try to support and integrate such students into smaller communities. Regional University is an institution in which students find few institutionally designed opportunities for social integration and guidance through the university as a whole; there is little systemic support for these particular students when they arrive on campus. But they have considerable support from financial aid services and individual faculty and staff; students encounter institutional agents who draw them into the institution, show them ways to navigate the university and welfare systems, teach them to advocate for themselves, and affirm their life circumstances through service delivery and in the classroom.

The results of positive institutional policies and of supportive institutional agents seem to be the integration of students into the college or university community, allowing student mothers to internalize identities as successful students (rather than seeing themselves as incompetent poor women), able to accomplish the academic and nonacademic tasks required for educational progress. The shift in social status from the negative stereotype of being a low income single mother, who is burdensome to society, to an intelligent, capable college student, who will contribute to society, is a powerful and compelling motivation for coming to, persisting in, and succeeding in college. Interacting with an institutional agent or program that teaches students how to be students and contributes to their sense of belonging to the educational community can be instrumental in transforming these students' identity. Many of the students describe how coming to college and finding institutional support were central to their feeling positively about themselves in general and about their ability to succeed in their educational endeavors. A connection with someone at the college or university means, as one student describes it, that she is being told, "'You can do it, just hang in there, I am behind you,' and then I internalize that too. Then it is like there is no stopping you." Another explains that the support she has received and has successfully translated into educational progress makes her feel "like I really have some self-worth. I always had to struggle and fight. My mother left me when I was eleven. Throughout my life I have been lied to, stolen from. Education empowers you. They can't take what I have learned. That's one thing they cannot steal from me." For a third mother on welfare, being a college student means,

Whenever people look at me, they see a positive influence as far as going to school, someone who is trying to make a difference in their career and in their life. . . . I think people see you differently being a college student. College gives me a sense of independence. My self-esteem is just wonderful. I feel so good about myself.

To be viewed as a contributing member of society and to sense the possibility of achieving one's goals are powerful explanations for what keeps many of these women from being overcome by their life experiences and responsibilities and what helps them fit into the college environment and persist in earning their degree, despite punitive welfare policy, child care problems and crises, day-to-day economic problems, gender and race discrimination, and negative family and peer voices.

It would be misleading to conclude that institutional size and demographics dictate the degree of institutional integration of low income mothers. Whether integration occurs is more an issue of institutional commitment, conscious program design, and everyday staff and faculty practices such as at Small College. A large, diverse institution can construct communities that teach first-generation students how to navigate the institution and facilitate access to social, financial, and educational resources, and Regional University has made attempts in this direction. The classroom domain, a domain in which all students necessarily participate, remains largely autonomous of university administrations, although the culture of the institution influences faculty recruitment and classroom practices. Pedagogies in all subject areas that connect systematic knowledge and skills to students' experience and everyday lives appear to resonate with first-generation, and perhaps all, students. The lessons we learn about what works with low income mothers are, arguably, lessons about what works with all students, and they are warnings not to allow colleges and universities, in the words of a staff member at Regional University, "to humiliate with our policies and procedures." We should dwell on the words of the Regional University graduate whose successful completion of college was largely a result of the support she found in and outside of the classroom. Accordingly, she concluded that "being in college was just a wonderful place to be because it expanded my mind with so many possibilities of things I can do and be."

REFERENCES

American Association of State Colleges and Universities. 1998. *Higher education and the labor market: AASCU special report.* Washington, D.C.: AASCU.

Education Resources Institute, The (TERI). 1995. *The next step: Student aid and student success.* Boston: The Education Resources Institute.

————. 1997. *Missed opportunities: A new look at disadvantaged college aspirants.* Boston: The Education Resources Institute.

Geske, Terry G., and Elchanan, Cohn. 1998. Why is a high school diploma no longer enough? The economic and social benefit of higher education. In *Condemning students to debt: College loans and public policy,* ed. Richard Fossey and Mark Bateman, 19–36. New York: Teachers College Press.

Gittell, Marilyn, and Sally Covington. 1993. *Higher education in JOBS: An option or an opportunity? A comparison of nine states.* New York: Howard Samuels State Management and Policy Center.

Gittell, Marilyn, Jill Gross, and Jennifer Holdaway. 1993. *Building human capital: The impact of post-secondary education on AFDC recipients in five states.* A report to the Ford Foundation. New York: Howard Samuels State Management and Policy Center.

Gittell, Marilyn, Margaret Schehl, and Camille Fareri. 1990. *From welfare to independence: The college option.* New York: Howard Samuels State Management and Policy Center.

Gittell, Marilyn, Kirk Vandersall, Jennifer Holdaway, and Kathe Newman. 1996. *Creating social capital at CUNY: A comparison of higher education programs for AFDC recipients.* New York: Howard Samuels State Management and Policy Center.

Mortenson, Thomas G. 1993, September. Family income backgrounds continue to determine chances for baccalaureate degrees in 1992. *Postsecondary Education OPPORTUNITY.* Available at http://www.postsecondary.org/.

Murnane, Richard. 1994. Education and the well-being of the next generation. In *Confronting poverty: Prescriptions for change,* ed. Sheldon Danziger, Gary Sandefur, and Daniel Weinberg, 289–307. Cambridge, Mass.: Harvard University Press.

Chapter 6

Student Financial Aid
and Low Income Mothers

Donald E. Heller and Stefani A. Bjorklund

If you're eighteen, able-bodied, and you have a high school diploma, that's all they care about. So when these things are written, they're not written to help anybody trying to get a college degree—whether it's a bachelor's degree or higher. . . . That's the new welfare reform. That's how it was explained to me.

—Kim, twenty-nine years old, mother of two,
graduate student, and welfare recipient

A recent report from the federal government (Advisory Committee on Student Financial Assistance 2001) found that financial barriers were a critical factor in the ongoing gap between the college participation rates of low income youth and those of their higher income peers. Even when one includes financial aid from all sources—the federal government, state governments, higher education institutions, and private organizations—and in all forms—grants, loans, and work-study—low income college students still face a gap of thousands of dollars per year between the cost of attending college and the resources available to them.[1]

In this chapter, we examine the role of financial aid in promoting college access and persistence of attendance by low income mothers. Although little research has been conducted on the specific financial aid requirements of low income mothers, there is a good body of knowledge regarding low income students in general. We begin by providing an overview of the knowledge regarding the effectiveness of financial aid, and then examine existing federal,

The authors wish to acknowledge the research assistance of Roger Geertz Gonzalez in the preparation of this manuscript. Epigraph quote is from Stefani Bjorklund, 1999. Paper presented at the annual meeting of the Association for the Study of Higher Education, San Antonio, Texas, November.

state, and institutional policies that are, at least in part, geared toward the need of this population of students. Next, we examine how the regulations included in the 1996 Personal Responsibility and Work Opportunity Reconciliation Act (PRWORA) have affected access to financial aid for low income mothers. We then provide a set of recommendations for improving the ways that financial aid policy and welfare policies can support the post-secondary participation needs of low income mothers.

DOES FINANCIAL AID WORK TO PROMOTE COLLEGE ACCESS?

The empirical research on college access has been fairly conclusive regarding the impact of financial aid on low income students. There is consistent evidence that financial aid, particularly in the form of grants or scholarships, does work to encourage the college enrollment and persistence of poor students, and that the effects of aid are stronger for these students than they are for wealthier ones (Heller 1997; McPherson and Schapiro 1991; Leslie and Brinkman 1988; Jackson and Weathersby 1975). For example, Manski and Wise (1983) model the effects of the Basic Educational Opportunity Grant program (BEOG) on college enrollments in the late 1970s.[2] They conclude that total college enrollments with BEOGs (compared to enrollments if BEOGs had not been put in place) were "60 percent higher among low income students, 12 percent higher among middle-income students, and 3 percent higher among upper-income students" (1983, 21).

Leslie and Brinkman (1988) review 124 studies of the effects of student financial aid on access and persistence in college. They conclude, "Student aid does work on behalf of the equal opportunity goal. Because of aid, more low income individuals have been able to study at the college level, attend relatively costly and prestigious institutions, and stay in school longer than would otherwise have been the case" (179–180). Heller (1997), in his review of the research conducted subsequent to the studies assessed by Leslie and Brinkman, finds "there is a relationship between income and sensitivity to tuition and financial aid. . . . [The college enrollment decisions of] poorer students are more sensitive to increases in net cost, whether those increases take the effect of tuition increases or financial aid decreases" (642).

Although this empirical evidence reveals the impact of financial aid on college attendance, little of this research has focused on low income mothers as a specific population. Most of the research on the effects of financial aid on college attendance and persistence are quantitative studies using single institution or cross-sectional datasets of students. Because the representation of low income mothers is so small in most samples, these students are generally overlooked as a demographic group in research studies.

Whereas scant quantitative research exists on the effects of financial aid on the college attendance of—or even how much financial aid is awarded to—low income parents, evidence that is available indicates that financial aid is important for low income parents. Eighty-five percent of the students receiving welfare who participated in Gittell, Gross, and Holdaway's study (1993, 32) agree "financial aid was indispensable [to their staying in school]." To that end, many welfare students have used their student loans to pay for expenses not directly related to school attendance (e.g., day care, rent) (Kaufmann, Sharp, Miller, and Waltman 2000; Bjorklund 1999). Terenzini, Cabrera, and Bernal (2001) caution, however, that financial aid is only one of several factors affecting persistence among college students with low socioeconomic status, and confounding influences must also be considered in attrition studies.

CURRENT STATUS OF FINANCIAL AID POLICIES IN THE UNITED STATES

An Overview of Financial Assistance for College

There is no single system of financial assistance for college in the United States. A complex structure of both providers and types of assistance is available to help subsidize the cost of college attendance. The providers include the federal and state governments, higher education institutions, private scholarship organizations, and employers. Types of assistance include grants, tuition waivers or vouchers (that generally function in a manner similar to grants), loans, and work-study assistance.

The College Board's annual, comprehensive survey of student financial aid reveals that over $74 billion in assistance was available for all levels of enrollment (including undergraduate, graduate, and nondegree programs)[3] in the 2000–2001 academic year (College Board 2001). Table 6.1 summarizes this total by source and type of aid. The federal government is the largest provider of aid, with the majority (73 percent) provided in the form of loans. The "other sources" category includes institutional and private grants, and loans provided by private-sector companies.[4]

Most of the assistance provided by the federal government uses financial need as the primary criterion for provision of aid. The federal programs—including Pell grants, Supplemental Educational Opportunity Grants, and the subsidized student loan programs, most of which were enacted as part of the Higher Education Act of 1965—originally focused on equalizing post-secondary educational opportunity.

Students who desire federal aid fill out a Free Application for Federal Student Aid (FAFSA), providing data about their income, assets, and other

TABLE 6.1
Sources and Type of Financial Aid, 2000–2001 Academic Year

| | Source of Aid | | | Type of Aid | |
	Total Amount ($ billions)	% of Total		Total Amount ($ billions)	% of Total
Federal government	$50.7	68.1%	Grants	$31.6	42.5%
State governments	5.2	7.0	Loans	41.7	56.0
Other sources	18.5	24.9	Work-study	1.1	1.5
Total	$74.4	100.0%	Total	$74.4	100.0%

Excludes employer-provided grants and institutionally provided waivers and vouchers.

Source: College Board (2001).

information, along with that of their parents if they are dependent students. People with children, as well as all students age twenty-four or older, are considered independent for purposes of determining eligibility for federal aid. The information provided on the FAFSA is used to determine how much each student should be expected to contribute to the costs of attending college, an amount labeled the "effective family contribution" (EFC). Although federally funded student aid is excluded in determining eligibility for welfare, medical assistance, food stamps, and child care co-pays—untaxed benefits (including welfare payments and veterans' noneducational benefits) are included in calculating a student's expected contribution.

The EFC is subtracted from the "cost of attendance" (the sum of tuition and fees, room and board, books and supplies, transportation and personal expenses) to determine the amount of financial assistance for which the student qualifies (U.S. Department of Education 2002). College financial aid officers then put together a package of assistance for each student consisting of various forms of federal assistance (grants, loans, and work-study), each of which has a maximum limit that can be awarded to each student. For example, in the 2000–2001 academic year, while the maximum Pell grant that could be awarded was $3,300, the average recipient received a Pell grant of $2,057 (College Board 2001).

Despite having the potential to receive substantial financial aid packages from the federal and state governments, low income mothers face greater financial obstacles than do most college students. Indeed, a family of two or three is more expensive to clothe and feed than is a single person. Costs unrelated to the completion of a student's course of study (e.g., child care), however, are not included in calculating a student's cost of attendance (U.S. Department of Education 2002). So, although the calculated cost of attendance and ensuing aid packages would likely be the same for a low income student and a low income student raising children, the parenting student would need to find additional funds for day care and other child-related expenses.

If asked, college or university financial aid administrators may take into account special circumstances when determining a student's cost of attendance. "Special circumstances" generally have included exorbitant medical bills or sudden unemployment (of the parent of a dependent student). The financial aid administrator might also take into account family expenses of low income parenting students, though no policies require them to do so. College financial aid administrators have the final authority to determine a student's cost of attendance; their decisions cannot be appealed to the U.S. Department of Education (U.S. Department of Education 2002). However, in many cases it is incumbent on the student applying for aid to ask for this special consideration.

Although the majority of state scholarships and grants are awarded using financial need criteria similar to those used in the awarding of federal Pell grants, the trend in recent years has been toward the abandonment of financial need and the adoption of academic criteria as the means of awarding aid. In the 1980s and through 1993, approximately 90 percent of the aid provided by states to undergraduate students annually was awarded based on demonstrated financial need. Since then, merit scholarships, spurred by the popularity of the Georgia HOPE Scholarship program,[5] have grown to the point that they represented 24 percent of all dollars awarded in the 2000–2001 academic year (National Association of State Student Grant and Aid Programs 2001). Studies examining these new merit scholarship programs have found that, in contrast to programs that award grants based on financial need, the benefits of merit aid programs flow disproportionately to higher income students (Binder and Ganderton 2001; Cornwell, Mustard, and Sridhar 2001; Heller and Rasmussen 2001).

Colleges and universities make their own decisions regarding the use of institutional scholarship aid, which is generally funded through gifts from donors, or through the recycling of tuition revenue from some students into aid for other students. Historically, financial assistance for undergraduate students was used primarily only by elite, private institutions whose policies mirrored those of the federal government in promoting equality of educational opportunity. In the past two decades, however, institutional aid has been used as an enrollment management tool with the awarding of grants based not on the financial circumstances of the student, but targeted instead at "desirable" students whom the institution wishes to enroll. These desirable students are generally those with high academic achievement (measured through high school class rank or scores on standardized tests such as the SAT or ACT), who will help move institutions upward in rankings such as those produced by *U.S. News and World Report*. Besides deciding who will receive scholarship aid, institutions can also practice "preferential packaging," in which they strategically use grants, loans, and work-study to attract desirable students.

The increasing use of merit as the key criterion for the awarding of grants by both state and institutional scholarship programs has limited the availability of college aid for poorer students and provided more aid for students with greater financial means. Although creating scholarships based on merit does

TABLE 6.2
State and Institutional Grant Awards by Family Income, 1992–1993 and 1999–2000

	State Grants		Institutional Grants	
	Income below $20,000	Income above $100,000	Income below $20,000	Income above $100,000
Percentage receiving grants, 1992–1993	22.8	1.9	17.0	11.2
Percentage receiving grants, 1999–2000	33.1	5.3	20.4	20.3
Percentage increase, 1992–1993 to 1999–2000	45.2	178.9	20.4	81.3
Mean grant received, 1992–1993	$1,502	$1,478	$2,740	$3,313
Mean grant received, 1999–2000	1,752	1,820	3,773	5,141
Percentage increase, 1992–1993 to 1999–2000	16.6	23.1	37.7	55.2

Source: Authors' calculations from Tuma, Geis, and Malizio (1995) and National Center for Education Statistics (2001).

not exclude welfare recipients from the pool of potential applicants per se, these awards often compete with need-based programs for a finite amount of state or institutional resources. In addition, most merit scholarships are awarded to full-time, traditional-aged college students (those making the immediate transition from high school to college).

Table 6.2 presents data from national surveys of undergraduate students conducted by the U.S. Department of Education. Shown are the percentages of dependent students receiving institutional and state grants (both merit and need-based), and the average grant sizes, for students in two income groups in the 1992–1993 and 1999–2000 school years. For both state and institutional grants, the proportion of higher income students receiving grants increased at a higher rate than did the proportion of lower income students. In addition, and again for both types of grants, higher income students saw more growth in the size of the average grant received.

The Problem of Unmet Need

Ideally, all of the financial resources available to a student—from her own income and assets and from student aid—would be enough to allow her to attend the higher education institution of her choice. The reality, however, is that lower income students in particular face large amounts of "unmet need"—the difference between the cost of attending college and the resources available to meet those costs. Low income mothers in post-secondary education likely experience even greater cost-resource discrepancies than nonparenting students because parents generally allocate any "extra" income to pay for family expenses rather than college costs.

A study conducted by the Advisory Committee on Student Financial Assistance, a governmental body established to advise the secretary of education and Congress on student aid policy, finds that unmet need is becoming a serious problem for lower income students. In the 1995–1996 academic year (the most recent year for which data are available), the average unmet need of a high income student attending a public, four-year institution was $400 per year. The same measure for a low income student was $3,800 annually (Advisory Committee on Student Financial Assistance 2001), and would likely be even greater for a low income student raising a family. At community colleges, the sector in which many low income mothers enroll, the average unmet need for low income students was $3,200 per year.[6] The reader should note that this is the level of unmet need after taking into account all types of financial assistance, including loans. Thus, even if the low income student were able to complete a degree in just four years—a daunting task for even the most academically prepared students—she would still have to find over $15,000 to close the gap between the cost of attending college and the resources available to her.

A subsequent report of the Advisory Committee examines the influence of unmet need on the progress of students through the pipeline from middle school through to attainment of a bachelor's degree (Advisory Committee on Student Financial Assistance 2002). Based on data from a national survey conducted by the U.S. Department of Education, the report compares how students with low unmet need (those students with little gap between college costs and financial resources) and those with high unmet need exited the educational pipeline at different rates. Figure 6.1 demonstrates that 95 percent of eighth grade students with low unmet need reported that they expected to finish college while only 70 percent of those with high unmet need reported the same expectation. At the end of the pipeline, almost half of students with low unmet need completed a bachelor's degree, but fewer than one in eight students with high unmet need were able to do so.

Welfare recipients "differ from most other college students. College students often rely on their families for help with housing, food, transportation, and tuition, but welfare recipients lack such support" (Carnevale and Sylvester 2000). Like other low income college students, parenting students use the financial aid packages available to them—including federal and state loans and grants, work-study and institutional support—to absorb educational costs and defray living expenses. Due to the costs incurred by raising children, however, low income mothers are more likely to experience greater "unmet need" than do other poor students.

But what are the costs of raising children? The U.S. Department of Agriculture (USDA) offers estimates of the annual child-rearing financial responsibilities for single and married parents of only children, two children, and three

FIGURE 6.1
Milestones to College Completion

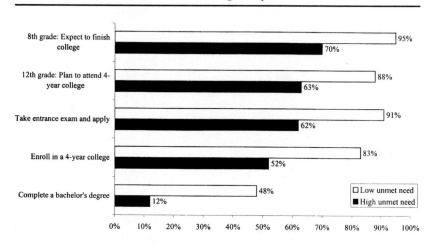

Source: Advisory Committee on Student Financial Assistance (2002).

or more children (Lino 2002). The annual estimates include expenditures for housing, food, transportation, clothing, health care, child care and education, and miscellaneous expenses. Based on the estimates and formulas provided in the report, the average annual cost for a low income, single parent[7] to raise one child in 2001 was $8,884; the cost of raising two children was $12,715. Poor, single parents of three children spent an average of $15,612 on child-rearing in 2001. Therefore, it appears that single, parenting students have at least $9,000 more annual expenses than do nonparenting students, yet financial aid officers can derive equal "cost of attendance" estimates for both types of students.

Studies investigating factors that influence welfare recipients' educational experiences indicate that supplemental subsidies such as medical assistance, food stamps, transportation, and affordable, quality child care are vital to students' success (Butler and Deprez 2000; Price 2000; Bjorklund 1999; Rooney 1998; Gittell, Gross, and Holdaway 1993; Kates 1991). The availability of additional financial support to defray the costs of books, tuition, and student fees also has been found to contribute to the persistence of low income mothers (Butler and Deprez 2000; Price 2000; Gittell, Gross, and Holdaway 1993; Kates 1991). Federal and state aid-granting agencies and universities generally include tuition and fees, room and board, books and supplies, transportation, and incidental or personal expenses—but do not include family expenses—in calculating a student's estimated costs of college attendance and aid package. The estimate for "incidental" or "personal" expenses generally includes clothing and entertainment, but is rarely sufficient to cover even clothes and entertainment for more than one person. Strawn (2000, 3) explains,

> [F]ederal student aid is not adjusted for family size, so that students with dependents do not receive more aid than other students with the same income but no dependents. In the past, the welfare system often provided a hidden subsidy to post-secondary education by supporting single parents enrolled in school, but with the shift to a work-based welfare system, in most states this subsidy no longer exists.

Although many welfare recipients must use part of their student loans (and any other resources they can muster) to pay for family and child care expenses, obtaining adequate child care is difficult, as it can be for all working parents (Gittell, Vandersall, Holdaway, and Newman 1996). The USDA report estimates that low income, single parents spent only between $300 and $720 per child per year on child care and education in 2001 (Lino 2002), yet quality child care generally costs at least that amount per child per month. Rochelle, a junior and mother of one daughter, said about day care, "I wanted to get [financial] help from the welfare office . . . but you have to work twenty hours a week in order to get any help from them. Which just doesn't make any sense to me because I'm a full-time student and if I work twenty hours that would be twenty more hours I wouldn't be with my daughter" (Bjorklund 1999).[8]

In child care programs nationwide, "spaces are limited, costs are high . . . infant care and evening or weekend care are generally not available" (Kaufmann et al. 2000, 14). Furthermore, due to the lack of quality day care, children of low income mothers often have been "placed in unsatisfactory and sometimes developmentally dangerous child care settings" (Kahn and Polakow 2000, 62). Despite having obtained a coveted spot for her infant son in campus day care, a twenty-two-year-old student, Jennifer, lamented about leaving him there: "On my first day when I had to leave him in day-care I was, like, in tears thinking, 'What am I doing? I'm leaving my kid with these people and I don't even know who they are. Oh god, I'm some bad mother. I'm leaving my kid in the day-care. . . . I always want him to know I'm his mother and I'm supposed to take care of him, not somebody else. I don't need somebody to do that for me" (Bjorklund 1999). When the lack of access to quality child care forces parenting students to choose between their academic aspirations and their children's well-being, college careers often are cut short.

THE NEXUS OF WELFARE REFORM AND STUDENT FINANCIAL AID

The 1996 PRWORA legislation, otherwise known as "welfare reform," replaced the open-ended federal program, Aid to Families with Dependent Children

(AFDC), with Temporary Assistance for Needy Families (TANF). Key changes created by the legislation included instituting new work requirements and a five-year lifetime limit on receiving welfare benefits. Replacing the federal guarantee of income to individuals with block grants to the states gave states increased flexibility in administering benefits to their residents.

At best, poor women relying on welfare for their families' survival struggled to stay in school before 1996 (Gittell, Vandersall, Holdaway, and Newman 1996; Gittell and Covington 1993; Gittell, Gross, and Holdaway 1993; Kates 1991). The 1996 reform legislation and financial aid guidelines, and the actual implementation of these policies, have affected welfare recipients' work and home lives (Meyers, Glaser, and Mac Donald 1998), and have negatively influenced the college persistence of low income mothers (Cox and Spriggs 2002; Institute for Women's Policy Research 2002; Kahn and Polakow 2000; Pandey et al. 2000; Rooney 1998). In fact, findings of a recent investigation analyzing data from the Urban Institute's 1997 and 1999 National Surveys of America's Families reveals that welfare recipients were 13 percent more likely to attend college than other poor women in 1996. By 1998, however, welfare recipients were 7 percent less likely to attend college than other low income women (Cox and Spriggs 2002). The research also suggests the decline in welfare recipients' college attendance was directly related to the 1996 welfare policies (the researchers held constant a number of other factors in their analyses) and that there "was not a simple shift of college attending welfare recipients into the pool of poor women attending college" (Cox and Spriggs 2002, 14).

The legislation's work requirements pose considerable challenges to college students who receive welfare. To maintain compliance with federal regulations, states must have demonstrated that one-quarter of their welfare recipients engaged in work-related activities by fall 1997, that work participation rates have increased by 5 percent each fiscal year, and that half of all adults on welfare were employed by 2002. Although states were given the latitude to define "work-related activities" to meet the levels of work activity requirements dictated by the federal legislation, many states chose not to include post-secondary education in their definitions.

Studies show the number of hours per week students are employed and students' enrollment status (whether enrolled full time or part time) influence their college persistence (Choy 2002; Bean and Metzner 1996; Astin 1975, 1972). Astin (1975) suggests that working fewer than twenty hours per week is positively correlated with college student persistence, and "most researchers agreed that employment in excess of twenty to twenty-five hours per week was negatively related to persistence" (Bean and Metzner 1996, 152).

Part-time attendance is also detrimental to persisting in college and attaining a degree. A recent report of the American Council on Education (ACE) indicates that whereas 52 percent of students who began a full-time bachelor's degree program in 1989 received their degree by 1994 (and 18 per-

cent were still working toward a degree), only 12 percent of students beginning in part-time status received their degree (and only 21 percent were still
enrolled) (Choy 2002).

Another ACE study, exploring the effects of students' financial decisions
on their academic success, finds that over half of the freshmen it tracked who
worked over fifteen hours per week and attended college part time quit school
within three years. In contrast, fewer than 10 percent of students who carried
full course loads and worked fourteen hours per week or less dropped out (King
2002). At this writing, most states require welfare recipients to be engaged in
twenty-five to thirty hours of work per week, and the Bush administration's
reauthorization proposal advocates more work hours per week. Increasing
the work requirements would compel low income parenting students to be
employed for more hours and enroll for even fewer college credits.

The work requirements' greatest influence on students' financial aid appears
to be that women who are working more hours per week are enrolling for fewer
credit hours per semester, thereby diminishing their eligibility for federal and
state financial aid. Strawn explains

> Federal student aid, by far the largest source of student aid, has several
> features that limit its availability to low income workers seeking to up-
> grade their skills. . . . [F]ederal student aid is not structured to support
> incremental approaches to low income workers acquiring skills because
> it is generally not available for individuals taking less than six credits a
> semester (two classes), yet many low-wage workers cannot manage to
> take more than one class per semester because they are already working
> full-time. This is especially true for working single parents who have the
> additional responsibility of caring for their children. (Strawn 2000, 3)

Although some of PRWORA's provisions discourage post-secondary participation by low income parents, it is also important to note that student aid
guidelines also can prevent these students from receiving financial assistance
and attending college. Federal student aid guidelines require students to enroll
half time to be eligible for most federally guaranteed and subsidized student
loans. Half-time enrollment is generally considered taking six credit hours per
semester (two courses), although post-secondary institutions determine what
number of hours meets the half-time requirement depending on the program
in which a student is enrolled. Pell grants are available to students enrolled in a
minimum of three credits; however, the grant amounts are lower to reflect the
fewer credits taken. Moreover, post-secondary institutions sometimes choose
not to process the paperwork necessary for students enrolled for less than half
time to receive a Pell grant because the paperwork outweighs the revenue generated. Campus financial aid officers who administer the federally funded,
campus-based programs (i.e., Supplemental Educational Opportunity Grants,

College Work-Study, and Perkins Loans) generally require students to enroll at least half time to receive any of these benefits. State-funded student aid may also prove elusive for students whose jobs prevent them from enrolling at least half time. States also establish their own credit-hour requirements for student aid eligibility, and their minimums often exceed the federal minimums.

Golonka and Matus-Grossman (2001) summarize the barriers to receiving financial assistance faced by "... welfare recipients and low income working individuals, particularly those desiring to attend school part time or participate in noncredit programs":

- Most financial aid programs do not support students in non-credit or non-degree programs or students who do not attend school continuously, but move into and out of the system.
- Many financial aid programs are geared toward full-time or half-time enrollees, and students attending less than half-time (that is, one course per semester) may not even be eligible. While less-than-half-time students are eligible for Pell grants (the largest federal need-based scholarship program), college financial aid offices sometimes seem reluctant to invest the time in processing grants for these students.
- Many potential low income students have previously defaulted on student loans, making them ineligible for many types of aid.
- Many financial aid programs cover only tuition and related expenses. Students who have to reduce work hours to attend college while continuing to support their family will likely need additional support for living expenses, child care, and transportation, which are often not covered by financial aid programs.
- Some programs that are intended to support low income students actually work at cross-purposes with each other. For example, individuals' income from state-funded work-study programs is counted in determining eligibility for Food Stamps and Medicaid. (Federal work-study income is exempt.) (22)

Although not directly affecting student aid, the five-year limit on receiving TANF benefits is expected to have a negative effect on student persistence as individuals beyond their five-year limit would be forced to work more hours outside the home—rather than attending classes and studying—to provide for their children, and as described earlier, part-time college attendance is a barrier to college persistence and degree attainment. In addition, a bachelor's degree generally takes a minimum of four years of full-time enrollment to earn. Because many welfare recipients attend college part time, these students generally spend more than four years pursuing a "four-year" degree. Because many grant programs have limits on how long students can receive the awards, students who attend college part time are penalized. Tanya, who participated in a

1999 study of low income, parenting students (Bjorklund 1999), did not receive any TANF cash assistance and, consequently, used her student loans to pay for child care. She asserted although she had to take nineteen credits and care for her daughter, "I have to graduate in the spring. I don't have any more loan money. And, that's my main source of income. There's nothing I can do about it. I have to graduate next semester." Although welfare benefits are paltry, receiving cash assistance beyond the five-year limit indeed could be a crucial factor in poor women's ability to attend college while supporting their families.

POLICY RECOMMENDATIONS FOR IMPROVING ACCESS TO FINANCIAL AID FOR LOW INCOME MOTHERS

The responsibility for improving access to financial aid for low income mothers rests on federal and state financial aid and welfare policy makers and on individual higher education institutions. Although post-secondary education policies have not been at the forefront of the minds of most welfare policy makers or implementers, scholars have begun calling attention to the ways education, student financial aid, and welfare policies are intertwined. For instance, whereas welfare benefits are counted in calculating a student's financial aid eligibility, federal student aid is not counted in determining eligibility for TANF, medical assistance, or child care co-payments. Golonka and Matus-Grossman (2001) propose combining federal, state, and institutional financial aid and TANF policies to create comprehensive aid packages for poor students pursuing college degrees. They suggest, "The various financial-aid entities . . . [ought to] articulate agreements . . . so that one source of financial aid does not count as income toward eligibility requirements for other sources of aid" (2001, 24).

Golonka and Matus-Grossman (2001) also recommend federal legislation to change some facets of existing federal programs to enable states and colleges to reach more low income families. These modifications include:

- Permitting rolling (not fixed) deadlines or additional deadlines for federal financial aid programs (many people cannot take advantage of Pell grants, for example, because they apply for college aid after the Pell deadlines have passed);
- Considering revisions to the Pell grant program so that tuition assistance could be provided for one class per semester or for non-credit courses that lead to a recognized certificate;
- Modifying Food Stamp and Medicaid rules so that state-level work-study aid or other forms of state financial aid do not count as income for purposes of determining eligibility [for assistance] (currently, only federal work-study income is exempt; states can apply for waivers, but changing federal rules would allow more states to

offer their own assistance packages to low-income families without jeopardizing their Food Stamp or Medicaid benefits). (26)

In fall 2001, the U.S. Department of Education awarded $10.5 million to colleges to provide day care for low income, parenting students. Four-year grants were awarded to 222 colleges that dispersed over $350,000 in Pell grants the previous year (U.S. Department of Education 2001). The additional funds have opened new campus-based child care centers, substantially lowered poor students' child care co-payments, and provided children with safe, quality care.

By including post-secondary education in their definitions of "work-related activities," states would increase the likelihood that low income mothers might take enough credit hours to be eligible for financial assistance.

States can also choose to use their federal TANF and Maintenance-of-Effort (MOE) funds—and resources not restricted by TANF regulations—to assist students in meeting educational expenses by providing cash assistance and sponsoring need-based tuition assistance and support services (e.g., work-study, child care, transportation, living stipends) for poor parents participating in higher education (Golonka and Matus-Grossman 2001; Friedman 1999). Greenberg, Strawn, and Plimpton (1999) describe individual states' current TANF policies and explain how states can support post-secondary education within or outside of their cash assistance programs using non-TANF and TANF-related funds. Three of the many examples they mention include states' options to: (1) use flexibility in defining "work-related activities" to include higher education; (2) use their federal TANF money and MOE[9] funds to support post-secondary education participation; and (3) use TANF funds to support post-secondary education outside the welfare system (e.g., fund work-study programs, and child care and transportation benefits).

Some states have developed programs that reflect these suggestions. For example, the California state legislature in 1997–1998 agreed to provide $65 million annually (in non-TANF funds) to 108 of the state's community colleges to bolster the schools' educational and support programs for their students on welfare. The schools also receive an additional $16 million in TANF funds (Mathur 2002). Research indicates that California's TANF program, Cal-WORKs, has helped welfare recipients attend and earn degrees from community colleges, and that CalWORKs students work more and earn more soon after completing a certificate or degree program (Mathur 2002).

Likewise, Pennsylvania recently allotted $750,000 of its TANF funds to implement a program to help welfare recipients pay for college tuition. The Pennsylvania Higher Education Assistance Agency administers the program, called the TANF Educational Award Program (TEAP), and "offers need-based aid of up to $1,200 per academic year to TANF recipients who are undergraduate students at an approved post-secondary school" (Friedman 2001, 4).

Educational institutions can support college attendance of low income mothers by designing flexible schedules, including offering night and weekend courses and compressed semesters, to enable students to complete required classes (Friedman 1999), and allow students to enroll for at least the minimum number of credits required to qualify for certain types of financial aid. Additionally, Golonka and Matus-Grossman (2001) suggest colleges pursue Pell grants for students taking as few as three credit hours. Although the grant amount may be small, adding it to the resources of an entire aid package may substantially improve poor students' persistence toward degree or certificate attainment.

CONCLUSION

The 1996 welfare legislation, based on work-first priorities, clearly does not support post-secondary education as a route out of poverty for low income mothers. Additionally, some politically conservative scholars and lawmakers argue that welfare recipients should not receive any support for enrolling in post-secondary education. Robert Rector, a senior research fellow at the Heritage Foundation believes "it is 'very inequitable' to ask taxpayers who may not be able to afford college tuitions to support the families of welfare recipients who take classes" (Schmidt 2002). However, lawmakers who create welfare policies that force recipients into low-wage work are shortsighted. A college student who receives welfare benefits aptly stated, "Institutionally, they have no concept. They don't seem to have an understanding that if you give someone an education, they're going to be paying more taxes because they're going to be earning more. They're going to pay back everything they take now . . . and more" (Bjorklund 1999).

Although recent debates in policy circles question whether welfare policies or student financial aid policies ought to address the financial barriers faced by low income mothers attending college, no simple answers have surfaced. Certain higher education scholars and policy makers have suggested states bear the primary responsibility for ensuring that financial aid is available for all of their college-eligible citizens and that the federal government take responsibility for providing need-based grants and loans as an advertisement in the *New York Times* on 7 March 2001 touted. Individuals and organizations working to eradicate poverty and women's rights advocates have argued that federal and state welfare policies ought to support post-secondary education within and outside of their TANF programs.

Whether welfare policies or student aid policies or a combination of the two address these issues, a more educated citizenry would certainly benefit the economy and society of the nation and of individual states. Therefore, no matter whether ensuring poor students' access to post-secondary education falls under the purview of "welfare" or "financial aid" policies, it is ultimately the responsibility of both the federal and state governments.

Coordinating the provision of both welfare benefits and student financial aid can only help to promote the college access and degree-attainment needs of low income mothers. Focusing on one set of policies, in isolation from the impact of the other, is not likely to address the needs of this population. There is a role for all parties involved—state governments, the federal government, higher education institutions, and students themselves—in ensuring this coordination is efficiently and effectively carried out.

Notes

1. Later in this chapter we provide more details on how financial aid officers calculate the cost of attending college.

2. Pell grants are the foundation of federal support for low income undergraduates. In the 2000–2001 academic year, eight billion dollars in Pell grants were awarded to 3.8 million students (King 2000). In the 1999–2000 academic year, over 90 percent of Pell grants were awarded to dependent students with parental income of under $40,000 and independent students with income below $30,000 (authors' calculations from National Center for Education Statistics 2002).

3. Excluded are federal and state tax credits such as the Hope and Lifetime Learning tax credits, targeted at college costs.

4. The College Board survey does not include any amounts borrowed by students or their families from credit cards or other than from standard student loan programs (such as home equity loans used to finance college costs).

5. The Georgia HOPE (Helping Outstanding Pupils Educationally) Scholarship program was started in 1993 as the nation's first, broad-based and state-sponsored merit scholarship program. It provides full-tuition scholarships for students to attend any public institution in the state, with a high school GPA of 3.0 required for awarding of the scholarship (and a college GPA of 3.0 for maintaining the scholarship while in college). Although the program originally had an income cap of $66,000 for the awarding of the grants, this cap was removed in the program's third year and there is no longer any means testing used (Heller 2002).

6. The unmet-need figures were calculated for full-time, dependent students. The major difference between these students and most low income mothers is that the latter are independent students and likely to attend college part time. Thus, it is likely that the total amount of the unmet need for low income mothers is less than for full-time students, but it is still as much a barrier toward college persistence and degree attainment.

7. The USDA report defines "low income" as single parents whose before-tax annual income was less than $39,000; the average annual income of low income, single parents was $16,400.

8. These quotes are from a qualitative study of low income mothers and their post-secondary educational experiences.

9. A state's Maintenance-of-Effort obligation refers to the level of spending a state must meet to receive its full federal TANF block grant.

REFERENCES

Advisory Committee on Student Financial Assistance. 2001. *Access denied: Restoring the nation's commitment to equal educational opportunity*. Washington, D.C.: U.S. Department of Education.

———. 2002. *Panelist briefing: Meeting of the Advisory Committee on Student Financial Assistance*. Washington, D.C.: U.S. Department of Education.

Astin, Alexander. 1972. *College dropouts: A national profile*. Washington, D.C.: American Council on Education.

———. 1975. *Preventing students from dropping out*. San Francisco: Jossey-Bass.

Bean, John P., and Barbara S. Metzner. 1996. A conceptual model of nontraditional undergraduate student attrition. In *College students: The evolving nature of research*, ed. Frances K. Stage, Guadalupe L. Anya, John P. Bean, Don Hossler, and George D. Kuh, 137–173. Needham Heights, Mass.: Simon and Schuster.

Binder, Melissa, and Philip T. Ganderton. 2001, December. Musical chairs in higher education: Incentive effects of the NM success scholarship. Paper presented at the meeting on State Merit Aid Programs: College Access and Equity, The Civil Rights Project, Harvard University, Cambridge, Mass.

Bjorklund, Stefani A. 1999, November. College and children: How welfare students make it work. Paper presented at the annual meeting of the Association for the Study of Higher Education, San Antonio, TX.

Butler, Sandra S., and Luisa Stormer Deprez. 2000, March. *Maine's Parents as Scholars program: Higher education post welfare reform*. Proceedings of Women's Lives, Voices, Solutions: Shaping a National Agenda for Women in Higher Education. Minneapolis: University of Minnesota.

Carnevale, Anthony P., and Kathleen Sylvester. 2000. As welfare rolls shrink, colleges offer the best route to good jobs. *Chronicle of Higher Education* 18 February: B6.

Choy, Susan. 2002. *Access and persistence: Findings from 10 years of longitudinal research on students*. Washington, D.C.: American Council on Education, Center for Policy Analysis.

College Board. 2001. *Trends in student aid, 2001*. Washington, D.C.: College Board.

Cornwell, Christopher, David B. Mustard, and Deepa J. Sridhar. 2001, December. *The enrollment effects of merit-based financial aid: Evidence from Georgia's HOPE scholarship*. Paper presented at the meeting on State Merit Aid Programs: College Access and Equity, The Civil Rights Project, Harvard University, Cambridge, Mass.

Cox, Kenya L. C., and William E. Spriggs. 2002, June. Negative effects of TANF on college enrollment. Available at http://www.nul.org/tanf/. Washington, D.C.: National Urban League Institute for Opportunity and Equality.

Friedman, Pamela. 1999. Post-secondary education options for low-income adults. *Welfare Information Network: Issues Notes* 3(12). Available at http://www.financeproject info.org/win/postseced2.htm.

———. 2001. TANF reauthorization and post-secondary education options for welfare recipients. *Welfare Information Network: Reauthorization Notes* 1(3). Available at http://www.financeprojectinfo.org/tanf/tanfreauth_postsecedreauthorization.htm.

Gittell, Marilyn, and Sally Covington. 1993. *Higher education in JOBS: An option or an opportunity? A comparison of nine states.* New York: Howard Samuels State Management and Policy Center.

Gittell, Marilyn, Jill Gross, and Jennifer Holdaway. 1993. *Building human capital: The impact of post-secondary education on AFDC recipients in five states.* A report to the Ford Foundation. New York: Howard Samuels State Management and Policy Center.

Gittell, Marilyn, Kirk Vandersall, Jennifer Holdaway, and Kathe Newman. 1996. *Creating social capital at CUNY: A comparison of higher education programs for AFDC recipients.* New York: Howard Samuels State Management and Policy Center.

Golonka, Susan, and Lisa Matus-Grossman. 2001. *Opening doors: Expanding educational opportunities for low-income workers.* New York: Manpower Demonstration Research Corporation.

Greenberg, Mark, Julie Strawn, and Lisa Plimpton. 1999. *State opportunities to provide access to postsecondary education under TANF.* Washington, D.C.: Center for Law and Social Policy.

Heller, Donald E. 1997. Student price response in higher education: An update to Leslie and Brinkman. *Journal of Higher Education* 68(6):624–659.

———. 2002. The policy shift in state financial aid programs. In *Higher education: Handbook of theory and research.* Vol. 17, 221–261. New York: Agathon Press.

Heller, Donald E., and Christopher J. Rasmussen. 2001, November. Do merit scholarships promote college access? Evidence from two states. Paper presented at the annual conference of the Association for the Study of Higher Education, Richmond, VA.

Institute for Women's Policy Research. 2002, 22 May. *Life after welfare reform: Low-income single parent families, pre- and post-TANF.* Washington, D.C.: Institute for Women's Policy Research.

Jackson, Gregory A., and George B. Weathersby. 1975. Individual demand for higher education. *Journal of Higher Education* 46(6):623-652.

Kahn, Peggy, and Valerie Polakow. 2000. *Struggling to stay in school: Obstacles to post-secondary education under the welfare-to-work regime in Michigan.* Ann Arbor: University of Michigan, Center for the Education of Women.

Kates, Erika. 1991. *More than survival: Access to higher education for low-income women.* Washington, D.C.: Center for Women Policy Studies.

Kaufmann, Susan W., Sally Sharp, Jeanne E. Miller, and Jean Waltman. 2000. *Michigan: A smart state for women? Women and higher education.* Ann Arbor: University of Michigan, Center for the Education of Women.

King, Jacqueline E. 2000. *2000 status on the Pell grant program.* Washington, D.C.: American Council on Education, Center for Policy Analysis.

———. 2002. *Crucial choices: How students' financial decisions affect their academic success.* Washington, D.C.: American Council on Education, Center for Policy Analysis.

Leslie, Larry L., and Paul T. Brinkman. 1988. *The economic value of higher education.* Washington, D.C.: American Council on Education.

Lino, Mark. 2002. *Expenditures on children by families, 2001 annual report.* Misc. publication no. 1528-2001. Washington, D.C.: U.S. Department of Agriculture, Center for Nutrition Policy and Promotion.

Manski, Charles, and David Wise. 1983. *College choice in America.* Cambridge, Mass.: Harvard University Press.

Mathur, Anita. 2002, May. *Credentials count: How California's community colleges help parents move from welfare to self-sufficiency.* Washington, D.C.: Center for Law and Social Policy.

McPherson, Michael S., and Morton O. Schapiro. 1991. *Keeping college affordable: Government and educational opportunity.* Washington, D.C.: Brookings Institution.

Meyers, Marcia K., Bonnie Glaser, and Karin Mac Donald. 1998. On the front lines of welfare delivery: Are workers implementing policy reforms? *Journal of Policy Analysis and Management* 17(1):1–22.

National Association of State Student Grant and Aid Programs. 2001. *NASSGAP 31st annual survey report 1999–2000 academic year.* Albany: New York State Higher Education Services Corporation.

National Center for Education Statistics. 2001. *National Postsecondary Student Aid Study: Student financial aid estimates for 1999–2000.* Washington, D.C.: U.S. Department of Education.

———. 2002. *National Postsecondary Student Aid Study: Data Analysis System.* Washington, D.C.: U.S. Department of Education.

Pandey, Shanta, Min Zhan, Susan Neely-Barnes, and Natasha Menon. 2000. The higher education option for poor women with children. *Journal of Sociology and Social Welfare* 27(4):109–170.

Price, Charles. 2000. *Welfare reform and the college option: A national conference.* Summary of conference proceedings. New York: Howard Samuels State Management and Policy Center.

Rooney, Bobbie J. 1998. Greedy institutions: A qualitative study of the competing demands of family, university and social services in the lives of low-income, single-parent students. Unpublished master's thesis, Miami University, Oxford, Ohio.

Schmidt, Peter. 2002. Bush proposes welfare changes to further emphasize work. *Chronicle of Higher Education* 8 March: A23.

Strawn, Julie. 2000. *Workforce development for the unemployed and low wage workers: The role of postsecondary education.* Working draft. Washington, D.C.: Center for Law and Social Policy. Available at http://www.clasp.org/pubs/jobseducation/lowwageand postsecondarydraft.htm.

Terenzini, Patrick T., Alberto F. Cabrera, and Elena M. Bernal. 2001. *Swimming against the tide: The poor in American higher education.* College Board Research Report no. 2000-3. New York: College Board.

Tuma, John, Sonya Geis, and Andrew G. Malizio. 1995. *Student financing of undergraduate education, 1992–93.* Washington, D.C.: U.S. Department of Education, National Center for Education Statistics.

U.S. Department of Education. 2001, October. *Paige announces grants to provide low-income college students with child care.* Available at http://www.ed.gov/PressReleases/ 10-2001/10052001f.html. Washington, D.C.: U.S. Department of Education.

———. 2002. Funding your education. Available at http://www.ed.gov/prog_info/ SFA/FYE/. Washington, D.C.: U.S. Department of Education.

Chapter 7

Credentials Count

How California's Community Colleges Help Parents Move from Welfare to Self-Sufficiency

Anita K. Mathur
with Judy Reichle, Julie Strawn, and Chuck Wiseley

Attending Lassen Community College has been a big milestone in my life.
The instructors challenged me to be the best that I could be. I always felt
like I was an important part of Lassen Community College. The instructors
gave me the self-esteem that I needed to reach my goal and make my
dreams come true.

—Janet Diestel-Hartzell, CalWORKs participant

INTRODUCTION

In August 1997, California's legislature and governor established the California
Work Opportunity and Responsibility to Kids (CalWORKs) program as the
state's version of welfare reform. Under CalWORKs, all adult participants must
work or participate in eighteen to twenty-four months of welfare-to-work activities to remain eligible for assistance. A participant's welfare-to-work plan
may include attendance at a California community college if the county welfare
department agrees that attendance will lead the participant toward unsubsi-
dized employment, and if the college affirms that the participant is making sat-
isfactory progress.[1] In the year 2000, 28 percent of California's 400,000 adult

Epigraph quote from California Community College Chancellor's Office CalWORKs
Unit, *California Community College CalWORKs Student Success Portraits* (Sacramento,
Calif.: CCCCO, October 2000), 8.

welfare participants enrolled in at least one course at one of the 108 community colleges in California.

While participating in a California community college program, Cal-WORKs participants must participate in welfare-to-work activities for a minimum of thirty-two hours per week. Classroom, laboratory, and internship hours count toward that requirement. Outside class preparation (study-time hours) may or may not count, depending on each county's policy. Other countable welfare-to-work activities include work-study, part-time employment, on-the-job training, and community service. The thirty-two-hour requirement means that many full-time students are also required to be in work activities for an additional twenty hours per week.

California community colleges are playing a critical and expanding role in the state's welfare reform system. With the introduction of the Cal-WORKs program in 1997, $65 million was allocated from the state General Fund to the California community colleges. This new funding was in addition to the $16 million allocated annually to the California community college system during the previous federal welfare program, Aid to Families with Dependent Children (AFDC). The California community colleges have used these funds to redesign their curricula and provide new services, such as child care, work-study opportunities, service coordination, and job-development and job-placement programs. These new resources help to accelerate training and credentialing within the time limits and constraints faced by welfare participants.

This chapter begins by describing in detail the many programs and services offered to welfare participants at college campuses through community college CalWORKs/TANF funds and other categories of funding from the state and federal governments. After describing these newly implemented support services, we provide an analysis of the educational, employment, and earnings outcomes of welfare participants who enrolled in credit coursework in the California community college system. To place the economic outcomes of these participants in context, their outcomes are contrasted with those of the general welfare population in California and with those of the general community college student body. Our data analysis of students who leave California community colleges shows that students receiving welfare who complete a significant amount of coursework work more and increase their earnings substantially in one to three years after exiting college. Those who obtain certificates and associate's degrees have the most substantial increases over time, and those who complete vocational programs see the highest overall earnings. Preliminary evidence also suggests that, even while in school, welfare participants who enroll in community college programs have higher earnings than the general population of welfare participants in the state of California. The chapter concludes by offering recommendations for relevant state and federal policies.

FACILITATING STUDENT PROGRESS: CALIFORNIA COMMUNITY COLLEGE CalWORKs SERVICES

The primary California Community College (CCC) CalWORKs programs and services funded by the additional money given to the California community college system in 1997 are child care, work-study, job development and job placement, and coordination of welfare-to-work plans that include education as an allowable activity. In addition, instruction, child care, and job-placement services are also offered to those who have recently left assistance, so that they might upgrade their skills and advance in a career. Since the beginning of new programs in 1997, the number of student welfare participants receiving CCC CalWORKs services has increased 57 percent, from 27,000 in 1997–1998 to 47,118 in 2000–2001. The number of students served through the CCC CalWORKs program represents approximately 14 percent of the adult welfare participant caseload in California and approximately 50 percent of welfare participants who attend California community colleges.

The following section describes the primary services provided to CalWORKs participants in the community college system, and presents the voices of a few students reflecting on these services.[2]

Child Care

Adequate child care is critical to the success of student welfare participants. CalWORKs students require child care that accommodates their varied circumstances and individual schedules, including night and weekend classes. State CalWORKs regulations guarantee child care coverage for the entire period that a welfare participant is engaged in welfare-to-work activities (thirty-two hours per week) plus travel time to those activities. County welfare offices typically provide funding to meet the full child care needs of CalWORKs students. However, child care services are often funded through the community colleges' CalWORKs program. California community colleges have a sizable budget for child care services, and typically services are available to meet these students' and their children's needs. CCC CalWORKs child care services were provided to 7,975 children in 2000–2001—nearly four times the number served when the program began in 1998. All California community colleges also have the capacity to offer child care vouchers through their CARE program and vocational education services. These supplements can bridge gaps in services.

Mary Varela, a successful CCC CalWORKs student, explains how CalWORKs child care helped her:

> Without [CalWORKs'] support, I would have been very limited in choosing my major, since transportation and child care put serious

limits on my time and availability for school. With the help of Cal-
WORKs in these areas, I was freed up to invest in a more demanding
career program. My associate's degree in the Health Sciences gives me
a competitive edge in the Silicon Valley economy, and increases my
earnings potential. The child care, especially, has allowed me to move
forward with my goals by providing backup day care when campus
child care is not available. This has let me work off-campus, gain on-
the-job experience, and take the occasional night class. . . . Having a
child care center right here on campus has allowed me to pursue my
educational goals, knowing that my child is close by and well taken
care of. For me, attending community college has meant that my
daughter and I now have a future. (CCCCO 2000, 16)[3]

Prior to the implementation of CalWORKs, there was a child care program
through Greater Avenues for Independence (GAIN). However, this program
was extremely limited in scope and was run solely by the counties. There were no
college or alternative payment provider network structures. The amount of child
care funding for GAIN participants was quite limited—in fact, the limited an-
cillary funds were why the numbers of students in GAIN had to remain small.
Although the Department of Education provided additional child care funding
through nonprofit agencies, waiting lists for child care through these agencies
were extensive. Today, through the combination of county and community college CalWORKs funding, child care services have been fully provided to student
parents during their first eighteen to twenty-four months of work activities and
can also be extended for the duration of their sixty-month lifetime limit.

Work-Study

Work-study funds are allocated to provide work opportunities that enable participant students to meet CalWORKs work requirements while pursuing an
educational program and to provide students with related work experience that
will make them more marketable when they finish their educational program.
Work-study funds can be used only if the total hours of education and employment are sufficient to meet both the state and federal minimum requirements
for qualifying work-related activities. Because earned income from any college
work-study program is exempt from welfare cash grant calculations, the opportunity to participate in work-study considerably raises the income level of the
CalWORKs student household.[4]

Typically, there is enough work-study funding for approximately one-
quarter of all CCC CalWORKs students. In 2000–2001, $15 million subsi-
dized eight thousand students. Federal work-study served nearly thirteen
thousand students at the colleges and dispensed nearly $22 million in work-

study awards/wages. The majority of students are placed in on-campus positions, but every college offers some off-campus work-study opportunities as well. Other work-study opportunities at the colleges are provided through the Extended Opportunity Programs and Services (EOPS) department (described later in the chapter), serving almost one thousand students with $1.2 million in awards. Therefore, the CCC CalWORKs work-study program is a significant source of income and work experience for large numbers of students.

CCC CalWORKs students who completed educational programs often speak of the importance of CalWORKs work-study:

> The CCC CalWORKs Program played a very big part in my success at Lassen Community College. The CCC CalWORKs Program made it possible for me to get the experience I needed by letting me work at the Child Development Center, and paying me to be there. . . . I was recently hired as a full-time teacher for Lassen College Child Development Center. I am planning on going back to school in a few years to work towards getting my Master's Degree in Early Childhood Education. . . . I would like to send a special thanks to the staff at the Child Development Center at Lassen Community College for giving me the chance to learn from such a wonderful group of people. (CCCCO 2000)[5]

> Attending community college has been a sound economic investment in my future, but has also helped me to grow in other areas. I have been able to explore my own interests and talents, and have found an economic sector that not only prepares me to financially provide for my family, but also one that allows me to express my creative potential. I am working toward a Certificate in Interactive and Multimedia Technologies. Attending Foothill College has introduced me to new ideas, inspiring people, and growth opportunities. For the past year, I have been a student employee in human resources at the District Office, and am now also working as an HTML tutor. (CCCCO 2000)[6]

Job Development and Placement

CCC CalWORKs funding for job development and placement serves several purposes. First, this program places CalWORKs students in work activities that enable them to meet their work-participation requirements. Such placements also provide students with additional income and make them more marketable when they complete their educational program. On-campus coordinators provide job-development and placement services to students in work-study programs, internships, community service, and other paid and unpaid work activities.

Job-development and placement services also provide career education and train students in job-seeking and job-retention skills. Approximately 18,000 students receiving welfare were helped by job development and placement services in 2000–2001, and 5,807 were placed in employment by college staff.

CCC CalWORKs Coordination

In addition to providing student services, CCC CalWORKs funding is also used to employ staff at each campus to coordinate referrals to the college from the county welfare offices, track student progress, refer students to various student support services, place students in appropriate academic programs, and ensure that welfare-to-work plans overall are viable. Campus coordinators also develop linkages with other local agencies including local workforce investment boards and one-stop centers. A distinct difference of the new CalWORKs program is the strong emphasis on funding direct student services rather than college staffing. However, the CalWORKs staff are often cited by successful students as key players in their academic progress. For example, two CalWORKs students write,

> I can't say enough about the CCC CalWORKs program. I would not have been able to make it through my educational program without it. The staff has been like a family to me. They have provided me with academic counseling, financial assistance, job assistance, and even an occasional word of encouragement when it was needed. I hope to one day help others the same way that they have helped me. (CCCCO 2000)[7]

> Without the CCC CalWORKs program I would not be attending Lassen Community College. I would not be able to look to the future with long-term goals and thoughts of furthering my dreams of a new career. All of the people and departments who have also worked so hard to help me and continue to support me in all the things I am doing now are what mean the most to me; without them I would have been lost. I feel that the only way I can truly show my thanks is to keep going and continue showing them that I am trying to be one person they can feel proud of and that I am worthy of all their combined efforts to help me succeed. So thank you! I bow to you all. (CCCCO 2000)[8]

OTHER SERVICE DEPARTMENTS WITHIN THE COLLEGE

CCC CalWORKs services were specifically established to supplement, not supplant, existing services at the California community colleges. Many service programs were well established when these new, extensive CCC CalWORKs services began; they are almost always used whenever CCC CalWORKs students are eligible. The major service programs are: Extended Opportunity Programs and Services (EOPS), and its adjunct program, Cooperative Agencies Resources for Education (CARE); Disabled Students Programs and Services (DSP&S); AmeriCorps; and academic counseling, transfer, and matriculation services. The primary goal of EOPS is to encourage the enrollment, retention, and transfer of students with language, social, economic, or educational disadvantages, and to facilitate the successful completion of the students' college objectives. EOPS offers academic and support counseling, financial aid, and other support services. EOPS recipients are required to be full-time students, that is, enrolled for at least twelve units per semester. The CARE program was established in 1982 to further assist EOPS-eligible students who are female, single heads of household, and welfare participants with a child under the age of fourteen in the household. Student eligibility for CARE grants and services is determined by their unmet financial need. Both CARE and EOPS offer academic counseling. Less than one-fourth of CalWORKs students each year have eligibility for EOPS and/or CARE services however, since most begin community college without the capacity for full-time credit coursework. DSP&S provide support services, specialized instruction, and educational accommodations to students with disabilities so that they can participate fully and benefit equally with their peers from the college experience.

There are three AmeriCorps Service Learning programs available at thirty-one of the CCC campuses (as of 2001). One program targets the involvement of CalWORKs participants while the other two AmeriCorps programs accept CalWORKs participants but do not specifically target their involvement. Matriculation services are available for all enrolled credit and noncredit students and include counseling, assessment and testing, orientation and follow-up services. The intent of these services is to assist students in planning and implementation of their educational and vocational programs, and in setting goals leading to their eventual success in the community college or a transfer institution. CCC CalWORKs services are coordinated with academic counseling, transfer, and matriculation services to ensure maximum utilization of these valuable campus services by CCC CalWORKs students.

FINANCIAL AID

CalWORKs participants are usually eligible to receive some form of state and/or federal financial aid available through a California community college campus financial aid office. The CCC CalWORKs program works with the financial aid office to coordinate student budgets and ensure that students are not "over-awarded" financial aid. The major forms of financial aid available to CCC CalWORKs participants are course fee waivers and federal grants.

The Board of Governors' (BOG) fee waiver program is designed to ensure that the California Community College fee policies ($18 per unit) are not a financial barrier to education for any California resident. Students who receive public assistance benefits are eligible to receive a BOG fee waiver to bypass fees for any credit course they take. Roughly two-thirds of CalWORKs students, compared to one-third of the general student body, receive this fee waiver.[9] In addition to the fee waiver, the state of California offers two "Cal Grants" that CCC CalWORKs students may be eligible to receive while attending community college. Cal Grant "B" awards provide grants (of approximately $1,550 each) to California residents attending any qualifying California institution offering undergraduate academic programs of not less than one academic year. Cal Grant "C" grants (in the amount of $600 annually) assist students enrolled in California occupational or vocational programs that are four months to two years in length. Approximately 3 percent of CCC CalWORKs students received Cal Grants "B" or "C" in 1999–2000. This low percentage is primarily a function of a limited application period, the Cal Grant program's focus on recent high school graduates, and the relatively small number of grants awarded. CCC CalWORKs students are more likely to receive vouchers (for books and other services) and grants through the EOPS and CARE programs at the colleges. Twelve percent of the CCC CalWORKs students received these types of grants in 1999–2000.[10] In addition to grants from the state and college, CCC CalWORKs students are also eligible to apply for need-based federal grants, loans, and scholarships. Approximately one-third of CCC CalWORKs students received federal Pell grants (in the amount of $4,000 per year) in 1999–2000 and 17 percent received other forms of federal financial aid or assistance.

Although there are many financial aid options available to students, there is insufficient funding allocated to the colleges to provide the outreach that would systematically and effectively inform potential and current students about available assistance. Whereas many CCC CalWORKs students receive fee waivers and some federal and/or state grants and loans, a substantial percentage of students receive only limited grants and loans or none at all. This relative lack of aid makes the CCC CalWORKs federal- and state-funded work-study jobs an especially critical aid supplement to the other programs.

CREDENTIALS COUNT: EDUCATIONAL AND ECONOMIC OUTCOMES OF STUDENTS ON WELFARE

Participants

Because of recent policy changes that have conditionally permitted welfare participants to count education as a work activity, it is important to document how student welfare participants fare educationally and economically over time. The remainder of this chapter tracks the progress of welfare participants who have enrolled in and exited from a California community college. To place the educational and economic outcomes of these participants in context, their outcomes are contrasted with those of the general community college student body and with those of the general welfare population in California.

For the majority of this study we look at the outcomes of all welfare participants in California who exited a California community college during the academic year 1996–1997. Although this group attended and exited college prior to the full establishment of welfare reform policy changes in California and prior to the implementation of the CCC CalWORKs program, the use of this pre-reform group allows us to track employment and earnings outcomes for a full three years after students exit from college.[11]

Educational Outcomes

Students receiving welfare who exited college in 1996–1997 were remarkably similar in educational attainment to members of the general student body who exited from college at the same time. A little over one-third of exiting welfare participants and the general student body left with more than twelve credits completed. Among those who left with twelve or more credits, welfare participants were equally likely as the general student body to leave with an associate's degree (about 17 percent each), and somewhat more likely to leave with a certificate (15 percent versus 11 percent respectively).

The vast majority (about two-thirds) of students receiving assistance and of the general student population that left college in 1996–1997 completed fewer than twelve units of coursework. Among this less-than-twelve-unit exit group, we did find differences between welfare participants and the general student body. A greater proportion of welfare participants in this population completed zero units upon leaving school.[12] Figures 7.1 and 7.2 illustrate the differences.

Welfare participants who left with zero units were more likely to be Hispanic than the zero-unit completers in the general student body and were also slightly more likely to be under age twenty. There was also some indication that the zero-unit welfare participant group may have included a larger proportion of those who enrolled without a high school diploma.[13] Among the students exiting in 1996–1997 with more than zero but fewer than twelve units completed (.01–11.99 units), there were similar demographic differences between the welfare population and the general student body. Welfare participant students with .01 to 11.99 units were far more likely to be ethnic minorities and not have a high school diploma at entry. Furthermore, although 70 percent of the welfare participant .01–11.99-credit group received tuition waivers, only 14 percent of the general student body leaving with .01–11.99 credits received tuition waivers. These characteristics indicate that welfare participants who leave

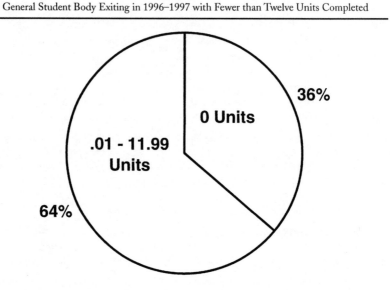

Source: CCCCO MIS Student Record Database with EDD and CDSS Match.

FIGURE 7.2
AFDC Participants Exiting in 1996–1997 with Fewer than Twelve Units Completed

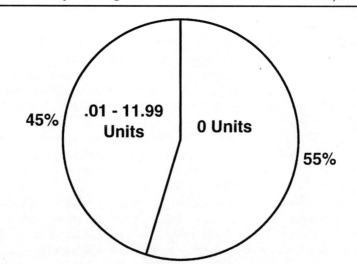

Source: CCCCO MIS Student Record Database with EDD and CDSS Match.

school having completed only a small number of units are more disadvantaged than the general student body who leave school with a similar level of educational attainment. Welfare participants are also more likely than the general student body to drop or fail courses.

These educational outcomes are for those students who did not immediately transfer into a public four-year California college. However, one of the primary missions of the California Community College system is to prepare students for transfer into four-year schools. The CCC Chancellor's Office collects data on exiting students who transferred into the California State University and University of California system (CSU/UC) within two years of exit. Data on the 1996–1997 exit group show that welfare participants are considerably less likely than the general student body to transfer into the CSU/UC system immediately after leaving community college. Of the 50,057 welfare participants who left college in 1996–1997, approximately 7 percent (3,334) transferred into CSU/UC within two years. This rate is less than half of the transfer rate among the general student body who left school in 1996–1997 (15 percent). However, transfer students from the welfare population completed full associate's degrees at about twice the rate of transfer students from the general student body.

Employment Outcomes

We find that the majority of California Community College welfare participants are employed in both the first and third years after they left school in 1996–1997, and that the employment rate for those employed in both years is higher for welfare participants who completed vocational degrees and certificates than for those who completed non-vocational degrees and certificates. We also find some indication that California Community College welfare participants have higher employment rates while in school than the general welfare population in the state of California, and that they are able to considerably narrow the employment gap with the general student body within three years after exiting college.

For purposes of this analysis, we define employment in a given year as having Unemployment Insurance (UI) wage records in at least one-quarter of that year. As Figure 7.3 shows, approximately 60 percent of all welfare participant students who left college in 1996–1997 were employed both the first year and the third year after leaving school. About one-quarter were employed in either the first year out of school or third year out of school, but not in both years. Approximately one-fifth remained unemployed in both the first and third years out of school.

Employment rates were typically higher for those who left school after completing vocational programs than for those who left after completing

FIGURE 7.3
Percent of Exiting AFDC Participants Employed First Year Out and Third Year Out of College

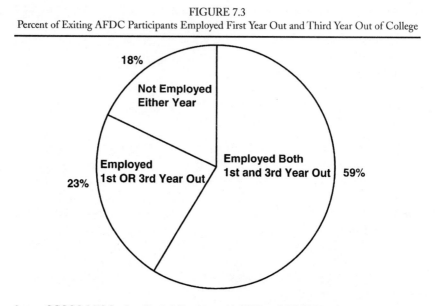

Source: CCCCO MIS Student Record Database with EDD and CDSS Match.

non-vocational programs. Although approximately half of the students who received non-vocational associate's degrees were employed both the first and third years out of school, 70 percent of those who received vocational associate's degrees were employed both years.

One argument against providing education and training to welfare participants is that it will distract from "real work." However, we find that our sample of student welfare participants had higher employment rates the last quarter they were in school than the general welfare population in California had in the same quarter. To compare student welfare-participant employment rates with employment rates of the general welfare population, we use the CCC Cal-WORKs group who exited community college in 1999–2000 rather than the CCC AFDC group who exited in 1996–1997. The last quarter that the CCC CalWORKs group was in school, 56 percent were employed. In comparison, 44 percent of the general welfare population in California were employed that same quarter. Community college welfare participants who enter college without a high school diploma still maintain higher employment rates than the general welfare population. During the last quarter in school, approximately 52 percent of student welfare participants who began school with less than a high school credential were employed, in comparison with 44 percent of the general welfare population in that quarter.

These data provide some indication that welfare participant students have comparable, if not higher, employment rates while in school than the general

FIGURE 7.4
Four-Quarter Employment Rates of AFDC and All Students Exiting Community College
in 1996–1997

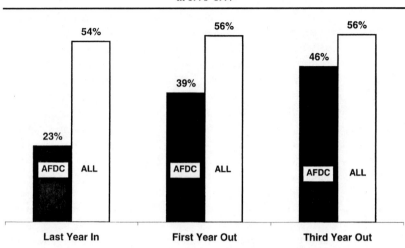

Source: CCCCO MIS Student Record Database with EDD and CDSS Match.

welfare population. But how do they compare to a more advantaged population? Although rates of steady employment are considerably lower among the welfare population than in the general student body, we find that welfare participant students who left school in 1996–1997 narrow this gap over time, as shown in Figure 7.4. To compare steady employment, we look at those who were employed all four quarters of the year as opposed to one or more quarters. The last year they were in school, only 23 percent of the total AFDC exit group was employed all four quarters of the year. The first year out of school, 39 percent of the AFDC exit group was employed all four quarters. By the third year out of college, 46 percent of the AFDC exit group was employed all four quarters of the year. With these increases, the AFDC group managed to close the four-quarter employment gap with the general student body from 31 percentage points to 10 percentage points in a relatively short period of time.

Vocational CCC AFDC participants increased four-quarter employment even faster with a 50-percent rate in the first year after college. The vocational AFDC group actually surpassed the general student body rate by the third year after college with 60 percent employed all four quarters.

Earnings Outcomes

To assess earnings outcomes, we compare the median annual earnings of welfare participant students who exited college in 1996–1997 and who were employed at least one quarter in both their first year and third year out of college. We compare actual earnings and earnings increases between student welfare participants and the general student body, and also look for differences in earnings by number of units completed, program type, and whether or not students came to college with a high school credential. We have four major findings. First, the more education welfare participants attain while in school, the greater their earnings increase in the labor market. This finding holds true even for those who entered college without a high school credential. Second, increases in earnings are similar for those in vocational and non-vocational programs, although actual earnings are higher for vocational students. Third, welfare participants' earnings after college grow faster than those of the general student body, allowing them to narrow the initial gap. Finally, welfare participants who attend college earn more while in school than the general welfare population, even if they began college without a high school credential.

The more education welfare participants attain while in school (number of courses, certificate, associate's degree), the greater the increase in median annual earnings from the first to third year in the labor market, as shown in Figure 7.5. AFDC participants who left college with an associate's degree in 1996–1997 had a 72 percent increase in median annual earnings between their first and third years in the labor market. This compared to a 48 percent increase for those who left with 12–23.99 units completed.

Actual earnings three years after leaving school were also higher among welfare participants who had taken a greater number of credits or left commu-

FIGURE 7.5

Percentage Increase in Median Annual Earnings from First Year Out to Third Year Out of School for AFDC Students Exiting Community College in 1996–1997

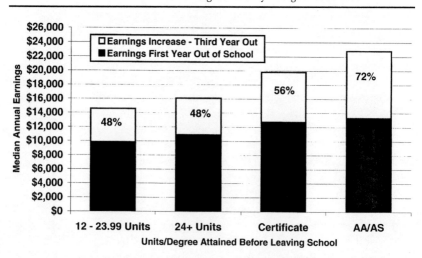

Source: CCCCO MIS Student Record Database with EDD and CDSS Match.

nity college with a degree. For example, those with an associate's degree made approximately $8,200 more per year their third year out of school than those who left with only 12–23.99 units.

The majority of welfare participants who attended and then exited community college in 1996–1997 held a high school degree when they first entered school (about two-thirds). However, the benefits of a community college education hold true even for those who entered without a high school credential. AFDC students entering college without a high school credential who exited with twelve or more credits increased their annual median earnings by 45 percent from their first year to their third year out of school. The more units with which these initially disadvantaged students left, the greater their earnings increase was during this period. Those who left with a certificate increased earnings by 55 percent and those who left with an associate's degree increased earnings by 77 percent. Although educationally disadvantaged students were able to make significant gains in earnings by their third year out of school, actual earnings of those who entered school without a high school degree lagged behind those who entered with a high school diploma under their belt, even at equivalent levels of educational attainment.

Earnings increases of non-vocational student welfare participants were on par with earnings increases of vocational student welfare participants from the first to third year out of college. Students who left school with at least twelve units of vocational and non-vocational coursework saw approximately a 60 percent increase in earnings from the first to third year out of school. However, despite similarity of earnings increases, vocational students retained substantially greater absolute earnings than non-vocational students over time. There was a $4,114 difference in median annual earnings between vocational and non-vocational AFDC participants with associate's degrees the first year out of school. By the third year out of school, welfare participants who earned a vocational associate's degree were earning $5,932 more than those who earned a non-vocational associate's degree.

Although welfare participants still earned considerably less than the general student body, student welfare participants who left school in 1996–1997 had greater earnings increases from the first to the third year out of school than the general student body. For example, welfare participants who left with an associate's degree realized a 72 percent increase in earnings between their first and third years in the labor market. In contrast, the general student body that left with similar credentials realized a 37 percent increase in earnings between their first and third years in the labor market.

After three years in the labor market, welfare participants who left community college in 1996–1997 narrowed their earnings gap with the general student body that left community college during the same time period. The general student body that left college with twelve or more credits made about 76 percent more than welfare participants with similar credits the first year out of school. However, the earnings gap narrowed to 51 percent by the third year out. Vocational welfare participants had the widest gap to close (an 85 percentage-point difference in median annual earnings the first year out of school) but managed to successfully close the gap to 53 percent by the third year out of school. Because there are large demographic differences between the welfare population and the general student body (particularly by gender), closing the earnings gap by this much in such a short period of time is a significant accomplishment.

Welfare participants with certificates and associate's degrees narrow the earnings gap with all community college students more quickly than do those without credentials. The first year out of school, student welfare participants who exited with certificates or associate's degrees still had a significant gap in median earnings with all community college students who exited with similar credentials (a 90 percent gap for those leaving with a certificate and a 62 percent gap for those leaving with an associate's degree). However, these welfare participant students were able to significantly close this gap by the third year out of school (by 33 and 32 percentage points respectively). By contrast, welfare participants who left school with twenty-four or more credits but no degree only decreased their gap with the general student body by 13 percentage points by the third year out, as illustrated in Figure 7.6. They did, however, also start out with a smaller gap the first year out of school.

Welfare participants who attend California community colleges appear to have higher quarterly earnings than the general welfare population in the state of California, even when only looking at the earnings of participants who

FIGURE 7.6
Percentage Greater Median Annual Earnings of All Students over AFDC Students
First Year Out (FYO) and Third Year Out (TYO) of Community College

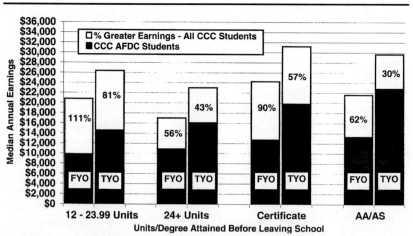

Source: CCCCO MIS Student Record Database with EDD and CDSS Match.

entered school at an educational disadvantage. Welfare participants who enter community college without a high school diploma have greater earnings while in school than the general California welfare population even though approximately half of the general California welfare population is estimated to have a high school diploma. Median earnings during the last quarter in school of employed welfare students who began college without a high school diploma was $2,616—22 percent higher than the employed general California welfare population that quarter. Taken along with our findings on employment rates, this comparison indicates that welfare participants who attend school do not necessarily suffer cutbacks on employment and earnings to pursue further education.

Although we do not yet have a longitudinal sample of the general California welfare population with which to compare our community college sample, we do know that the longer our student leavers are out of school, the more their earnings increase relative to the general welfare population. The first quarter that 1999–2000 CCC student welfare participants (who entered without a high school degree but exited with at least twelve units completed) were out of school, they made 50 percent greater earnings than the general welfare population made that same quarter. By their fourth quarter out of school, the earnings gap with the general welfare population increased to 80 percent.

IMPLICATIONS FOR STATE AND FEDERAL POLICY

California community colleges play a critical and expanding role in the state's welfare reform system. Each college provides education, training, and work experiences—all essential components of a welfare-to-work plan that can result in welfare participants gaining employment at a family-supporting wage. Community colleges provide a return on investment in a few short years due to increased tax revenues generated from the higher earnings of workers who attended a community college and the long-term employment they obtain. The data show that welfare participant students who complete a significant amount of coursework work more quarters of the year and increase their earnings substantially in one to three years after exiting college. This wage increase is especially true for those who are in vocational programs or who obtain an associate's degree. Preliminary evidence from this study indicates that welfare participants who enroll in community college academic programs see greater earnings than the general population of CalWORKs participants. These findings are consistent with recent national research that showed one of the most successful welfare-to-work programs ever studied—the Portland, Oregon, Job Opportunities and Basic Skills (JOBS) program—greatly increased participation in college and receipt of occupational certificates (Hamilton et al. 2001). This was probably an important factor in the program's ability to help welfare participants find better and longer-lasting employment than they would have found on their own.

Because post-secondary education and training play an important role in improving economic outcomes for welfare participants, states should be encouraged to advocate post-secondary education as a welfare-to-work activity and to increase funding of critical on-campus support and employment services for participants. Welfare reform implementation in California brought additional child care dollars to the community colleges, doubled campuses' ability to offer work-study opportunities, and expanded the scope of these new work-study opportunities by aligning them with students' career goals. With strict welfare regulations regarding work participation and time limits, the college service coordinators are particularly critical. Through state education CalWORKs program funding, every community college campus in California employs a CalWORKs coordinator and additional staff to help students choose and navigate through a course of study that not only meets welfare requirements but also helps them move toward self-sufficiency. Using on-campus coordinators to provide child care, work-study, and job-placement services ensures that student welfare participants receive the kind of support and employment-related education that pays off in higher-paying employment.

Interviews with welfare participant students indicate that the specific support and employment services offered through CCC CalWORKs programs are often key factors in their successful transition. However, future funding for these types of services is tenuous at best. With the downturn in the California economy in 2002, the budget for Community College CalWORKs services was decreased from $81 to $63 million. Twenty million of the new amount would be stipulated through a local district one-for-one dollar match. At the time of this writing, overall education funding, including the California Community College's overall 2003 budget as well as the CalWORKs budget, is anticipated to be cut even further due to lack of statewide revenues.

Despite the large increase in employment and earnings that a community college education and support services provide, welfare participant students who do not complete certificates or degrees remain somewhat disadvantaged in the labor market. The majority of welfare participant students, and indeed the majority of all community college students, take three-and-a-half years or longer to complete an associate's degree. Considering the additional barriers that welfare participants face, namely raising children on limited resources, it is not surprising that they take longer than the traditional two-year time frame to complete an associate's program. Given the current eighteen-to-twenty-four-month time limits imposed by welfare reform, the average CalWORKs student who is trying to complete an associate's degree will ultimately have to face a decision to leave school before her program is completed, or be ineligible for cash assistance. CalWORKs participants clearly need more time than is currently allowed to obtain an associate's degree. Although many community colleges have used CalWORKs funding to develop short-term programs that will accommodate time limits, programs that lead to self-sufficiency[14] wages require academic courses that are, for most students, usually unattainable within a two-year period.

At the national level, federal welfare policy should allow and encourage the balanced approach that California uses to provide a mix of employment and quality education and training services in welfare-to-work programs. Research has shown repeatedly that this method is by far the most effective welfare-to-work strategy (Gueron and Hamilton 2002). Toward this end, federal policy should ease restrictions on counting education and training participation toward meeting federal work requirements. Easing those restrictions would encourage states to provide a mix of employment and skill-upgrading activities to TANF participants. In addition, policies should allow sufficient time for welfare participants to obtain a variety of post-secondary education ranging from occupational certificates and associate's degrees to four-year college education. Policies should also offer incentives for states to provide support services and work-study positions to low income student parents to facilitate their success in school. Finally, welfare policies should make it easier to balance work, family, and school by keeping the overall number of work hours required at an attainable level, clarifying that student work-study is a countable activity toward work-participation rates, and examining how federal student aid policies can better support both unemployed parents and low-wage workers in school.

The long-term success of welfare reform, and the well-being of the families aided by it, depend on basing state and federal policy decisions on sound research and proven welfare-to-work strategies. Employment-focused post-secondary education and training, together with the supportive services that allow parents to succeed in school, are essential components of a welfare reform policy that will improve the lives of low income parents and their children and reduce the welfare caseload over the long term.

NOTES

1. Individuals referred to education programs by county welfare departments are often encouraged to enter short-term programs, less than a year in length, rather than to complete an associate's degree. However, if a participant is already enrolled in college on her own initiative when she begins her welfare-to-work plan, the student may continue in the educational program as part of her plan. Roughly one-half of welfare participant students at the colleges are self-initiated.

2. These interviews should not be seen as representative of the experiences of all CalWORKs students. Students who offered their comments were typically those who successfully completed programs and were thus best served by the CalWORKs program. Nonetheless, their stories can help illuminate how additional support services can help students succeed in school.

3. Mary Varela, Foothill Community College, *Student success portraits* (CCCCO 2000, 16).

4. Work-study aside, the state CalWORKs program allows all participants to disregard a higher level of earnings than was the case under the GAIN program. During the

GAIN program, the income disregard was figured according to this example: On $500 gross income, subtract $30. Then count 2/3 of the remainder ($313.33) against the grant. Total income kept = $186.67. With the CalWORKs program, a much higher disregard was allowed. For example: on $500 gross income, subtract $225. Then count 1/2 of the remainder ($137.50) against the grant. Total income kept = $362.50.

5. Janet Diestel-Hartzell, Lassen Community College, *Student success portraits* (CCCCO 2000, 8).

6. Sheri Cole, Foothill Community College, *Student success portraits* (CCCCO 2000, 20).

7. Linda Allen, Palomar Community College, *Student success portraits* (CCCCO 2000, 15).

8. Tracy E. Sant, Lassen Community College, *Student success portraits* (CCCCO 2000, 22).

9. Students may enroll in a combination of credit and noncredit coursework, but will receive the fee waiver only for credit coursework. Part of the reason a greater percentage of CCC CalWORKs participants do not receive the BOG fee waiver may be that many CCC CalWORKs students begin by taking solely noncredit courses and therefore do not initially meet the BOG fee waiver eligibility requirements.

10. EOPS grants that are awarded are coordinated through the financial aid office and assist in meeting students' unmet financial need. Vouchers for books and other services are distributed directly from the EOPS and CARE offices but disbursement of grants must be reported to financial aid offices to coordinate the benefits with all other aid programs as required by federal and state law.

11. The data for this study come from three sources. The first data source is student enrollment records for all 108 California campuses; the second is state welfare records; and the third is state unemployment insurance (UI) wage records. By linking these three sources of data together by social security number, we are able to track the education, employment, and earnings outcomes of welfare participants who attended a community college and then exited without returning to a community college for at least one year and without transferring to a four-year California college or university for at least a two-year period. We compare the earnings and employment outcomes of exiting student welfare participants to an exiting group made up of the entire community college student body and to the general population of welfare participants in the state of California. (Although the general student body is a combination of welfare and non-welfare participants, welfare participants are only about 5 percent of the total student body who leave school in a particular year; including welfare participants in the comparison group, therefore, is unlikely to bias the percentages very much.) The California Department of Social Services (CDSS) provides information to the public on the quarterly earnings of all welfare participants in the CalWORKs Adult Participants Quarterly Wage Earnings Reports. Data is publicly available from 1997–2001 and can be compared to the quarterly earnings of student participants who left college in 1999–2000.

We use two groups of student welfare participants in this analysis. The most recent group of students for which we have one year of follow-up wage data exited college in 1999–2000. We refer to this group as the CCC CalWORKs group because they received state CalWORKs income support, were fully subjected to other welfare reform regulations regarding work requirements and time limitations, and about half of them accessed college-provided California Community College CalWORKs programs and services mentioned in the preceding section. Because the 1999–2000 exit group has only one year of follow-up wage and employment data currently available, we only use the 1999–2000 exit cohort to look at the employment and earnings of student welfare participants in comparison to the general welfare population in California. To evaluate changes in student welfare participant earnings and employment over time, we examine a pre-CalWORKs group—referred to as the CCC AFDC group—that left college in 1996–1997 and for which three years of follow-up wage data are available. While comparable to the 1999–2000 cohort in many ways, the 1996–1997 cohort was not subject to state CalWORKs work requirements nor did they have access to CalWORKs support services that began to be offered through the community colleges in 1997–1998. They did, however, have access to new services being provided by the counties such as child care subsidies and higher earnings disregards that were not available to welfare participants prior to 1996. Overall, the demographic background and educational and economic outcomes of the two exiting welfare participant student groups are similar enough to be used somewhat interchangeably in making comparisons to the general student body and the general welfare population.

The goal of our comparison of CCC student welfare participants to the general CCC student body is to see how welfare participants who earn similar academic credentials compare with more demographically advantaged students over time. One would expect to see higher employment and earnings both in school and out of school for the general student body than for welfare participant students, given that the general student body generally has fewer potential barriers to academic and employment success. Welfare participant students are parents and more likely than the general student body to be women and ethnic minorities, especially African Americans. Furthermore, welfare participant students are about twice as likely as the general student body to lack a high school diploma at entry to community college.

Although comparing community college welfare participants to themselves and to the general student body over time has value, it does not answer the question of whether providing welfare participants access to a community college education rather than straight employment is economically beneficial. A comparison with the general welfare population in California will come closer to this type of analysis. To make this comparison, we examine the median earnings of welfare participants during the last quarter they were in school and the median earnings of the general welfare population during the same quarter. There are several caveats about this comparison. First, we do not yet have data available on the sample of the general welfare poupulation that would tell us what percentage of those participants were in fact in community college programs or allow us to control for other demographic factors, such as age or ethnicity. Second, the general welfare population is composed of a different group of participants each quarter. This means we are unable to look at how the earnings of a cohort of the general welfare population changes over time as we are with the CCC welfare cohorts. Third, the general welfare sample is a selection of participants receiving assistance for all three months of the quarter. We do know that student welfare participants received public assistance at some time during the last year they were in school, but we do not know the exact fiscal quarter. We do not know whether they are receiving aid in the quarters following exit from college. Therefore the CCC sample is less restrictive on assistance receipt than the CDSS sample.

12. Completing zero units means that the participant enrolled in a credit course but then either dropped or failed the course and therefore did not pick up credits.

13. It is not possible to accurately estimate education at entry for the zero-credit AFDC group because 23 percent were unknown on this characteristic.

14. Self-sufficiency income standards have been established for every county in California and for seventy different types of families based on a variety of variables that include family size, ages of children, and geographic location. The Self-Sufficiency Income Standard is designed to reflect what a family needs in order to adequately meet living expenses without public or private assistance. Costs contained in the standard include housing, child care, food, transportation, health care, and net taxes after relevant tax credits are applied (Pearce and Brooks 2000).

REFERENCES

California Community College Chancellor's Office (CCCCO), CalWORKs Unit. 2000, October. *California community college CalWORKs student success portraits.* Sacramento, Calif.: CCCCO.

California Department of Social Services, Research and Development Division. 2002. *CalWORKs adult participants quarterly earnings reports.* Retrieved 23 November 2002. Available at http://www.dss.cahwnet.gov/research/CalWORKsAd_402.htm.

———. 2002. *CalWORKs characteristics survey federal fiscal year 2000: October 1999 through September 2000.* Retrieved 23 November 2002. Available at http:www.dss. cahwnet.gov/research/res/pdf/CalWKsCharFFY2000.pdf.

Gueron, Judith M., and Gayle Hamilton. 2002. *The role of education and training in welfare reform. Welfare reform and beyond.* Policy Brief #20. Washington, D.C.: Brookings Institution.

Hamilton, Gayle, Stephen Freedman, Lisa Gennetian, Charles Michalopoulos, Johanna Walter, Diana Adams-Ciardullo, Anna Gassman-Pines, Sharon McGroder, Martha Zaslow, Jennifer Brooks, and Surjeet Ahluwalia. 2001, December. *National evaluation of welfare-to-work strategies: How effective are different welfare-to-work approaches? Five-year adult and child impacts for eleven programs.* Washington, D.C.: U.S. Department of Health and Human Services and U.S. Department of Education.

Pearce, Diana, with Jennifer Brooks. 2000, November. *The California self-sufficiency standard.* Washington, D.C.: Wider Opportunities for Women.

Chapter 8

"This Little Light of Mine"

Parent Activists Struggling for Access to Post-Secondary Education in Appalachian Kentucky

Christiana Miewald

INTRODUCTION

This chapter examines the intersection of welfare reform, post-secondary education, and political activism in Appalachian Kentucky. It explores how parent activists—women who were both recipients of public assistance and members of welfare rights organizations—fought to expand the state's definition of "work" in Kentucky's Transitional Assistance Program (K-TAP) to include participation in post-secondary education. The result was the passage of Kentucky House Bill 434 and other policy changes that increased access to education. This case study is instructive because it highlights the process by which local realities and experiences are translated into public policy through activism.

Garkovich, Hansen, and Dyk (1997) argue that much of the debate preceding passage of welfare reform nationally and in Kentucky revolved around a series of assumptions about people who live in poverty and rely on public assistance programs. These assumptions—that work will move people out of poverty, that no job is a bad one, and that women not in the labor market are not "working"—were typically reproduced in state plans across the country. These welfare myths, translated into policy, created and continue to create contradictions for people, agencies, and communities particularly in specific local contexts, including Appalachian Kentucky.

A depressed economy, high rates of unemployment and poverty, a need for improved social services, and a severe shortage of opportunities to earn a living wage make the emphasis on "work first" incorporated into Kentucky's welfare program, K-TAP, particularly difficult for Appalachian Kentuckians. With the region's projected job growth during the next six years at 11 percent, half the rate of Kentucky's urban areas, the prospects for welfare recipients trying to

find work in Appalachia are uncertain at best. Further, forcing K-TAP participants to find a job or enter workfare placements does not take into account the
local economy of care—the kinship and child care work that women do within
their communities. In Appalachian Kentucky, networks of kin, neighbors, and
friends provide an important social safety net that is threatened by pressures to
enter the wage labor market (Miewald 2000). Finally, Kentucky's work-first
policies are likely to place additional stresses on local economies, possibly in-
augurating a new mass migration from Appalachia to industrial centers in the
northeast and southern United States.

The people who live in the coalfields of Appalachian Kentucky have experienced decades of resource extraction, economic and political marginalization, and persistent poverty. Appalachian Kentucky, the rural southeastern
counties of Kentucky, has been historically exploited by absentee owners of
minerals rights and land, who emphasized short-term profits rather than long-
term, sustainable, locally controlled development. Households in the region
traditionally relied on male breadwinners with unsteady and dangerous work in
the coal industry, with women resiliently struggling to sustain families through
informal labor and more recently through low-wage service jobs. With the di-
vestment from the coalfields in the 1950s, the area's chronic poverty has intensified, forcing a significant percent of the area's residents to rely on public
assistance. In addition, both poverty and external economic and political power
weakened the civic infrastructure and political representation of the region.
Welfare reform is only the latest in a long history of policies imposed by outsiders who understand little about the culture, economics, or politics of the region. The current round of welfare reform presents a new set of challenges for
communities, and many in the region fear that the loss of federal assistance will
result in negative effects on already severely compromised community health
and well-being.

Following the federal trend toward devolution, Kentucky emphasized local
citizen involvement in policy formation. However, locally generated calls to end
the five-year time limit on assistance, eliminate work requirements for students,
or to provide more educational opportunities and living-wage jobs were met
with resistance by state agents who cited budgetary constraints and pressure to
comply with federal regulations. K-TAP, according to officials, was neither an
antipoverty nor education program but an effort to move recipients from welfare to work. Ironically, "local solutions," emphasized in federal policy debates
and in devolution provisions of the federal legislation, have only been allowed
when they are consistent with the dominant tenets and assumptions of federal
welfare-reform initiatives. States have been pressured to meet federal regulations, especially work-participation rates. States and counties are therefore
caught in a bind between following federal regulations and trying to adequately
address local needs. Thus, the Kentucky Works Program, which mandated
the hours and types of work K-TAP participants were required to engage in,

dictated that all activities must lead to employment. Such activities included short-term training and workfare, but not post-secondary education after twelve months, or work done raising children, maintaining kinship relations, or caring for sick or elderly family members.[1]

In fact, Kentucky's Transitional Assistance Program (K-TAP), the state's Temporary Assistance for Needy Families (TANF) program, became a political space in which different policy actors contested the meaning and impacts of "welfare reform" in relation to economic restructuring, gender relations, and the nature of "work." Several activist groups translated local needs and lived experience into public policy through a variety of tactics aimed at dismantling the myths of welfare. From 1997 to 1998, I explored this policy contention and policy community—including policy makers, advocates, parent activists, and community members—through a multisite ethnography that traced connections between different organizational and everyday worlds (Shore and Wright 1997), particularly between the formal "policy arena," represented by the governor, the Kentucky Cabinet for Families and Children, and state legislators, and the everyday lives of women experiencing economic and social restructuring in Appalachian Kentucky.

Fighting to increase access to education for low income Kentuckians was one way in which parent activists and welfare advocates struggled to shape policy in accordance with their lived experiences of local needs.[2] Together, they challenged the dominant paradigm of welfare reform by listening to, recording, and presenting the lived experience of women on public assistance to policy makers. In these efforts, K-TAP participants went beyond telling their stories; they were involved in all aspects of policy creation, including meeting with legislators and agency staff and helping to research and write legislation. They used their positions as workers and caregivers to challenge the restrictive work requirements and economic development policies that did not address their lived experiences of poverty and excluded access to education (East 2000; Herda-Rupp 2000). They were particularly motivated to do so as they withstood increasing workloads and reductions in public assistance while maintaining their caregiving responsibilities. While bringing to bear their experiences on the welfare debates, women were also engaged in a process of personal transformation as their efforts to reshape welfare reform reshaped them. They came to see themselves as people "with brains in their head," brains that could be used to shape public policy and their communities.

FIGHTING BACK AGAINST WELFARE REFORM

Despite the apparent hegemony of welfare myths and the political marginalization of K-TAP recipients, devolution and reconfiguration of public assistance created unlikely allies and possibilities at the local level. The welfare system has "helped to create new solidarities and has also generated the political issues that cement and galvanize these solidarities" (Piven 1990, 260). For example, the inclusion of the local perspective into the planning process has created new pathways for the inclusion of previously marginalized perspectives. County officials fearful of losing transfer payments; community colleges, which stand to see a decline in enrollment; and social service workers, whose jobs are threatened by privatization, find common ground with parents and welfare advocates in contesting state policy.

The economic and social burden placed on local institutions in Appalachian Kentucky has served to demystify welfare and highlight the linkages between public assistance programs and community survival. Therefore, it is possible for local communities and activist groups to come together to create the structural space to articulate their alternative vision of welfare policy. As welfare policy is developed and implemented in Kentucky, the potential economic and social fallout encompasses ever-increasing numbers of people and organizations, creating the possibility for new alliances on the local level as well as across geographic scales. New welfare policies were therefore often critiqued by Appalachian Kentucky politicians, activists, and residents as a threat to the region's economic and social well-being. This was accomplished through "backtalking"—challenging negative stereotypes about poverty in Appalachia (Stewart 1990)—and the creation of "free space" that "foster[ed] the discovery of new democratic potential among people and new political facts about the world" (Couto 1993, 166).

Part of the negative response to K-TAP came from several regional and statewide organizations, many of which had been involved in welfare rights issues prior to the Personal Responsibility and Work Opportunity Reconciliation Act (PRWORA). These groups, which had overlapping membership, sometimes separately and often as a loose coalition devised a number of tactics aimed at altering the public and political perceptions of public assistance. Among these organizations were Kentuckians for the Commonwealth (KFTC), a grassroots social justice organization; the Kentucky Welfare Reform Coalition (KWRC), a coalition of mostly professional advocates and academics; and Appalshop, a community-based media collective.[3]

To create policy that addresses the needs of localities, both the public and policy makers require an alternative to the "culture of poverty" construct, the idea that those in poverty suffer from a culture of passivity and work aversion, transmitted across generations resigned to low expectations and few resources. Without the power to develop alternative representations of welfare, it is difficult for local groups to influence the process by which policy is formulated. Instead, they must wait for strategic openings within the decision-making process, although this usually occurs after policy has already been formulated (Churchill 1995). Thus, it is important to examine the structural spaces or "cracks" that are occurring as a result of devolved public policies: places where local power may be useful in challenging poverty and economic development policy. These spaces may emerge as opposition to attempts to move from a welfare to a workfare state, providing the possibility for new interpretations of the causes of poverty (Maxwell 1996).

Free space for participants to reshape welfare can be difficult to create, particularly in situations in which overt class and gender inequalities limit access to the policy-making process, as they have in Kentucky. Kentuckians for the Commonwealth (KFTC) meetings were one free space that allowed the women of Appalachia to discuss their concerns and work on issues that were of concern to them. Within the context of KFTC, women were not only able to voice their opinions and share experiences but also take an active role in contesting K-TAP policy. To address a range of issues and to promote leadership in the region, KFTC involves all of its members in leadership and organizing skills training. Much of this training is devoted to teaching members how to communicate KFTC's message through lobbying, letter writing, talking to the press, holding public forums, and "direct actions"—creative protests designed to dramatize issues and educate the public and policy makers. KFTC often holds training sessions in conjunction with other social justice organizations, which allow for linkages between Appalachian Kentucky and other rural and urban places.

One parent activist, who had recently returned from a national meeting for social justice organizations, explained how this experience shaped her perspective.

> It's real funny when you get together in a big group of people and you hear all the same concerns. It's like, wait a minute, I figured if I got out of eastern Kentucky, there's a better life out there. [But] here I am talking to people from all over the country and they're telling me exactly what I'm finding here. So, rather than just an area, I think it's a class [of people] that they're trying to hold down. (Appalshop 1996)

Although social services had been an issue in Appalachian Kentucky for several decades, PRWORA created new concerns among parent activists, particularly those who were either current or former public assistance recipients. Many of these concerns were articulated by a group of K-TAP participants attending a local community college. The new work requirements and the reduction in the amount of time available for educational activities were particularly troubling to women who felt that an education was the only way to find a living-wage job in the area. During one informal discussion with several K-TAP participants who were attending the college, they discussed their concerns with the direction of the commonwealth's public assistance policies. These women were particularly proud of their educational achievements: "The majority of us have a 3.5 GPA or better and many of us are members of Phi Beta Kappa, those that can afford the $40 fee. That's pretty good for a bunch of welfare moms."

Several of the women at the community college had plans to continue their education but were afraid that the twenty-hour work requirement would limit their ability to do so. A major concern was with increasingly punitive policies, including sanctions, which were leaving women with little option about working. One woman noted, "Welfare reform means slave labor." Another equated the local boom in prisons with the effects of welfare reform on families: "They're building orphanages in eastern Kentucky to take our children away and they're building prisons to lock up women when they start stealing to feed their kids. They're taking money away from us so that they can take away our kids." This woman also felt betrayed by a system that was supposed to help them overcome negative situations but, more often than not, was simply interested in removing them from the welfare rolls.

Other women made very specific critiques against the work-first philosophy of K-TAP in light of the economic conditions in the mountains. Teresa, for example, found a job as a waitress, but still could not make ends meet.

> I was working, making minimum wage, but I just couldn't make it. It was just enough to buy the staples . . . shampoo and soap for my kids. So I quit and went back to welfare full-time and my caseworker said, "It's a shame you had to quit that job, you were doing so well." (Miewald 2000)

Teresa rolls her eyes and shakes her head at this statement and goes on to discuss economic development. Teresa's experience is supported by self-sufficiency standards that suggest that a single woman living in Appalachia with two children (one preschooler and one school age) would need to make around $13.00 an hour to be self-sufficient (Pearce 2001).[4] Yet, according to an evaluation of K-TAP leavers, the average hourly wage is only $7.92 (Barber et al. 2001; see also Fitzpatrick 1999). At the same time, potential employees who lack a high school diploma or GED are severely disadvantaged in the labor market and are likely to earn significantly lower wages than more educated workers. According to Fitzpatrick (1999, 14), "Working parents with less than a high school education are twice as likely as more educated workers to have low hourly earnings and are six times more likely to be poor." However, Appalachian counties continue to lag behind the rest of Kentucky in both secondary school completion and post-secondary training (Eller et al. 1994; Haleman et al. 2000). A number of studies indicate that whereas work-first approaches may move people into jobs quickly, they do not necessarily result in moving them out of poverty (Cummings and Nelson 1999; Zimmerman and Garkovich 1998). Education, however, does appear to increase the likelihood that a person will be able to find a living-wage job (Martinson and Strawn 2002). It is with the concerns of these women and these social realities in mind that KWRC began its legislative campaign.

Fighting the Good Fight: House Bill 434

In August 1997 members of the Kentucky Welfare Reform Coalition (KWRC) met to develop a legislative strategy for the 1998 Kentucky General Assembly, a strategy that included the lived experience and concerns of the students and other low income mothers. The initial result was the Kentucky Education Access for Parents (KEAP), or HB 434, a draft bill. KEAP proposed the creation of a separate, state-funded public assistance program, using Maintenance of Effort (MOE) dollars, for low income students.[5] Because such a program would not be considered TANF assistance, participants would not be subject to federal time limits or work requirements, according to "Bill Would Help College Students on Welfare Rolls," an article in the *Lexington Herald-Leader* on 20 February 1998. This provision would allow K-TAP participants to engage in post-secondary education without having the additional burden of waged or unwaged labor. HB 434 also called for a "bill of rights," guaranteeing that TANF participants would be informed of their right to attend a college or post-secondary program and creating an advisory commission to monitor and expand the program in the future.

It was not surprising to members of the Kentucky Welfare Rights Coalition that the bill met immediate resistance from the Cabinet for Families and Children, who argued that if HB 434 were passed with the separate MOE program, it might result in federal sanctions against the state for not meeting its work-participation requirement of 25 percent of the total caseload (Center for Community Change 1998). To keep portions of the bill, KWRC began negotiations with the Cabinet at the same time as they began mobilizing political and public pressure in support of their cause. KWRC held several lobby days including one in which parent activists dressed in caps and gowns and rallied in the capitol rotunda, circulated a petition of support for the bill, and wrote letters to the editor supporting the bill.

In one effort to support HB 434, Kentucky Youth Advocates, a research and policy center concerned with the well-being of children, developed, in conjunction with Kentuckians for the Commonwealth, a series of community meetings in which K-TAP participants, and others, were invited to share their stories about how welfare changes would affect them, their families, and their communities. Appalshop filmed these meetings as part of the Community Media Project (Appalshop n.d.). The forums provided a space within which K-TAP participants from different parts of the state could find a common voice and goal, despite the geographic differences. Many of the stories highlighted the frustration K-TAP participants felt with the state's emphasis on work over education. One twenty-two-year-old mother and community college student explained her reasons for staying on public assistance and not entering the workforce.

I'm very proud of being a student here at LCC; I've been here for four semesters and I've got a real good GPA. I'm very proud of that but . . . if you get a part-time job it really doesn't help you. I would rather be on welfare and further my education so I could have a better job, so I could take care of my son so he won't have to think that welfare is a way of life, because it isn't. (Pickering 1997)

This and similar statements were important in making clear that education was something that should be at the center of the Kentucky Welfare Rights Coalition's legislative agenda. According to one KWRC advocate, "People at forums and so forth spoke very strongly to [access to education] and that pushed it along to the point that we started looking at the options, the points of state flexibility" (Pickering 1997).

Segments of the forums were compiled into a short videotape that was disseminated to state legislators, as well as to local television and newspapers. This was part of an effort by Appalshop, Kentuckians for the Commonwealth, and Kentucky Youth Advocates to garner public and political support for House Bill 434. By giving "legislators and the citizens of Kentucky an opportunity to hear the stories of fellow citizens that they might not ordinarily hear," Appalshop and welfare rights activists were able to garner political and public support for the implementation of a policy that provided alternatives to the work-first rhetoric. Activists viewed educating legislators as the primary hurdle to advancing their cause; they often felt that legislators did not fully understand K-TAP regulations or the effects they would have in Appalachian Kentucky. Members of KFTC from Appalachian Kentucky made regular trips to Frankfort, the capital, while the general assembly was in session, to lobby legislators, meet with legislative staff, provide testimony during hearings, and stage "creative actions" to publicize their position. Convincing policy makers of their position was often a difficult and trying process for the women, particularly in a political environment that favored more stringent welfare programs. "Oh, I know they don't want to listen," explains one parent activist, "but we've caught 'em in the hallways and took a hold of their hands to introduce ourselves and hang on and stay hanging on until we get done saying what we got to say. We make them face our issues." Despite resistance by legislators and cabinet staff, parent activists eventually came to see themselves as players on economic justice and welfare issues. In particular, the experiences of parent activists were crucial in how the bill was developed. As one member of KWRC and a welfare rights advocate noted, parent activists were often the most careful about how to craft legislation.

One of the interesting things in all these discussions was that as the policy wonk, I wasn't the one that was thinking in the greatest level of policy detail. Because parents had particular experiences and frustrations with programs, they wanted to make sure some very detailed things got addressed in how those programs were run. (Miewald 2000)

The strategies used by Appalshop, the Kentucky Welfare Rights Coalition, and Kentuckians for the Commonwealth were similar to those employed by a number of other progressive organizations to destabilize political rhetoric and public opinion about welfare (see, for example, Dujon and Withorn 1996). These entities challenged welfare policies by backtalking the national rhetoric and state policy on public assistance. Stories that focused on the need for education, the value of providing care, and the daily struggles of parents were used as the foundation for alternative policy.

Because of the growing political and public support for HB 434, the cabinet agreed to a compromise proposal. The final version of HB 434 did not include a state-funded education program. It did, however, add language to Regulatory Statutes requiring that K-TAP participants be informed of their right to engage in educational activities as part of their self-sufficiency plan, and that they be provided with supportive services while in school. The bill also stipulated that there could be no cap on the number of Kentucky Works parents engaged in post-secondary education. It also established an advisory board to make further recommendations to increase educational opportunities for low income Kentuckians.

Although the compromise wording of the bill did not provide parents with the separate education program they wanted, most coalition members considered it a victory. One parent activist from Kentuckians for the Commonwealth summarized the experience in these words:

> The government has hurt people so bad with this welfare reform, we've been working to ease the blow a little bit, and we'd like to ease it a whole lot more than what we've done. Working with KWRC and KYA and different organizations, we might have softened it a little. We're gonna keep on working, try to soften it a little bit more so that people can get an education to get off welfare not just forced into slave labor. (Miewald 2000)

There is ample evidence that the efforts begun in 1997 to improve access to post-secondary education continue to affect Kentucky's welfare policies. In April 1999, the Kentucky Cabinet for Families and Children announced that the state would allow twenty-four months of post-secondary education without any additional work requirement for full-time students. In addition, student parents will be allowed to count ten hours of class toward the thirty-hour work requirement after twenty-four months (Kentucky Cabinet for Families and Children 2001). Additionally, the Cabinet for Families and Children now offers a one-time bonus of $250 to those who earn a post-secondary degree. In

2001, approximately 9 percent of Kentucky Works participants were engaged in post-secondary education (Kentucky Youth Advocates 2001). In this sense, Kentucky has become a leader in using state flexibility to meet the needs of its low income residents. Yet, some parents continue to feel that they are being steered away from education and into low-wage jobs, and welfare rights organizations point out that the cabinet was unwilling to adopt policies that would stop the five-year time clock for parents who attend school (Kentucky Youth Advocates 2001).

"This Little Light of Mine": Women's Political Activism as Transformative Work

The story of resistance to welfare reform in Appalachian Kentucky is only partially reflected in the struggles that occurred in the policy-making arena. There is another story here, which concerns what happens to individuals when they become involved in a political movement aimed at subverting dominant beliefs related to class and gender hierarchies (Herda-Rupp 2000). The women who were involved in the fight for HB 434 both influenced and were affected by the process. Although many of the women began their involvement with Kentuckians for the Commonwealth out of concern for how welfare legislation would affect them and their families, they quickly became more politicized, developing a critical consciousness in which "elite beliefs and official stories . . . are continuously scrutinized" and actively challenged (Seitz 1995, 221). Through lobbying, helping to write legislation, and organizing protests, these women went beyond their traditional roles as supports of men's class struggles, transgressed local norms of political participation prescribed for low income women, and developed their own critiques of class and gender inequality (see also Mele 2000; Stack 1996). To do so, however, they had to overcome a number of barriers. These women were often caught in circumstances beyond their control. Unemployed husbands, domestic abuse, single parenthood, limited education, and the lack of jobs left them with few options but to receive public assistance. They rejected policies that told them "any job is a good job" and instead argued that education is the only way they could support their families.

Involvement in politics, for these women, meant many different things—many saw their activism as a means of survival for themselves and their families. In public forums and rallies, parent activists would often argue that access to education would provide them with the resources to provide for their children, while working at a low-skill, low-wage job would simply keep their families in poverty. Parent activists also engaged in critiques of larger structures of gender and class inequality (Ward and Pyle 1995; Ward 1990). They would point out that policies were almost entirely created by politicians who knew little about the realities of being a poor woman in Appalachia. Thus, rather than solely the result of their social positions as mothers, wives, and caregivers, women's political activism was a means of acting on their multiple interests and relationships "as women, as wives and as mothers, as members of neighbor-hoods and communities, and as members of particular race, ethnic and class groups" (Morgan 1988, 111; see also Mele 2000).

As parent activists explored the causes of their everyday problems, they discussed the shared general economic crisis, the absence of good jobs for men and women, the poor quality of schools and community services, and the shrinking social safety net, all of which made it impossible for them to main-tain their households. For many of the women there was a clear connection be-tween the changing economic and political situation and their involvement. The declining coal industry and general lack of employment for men, tradi-tionally the main breadwinners, often put emotional or financial stress on the family. These women, in turn, subverted traditional gender roles—often with assistance from the state public assistance system—by going back to school in hopes of eventually finding a good paying job that would make a central con-tribution to the household. Through this experience, they came to value educa-tion, both as a way for them to make a living and because it gave them the confidence to take their lives in directions that were previously unavailable to them. When the state, with its K-TAP regulations, threatened to take away the ability to get an education, thereby consigning them to menial, low-wage work, these women were able to translate their individual needs into political action. Thus, according to Seitz (1995), women in Appalachia, as they do elsewhere, battle for access to resources needed for daily survival as well as for their voices to be heard within the political and economic discourse of the region.

Belinda was one parent activist who had become increasingly involved with KFTC's effort to improve the state's welfare policies and who was changed by her experiences of both education and political involvement. When I first met Be-linda, she was a divorced mother who struggled to balance work, going to school, and caring for her thirteen-year-old son. She had recently graduated from a local community college, where she had been the president of the Phi Beta Kappa Honor Society. She had received a scholarship to attend Morehead State Uni-versity, which was some ninety miles from her home. After her first semester there, however, Belinda stopped taking classes and took a job in a local restau-rant as a cook because of the K-TAP policy that required students to work after twelve months.[6] Working, going to school, and taking care of her son would have simply been too much for her. Therefore, instead of continuing her education, she took a job that paid $6 an hour and offered no benefits. She continued to receive food stamps and a transitional medical card, which were to run out in another six months. At the same time, the rent on her subsidized apartment increased be-cause she was receiving a paycheck. Despite these difficulties, Belinda does not mind working, but she wants a job at which she can make a living and use her in-telligence. "I don't want to sound boastful but I've got a few brains in my head and I'd like to put them to use, other than reading a recipe or somebody's ticket for dinner." Regardless of her unresolved personal difficulties, Belinda feels that Kentuckians for the Commonwealth is a valuable part of her life. For her, KFTC provided the resources and power—unavailable to her as a woman who had few family ties—to challenge the system. Through her experiences with KFTC, she has accomplished more than challenging an unjust system; she has come to view herself as a powerful person.

> Sometimes it might take an organization like KFTC to help you see your own true worth and help you realize it. Before KFTC, I did feel quite useless. . . . There was no place to turn to until KFTC and since joining them, I feel a lot stronger. If nothing else they're listening to me and they're really listening, it isn't in one ear and out the other. My opinion matters to them. I don't feel quite so useless and I don't sit back and take it anymore like I used to. I used to be the kind that just sat back and never said nothing but I don't think anybody would say that about me no more. I'll fight back for what's right. I was beat down for so long but I'm not anymore. I'm fighting back. (Miewald 2000)

Belinda's story, like those of many other women who joined KFTC, is an illustration of politics as self-transformation—how involvement in politics can make a difference in women's lives and identities that goes beyond changes in material conditions. Although some of these women went on to find employment in social or political activism, not all saw improvements in their own lives. In a very real sense, however, they were not only fighting for themselves but also for other women who were in similar situations but because of a variety of circumstances were unable to challenge the system.

Conclusion

The experience of low income women and their allies in Kentucky fighting against work-first stereotypes and for educational opportunities represents only one small part of a much larger story of women fighting back against punitive public assistance policies (Kushnick and Jennings 1999; Maggard 1999; Abramovitz 1996; Dujon and Withorn 1996; Mandell and Withorn 1993). In Kentucky, parent activists combined oppositional tactics such as protests and "backtalking" with creating legislation and lobbying. Although this combination of strategies was neither easy nor without conflict, it did allow for a number of different perspectives to be heard and ultimately resulted in welfare policies that are more sensitive to the needs of low income parents.

There are several implications that can be drawn from this story of parent activists struggling to improve their access to education. First, these efforts not only resulted in policy changes at the state level, but also provided parent activists an opportunity to have their visions of social support included in the current debate. According to Brown and Ferguson (1995), it is often women's everyday experiences as mothers and housewives and their caring responsibilities that extend from the household into the community that motivate their participation in social change. In this example, by working with state and regional organizations, parent activists were able to translate their experiences of family care and community involvement into a concrete set of demands related to welfare reform.

Furthermore, fighting for access to education became important to parent activists on a personal level as part of an emerging identity for women in the region. Parent activists understood that simply finding a job would not result in a better life for themselves or their families. Education, for many women in Appalachia, has become a path to economic and social independence. It is more than simply a degree; it is part of an emerging identity for women in the region—part of a social transformation from housewife and mother to student and breadwinner. Although education itself may not solve the multiple barriers these women often face, including a declining economy, the very process of being engaged in the political process (rather than simply being the targets of policy) has resulted in increased self-confidence for many of the women.

Finally, there were the changes in policies that assisted not only those women who protested and lobbied, but also countless others who will go on to obtain a degree. This does not mean, however, that the struggle is over. As of summer 2002, access to post-secondary education remained as part of Kentucky's TANF state plan (Kentucky Cabinet for Families and Children 2001). Yet, there is always the possibility that this too will change if states are faced with stricter regulations. If this occurs, will the women who so courageously stood up to politicians and state agencies be able to continue their efforts? There is an enormous amount of labor that needs to go into making even the smallest of changes to the system. As women are increasingly forced into ever more restrictive definitions of "work," there is the danger that few will be left to fight for a future that is more than a paycheck.

NOTES

1. This definition of allowable work activities is based on pre-1999 regulations.

2. Advocates are defined as experts, academics, lawyers or lobbyists, who help others by speaking or acting on their behalf.

3. KFTC was founded in 1981 as Kentucky Fair Tax Coalition, a group primarily concerned with stopping coal companies from using broad form deeds to strip mine property owners' land. The organization has since evolved into a multi-issue "citizens' social justice group" (Szakos 1993, 102), which is currently addressing a number of

state and local issues, including mountaintop-removal mining, recycling, timber regulations, and welfare reform. KWRC is an organization composed of representatives from several distinct organizations including KFTC, Kentucky Youth Advocates, the Kentucky Domestic Violence Association, the Kentucky Task Force on Hunger, the Homeless and Housing Coalition of Kentucky, the AFL-CIO, and Catholic Social Services. KWRC has also developed relationships with state legislators who are sympathetic to their position and are willing to support KWRC's legislative efforts. In addition, KWRC has linkages to national welfare organizations, such as the Center for Law and Social Policy (CLASP), who provide advice on addressing specific concerns such as access to post-secondary education.

Appalshop has been on the forefront of reshaping the welfare debate from the perspective of local residents and activist groups. Begun in 1969 as a community development project of the War on Poverty, Appalshop has grown into a nationally recognized media collective (see Gaines 1989). Through film, theater, and radio, Appalshop utilizes media to contest "hillbilly" stereotypes and to educate "outsiders" about Appalachia's heritage and problems.

4. The Self-Sufficiency Standard measures how much income is needed, for a family of a given composition in a given place, to adequately meet their basic needs—without public or private assistance.

5. Under TANF, states are required to maintain a certain level of state spending—known as Maintenance of Effort or MOE—on services or other assistance to low income families to receive their full TANF block grant. These funds may be spent on separate, non-TANF programs, referred to as a "separate state program." MOE-funded programs, such as the one proposed in KEAP, are not subject to TANF time limits, work participation requirements, or assignment of child support payments (Greenberg 1999).

6. These requirements have since changed, allowing students involved in full-time education to count that toward their work requirement for twenty-four months.

References

Abramovitz, Mimi. 1996. *Under attack, fighting back: Women and welfare in the United States.* New York: Monthly Review Press.

Appalshop. n.d. Community Development Project Grant. Unpublished Document. Whitesburg, Ky.: Appalshop.

———.1996. WMMT's mountain talk with KFTC members, transcript. Whitesburg, Ky.: Appalshop.

Barber, Gerard M., Daniel McAdam, Stacy Deck Shade, and Eric Schneider. 2001. *From welfare to work: Year 2001 panel study of families and children.* Frankfort: Kentucky Cabinet for Families and Children.

Brown, Phil, and Faith Ferguson. 1995. "Making a big stink": Women's work, women's relationships, and toxic waste activism. *Gender and Society* 9(2):145–172.

Center for Community Change. 1998. Kentucky legislature passes bill to allow post secondary education. Issue 8. Available at http://www.communitychange.org/organizing/Ky8.htm.

Churchill, Nancy. 1995. Ending welfare as we know it: A case study in urban anthropology and public policy. *Urban Anthropology* 24:5–35.

Couto, Richard A. 1993. The memory of miners and the conscience of capital: Coal miners' strikes as free spaces. In *Fighting back in Appalachia: Traditions of resistance and change*, ed. Stephen L. Fisher, 165–194. Philadelphia: Temple University Press.

Cummings, Scott, and John P. Nelson. 1999. *Kentucky transitional assistance program: A statewide and regional welfare reform evaluation*. Louisville: Center for Policy Research and Evaluation, University of Louisville.

Dujon, Diane, and Ann Withorn, eds. 1996. *For crying out loud: Women's poverty in the United States*. Boston: South End Press.

East, Jean F. 2000. Empowerment through welfare-rights organizing: A feminist perspective. *Affilia* 15(2):311–328.

Eller, Ronald D., Phil Jenks, Chris Jasparro, and Jerry Napier. 1994. *Kentucky's distressed communities: A report on poverty in Appalachian Kentucky*. Lexington: Appalachian Center.

Evans, Sara M., and Harry C. Boyte. 1986. *Free spaces: The sources of democratic change in America*. New York: Harper and Row.

Fisher, Stephen, ed. 1993. *Fighting back in Appalachia: Traditions of resistance and change*. Philadelphia: Temple University Press.

Fitzpatrick, Christina Smith. 1999. *Poverty despite work in Kentucky*. Washington, D.C.: Center on Budget and Policy Priorities.

Gaines, John. 1989. Appalshop documentaries: Inventing and preserving Appalachia. *Jump Cut* 34:53–63.

Garkovich, L., G. Hansen, and P. Dyk. 1997. Welfare reform and its implications for Kentucky's families on the economic edge. *Social and Economic Education for Development*. Lexington: University of Kentucky's Cooperative Extension Service.

Greenberg, Mark. 1999. The TANF Maintenance of Effort requirement. Washington D.C.: Center for Law and Social Policy. Available at http://www.clasp.org/TANF/moerev.htm#top.

Haleman, Diana L., Matthew Sargent, Julie N. Zimmerman, and Dwight Billings. 2000. *The impact of welfare reform on Kentucky's Appalachian counties*. Lexington: University of Kentucky Appalachian Center.

Herda-Rupp, Ann. 2000. The impact of social activism on gender identity and care work. In *Care work: Gender, labor, and welfare states*, ed. Madonna Meyer, 45–64. London: Routledge.

Kentucky Cabinet for Families and Children. 1999. *Kentucky Transitional Assistance Program (K-TAP)*. Frankfort, Ky.: Cabinet for Families and Children.

————. 2001. Temporary Assistance for Needy Families (TANF) Title IV-A State Plan. Frankfort: Cabinet for Families and Children.

Kentucky Youth Advocates. 2001. Kentucky welfare reform assessment project. Available at http://www.kyyouth.org/Publications/kwrap1.pdf.

Kushnick, Louis, and James Jennings, eds. 1999. *A new introduction to poverty: The role of race, power, and politics.* New York: New York University Press.

Maggard, Sally. 1999. Coalfield women making history. In *Confronting Appalachian stereotypes: Back talk from an Appalachian region,* ed. Dwight Billings, Gurney Norman, and Katherine Ledford, 228–250. Lexington: University Press of Kentucky.

Mandell, Betty Reid, and Ann Withorn. 1993. Keep on keeping on: Organizing for welfare rights in Massachusetts. In *Mobilizing the community: Local politics in the era of the global city,* ed. R. Fisher and J. Kling, 128–148. Newbury Park: Sage.

Martinson, Karin, and Julie Strawn. 2002. *Built to last: Why skills matter for long-run success in welfare reform.* Washington, D.C.: Center for Law and Social Policy.

Maxwell, A. H. 1996. Human rights and social welfare policy reform, views from the field: A discussion. *Urban Anthropology* 25: 211–219.

Mele, Christopher. 2000. Asserting the political self: Community activism among black women who relocate to the rural South. *The Sociological Quarterly* 41(1): 63–84.

Miewald, Christiana E. 2000. Women's work? Caring, kinship and community in Appalachian Kentucky. Unpublished diss. University of Kentucky, Lexington.

Morgen, Sandra. 1988. "It's the whole power of the city against us!": The development of political consciousness in a women's health care coalition. In *Women and the politics of empowerment,* ed. Ann Bookman and Sandra Morgen, pp. 97–115. Philadelphia: Temple University Press.

Pearce, Diana (with Jennifer Brooks). 2001. *The self-sufficiency standard for Kentucky: Real budgets, real families.* Louisville: Kentucky Youth Advocates.

Pickering, Mimi. 1997. Testimony on education and welfare reform. Video recording. Whitesburg, KY: Appalshop.

Piven, Frances Fox. 1990. Women and the state: Ideology, power and welfare. In *Women, the state and welfare,* ed. L. Gordon, 250–265. Madison: University of Wisconsin Press.

Seitz, Virginia R. 1995. *Women, development and communities for empowerment in Appalachia.* Albany: State University of New York Press.

Shore, Chris, and Susan Wright. 1997. Policy: A new field of anthropology. In *Anthropology of policy: Critical perspectives on governance and power,* ed. C. Shore and S. Wright, 3–39. London: Routledge.

Stack, Carol B. 1996. *Call to home: African Americans reclaim the rural South.* New York: HarperCollins.

Stewart, Kathleen. 1990. Backtalking the wilderness: Appalachian en-genderings. In *Uncertain terms: Negotiating gender in American culture*, ed. Faye Ginsburg and Anna Lowenhaupt Tsing, 43–58. Boston: Beacon Press.

Szakos, Joe. 1993. Practical lessons in community organizing in Appalachia: What we've learned at Kentuckians for the Commonwealth. In *Fighting back in Appalachia: Traditions of resistance and change*, ed. Stephen L. Fisher, 101–122. Philadelphia: Temple University Press.

Ward, Kathryn, ed. 1990. *Women workers and global restructuring*. Ithaca, N.Y.: Ilr Press.

Ward, Kathryn, and Jean L. Pyle. 1995. Gender, industrialization, transnational corporations and development: An overview of trends and patterns. In *Women in the Latin American development process*, ed. C. Bose and E. Acosta-Belen, 37–64. Philadelphia: Temple University Press.

Zimmerman, Julie N., and Lorraine Garkovich. 1998. *The bottom line: Making ends meet in rural Kentucky*. Lexington: Kentucky Cooperative Extension.

Chapter 9

College Access and Leadership-Building for Low Income Women

Boston's Women in Community Development

Deborah Clarke and Lynn Peterson

INTRODUCTION

Women in Community Development (WICD) is a college-access and leadership program for low income women located in Boston, Massachusetts, and affiliated with the nonprofit Women's Institute for Housing and Economic Development. It developed from the practices of the Women's Institute and a small-scale participatory-action research project on homelessness, and it aims to empower low income women through education to develop themselves, support each other, and serve their communities. Established in 1997 as a collaboration among the College of Public and Community Service at the University of Massachusetts in Boston, Project Hope, and the Women's Institute for Housing and Economic Development, WICD has so far involved about thirty students whose stories illustrate the importance and benefits of post-secondary education, not only for individual families but also for community development.

WICD represents one path through which small numbers of low income mothers can gain access to post-secondary education in Massachusetts. As in many other states, Massachusetts women on assistance or with very low incomes face nearly insurmountable barriers. In Massachusetts, education and training do not count toward mandatory work requirements, although work-first welfare reform without education and training and adequate child care does nothing to address the social ills it was meant to eradicate. The only choice open to women who are motivated to earn a college degree while receiving welfare is to pursue their education in addition to mandated work and without child care assistance for school hours. This places a heavy burden on women and their families. In fact, it may even put families at greater risk because mothers who are working and going to school are under more stress and have less time to supervise their children. Since welfare reform was enacted, the community colleges and the College of Public and Community Service at the University of Massachusetts in Boston have seen significant declines in enrollment.

Massachusetts embraces a work-first stance that says a job, any job, is the way out of poverty. In truth, however, getting a job is no longer a guarantee against poverty: It takes two-and-a-half full-time jobs at minimum wage to afford a modest two-bedroom apartment in Boston.[1] According to the Family Economic Self-Sufficiency Standard, developed by Washington, D.C.–based Wider Opportunities for Women and employed in states including Massachusetts, a one-parent, two-child family needs approximately $18/per hour to afford the average-priced two-bedroom apartment, child care, and other basic necessities with no subsidies.[2] Numerous studies document that the level of a mother's education impacts her children's school readiness and performance.[3]

What is also missing from the portrait of low income women painted by the media and policy makers are the courage, commitment, and strengths that low income women bring to their families and communities. By discussing the WICD program and the lives of some of its participants, this chapter attempts to illustrate how the talents of low income women are a precious resource that can and should be valued and supported—through better welfare reform, increased financial aid, and the availability of high-quality child care and after-school programs—rather than squandered. Investments in low income women will have long-term financial and social benefits for both individual families and the larger society.

EARLY BEGINNINGS OF WICD: THE WOMEN'S INSTITUTE FOR HOUSING AND ECONOMIC DEVELOPMENT AND PARTICIPATORY-ACTION RESEARCH

Women in Community Development (WICD) evolved from two primary sources: the work of the Women's Institute for Housing and Economic Development (WIHED) and a specific participatory-action research project that it supported. WIHED is a nonprofit organization, founded in 1981, the mission of which is "to build supportive communities that work for low income women and families." Since its founding, WIHED has worked with forty organizations to develop over four hundred units of innovative, supportive housing that include on-site family support programs, and in some cases, child care and community space. In addition to increasing the supply of service-enriched affordable housing, the agency works to build economic security for low income women. WIHED coordinates tenant services at a large, mixed-income public-housing development in Boston. Over the past eight years, WIHED has created and offered economic literacy classes, family child care provider training, women's business training, and the WICD college-access program.

The Women's Institute, committed to validation of women's knowledge of their own lives, to participatory practices that developed the abilities and capacities of low income women, and to secure housing for low income women, in 1994 supported the involvement of homeless women in the City of Boston's planning and program design in the areas of homelessness and affordable housing. As a group of government and nonprofit staff convened to develop recommendations to the City of Boston regarding programs for homeless women, the Women's Institute and others convinced the planning group to allow homeless women themselves to conduct research and participate in planning. Because its faculty had experience with participatory-action research—that is, projects in which researchers reflect the population they are studying and conduct research as part of a program of social action—the College of Public and Community Service (CPCS) at the University of Massachusetts was enlisted to assist. Roofless Women's Action Research Mobilization (RWARM) emerged. Through an arrangement with CPCS, women in the Roofless Women project were also given the opportunity to earn college credit for the research project. In fall 1994, six formerly homeless women were enrolled in CPCS, and one became an office intern at the Women's Institute.

Under the guidance of the College of Public and Community Service, the women designed a research instrument that they administrated to 126 women across the state of Massachusetts, and they conducted four focus groups. Women respondents came from a variety of situations—the street and shelters in city, suburban, and rural areas. In spring 1997, the project published its results in a report, *Lifting the Voices of Homeless Women,* and released its findings to legislators, educators, and service providers at the statehouse. They also produced four pamphlets, less formally written than the policy material, from the perspectives of women who were homeless: *Raising Children under Someone Else's Roof; Homeless Women—On Our Own; Domestic Violence;* and *Homeless Rights.*

As the Roofless Women project was ending, it became apparent that the project had provided a valuable structure for the students, all of whom had faced the challenges and strains of low income student parents; the project had provided peer support on personal and academic issues, educational and skill-building experiences, and leadership opportunities. Community agencies, including WIHED and Project Hope, and the University of Massachusetts in Boston therefore, in 1997, established WICD as a more permanent program that could continue to provide the experiences and relationships of RWARM. Project Hope is a community agency located in Dorchester, Massachusetts, that operates a family shelter, adult education program, mentoring program, child care center, and food pantry and is involved in community organizing. Many of the first WICD participants came from Project Hope staff and program graduates, along with some of the RWARM members who were working toward completing their degrees.

Women in Community Development (WICD): College Access and Leadership

WICD is a college-access and leadership program created as an economic development strategy to lift women out of poverty and as a community development approach to build the leadership capacity of low income women. The goals of Women in Community Development are to enrich the fields of human services and community planning with women who have used services or who live in disinvested communities; provide opportunities for low income women to earn a college degree; increase the earning potential of low income women, including those who have received welfare; develop the leadership abilities of low income women to better serve their communities; and create a support network among the participants. According to the group's mission statement, "We are grassroots women building a movement to empower ourselves and to develop our communities by achieving educational advancement, sharing the wealth of our knowledge, lifting our voices to break economic barriers of poverty, and moving forward as leaders in our community" (WICD 1998).

The WICD program operates with foundation grants and in-kind contributions. Participants in the program receive three benefits: financial assistance, peer support, and professional and leadership development. WICD provides financial assistance to eligible participants in the form of tuition waivers, grants to cover student fees depending on what participants need after securing financial aid, and book stipends. The tuition waivers are granted from the College of Public and Community Service to the Women's Institute as part of an agency agreement. The agency receives four tuition waivers for each course taught by its staff, which in turn are granted to the WICD participants. Foundation grants are used to pay student fees not covered by tuition waivers. Workshops and peer-group meetings are held monthly at Project Hope, a shelter and adult education center, where child care and refreshments are provided.

Participation in WICD has led to professional development opportunities for members. Several members have acquired employment in their fields through referrals made by other participants and agency collaborators. Participants are often invited to speak at workshops, provide testimony at legislative hearings, and join boards of directors of local agencies. For example, Women in Community Development members were invited to create a workshop at the Paths out of Poverty conference sponsored by Wider Opportunities for Women in Washington, D.C., in 1999 and locally in 2000. The interactive and informative workshop "Let's Get Real: Educate!" demonstrates the need for higher education, explains the barriers to attaining education, and offers recommendations for improving access to education. Members have also presented workshops at the Planners Network conference in New York, at a McAuley Institute conference in Washington, D.C., and at a roundtable at Harvard University.

The program is highly participatory and continues to evolve with participant feedback. For example, the Women's Institute received a grant from the Paul and Phyllis Fireman Charitable Foundation to pilot an individual development account, a savings program with a match. At the urging of WICD participants, the Women's Institute chose to launch this two-year demonstration program with WICD members. The grant provides a three-to-one match toward a participants' savings account over a two-year period. They may receive a match up to $7,400 and apply the funds toward purchasing a home, continuing their education, or starting a business. Attendance at monthly economic literacy workshops is mandatory.

Women in Community Development also received a grant from the Nellie Mae Education Foundation to conduct a process-and-outcome evaluation of the program. The grant was also used to examine similar college-access programs for low income, nontraditional-aged students across the county. Conducted by Fern Marx, senior associate at the Center for Research on Women at Wellesley College, *Grassroots to Graduation: Low-Income Women Accessing Higher Education* was released in April 2002. The results inform WICD expansion and replication, and are used for public policy advocacy. WICD has also joined forces with the Welfare Education Training Access Coalition (WETAC) to advocate for higher education under the Temporary Assistance for Needy Families (TANF) reauthorization.

THE STORIES OF WICD PARTICIPANTS

At the time of writing, ten women have graduated, including one with a master's degree. Sixteen are enrolled in a bachelor's program and eight are in graduate programs. Forty-six percent of the women are married, and a majority are between thirty-five and forty-five years old. All are self-defined as low income; several have received welfare in the past, and most work full time.

The stories of four WICD participants, one graduate and three current students, illustrate the individual strengths of low income parents and the collective vision and mission of WICD. Each elected to pursue a college degree despite the challenges of being older and having work and family responsibilities. The stories contain a range of community activism—from leadership in a school council, to community organizing, to service on agency boards of directors.

Joyce

Joyce and her family left Africa and arrived in the United States when she was twelve. She quickly became "American," learning English and graduating from high school. As the oldest of four children, Joyce took care of the household and her younger siblings while both her parents worked. She became pregnant at age eighteen, married the father of her child, and had two more children. When Joyce had to leave her failing marriage, she and her children became homeless. She was able, however, to access shelter for her and her family in a transitional housing program in Boston. Her quick wit and positive outlook made her a leader among the other women with whom she was housed. Temporarily without income, Joyce applied for welfare while simultaneously aspiring to long-term self-sufficiency. When Joyce saw an opportunity at the shelter to take a course on starting your own business, she signed up. The course was co-taught by staff from the Elizabeth Stone House and the Women's Institute for Housing and Economic Development.

Joyce learned how to assess a business idea and develop a business plan. Part of the class focused on personal finance: setting goals, establishing good credit, understanding taxes, and understanding the systemic issues of poverty. She talked to the instructors about how valuable the personal finance information was. This feedback resonated with the feelings of other women, and the two agencies collaborated to create an Economic Literacy Program to teach personal finance to other homeless women. Joyce became the assistant instructor.

Realizing a high school diploma would not allow her to support her family and that she needed more education, Joyce joined WICD in the first semester it started, January 1997. Joyce's enthusiasm for learning couldn't be contained; she registered for an overload of courses and juggled school with caring for her three children. Her family support, particularly that of her brother who became a father figure to her children, made it possible for her to go to school.

While in school, Joyce was elected to the student senate and participated in a leadership-training program. She joined the Women's Institute board of directors, and served as president of the parent council at her children's school. She emerged as a leader within WICD, and proposed to the Women's Institute that they create a peer coordinator position, which she volunteered to fill. Her proposal was based on her feelings that the women needed their own meetings to vent, inspire one another, work through personal issues, and share advice on getting through school. Additional funds were raised and Joyce was hired on a part-time hourly basis as the peer coordinator. In addition to providing peer support, she worked with the members to shape the program. She led them in a process to develop a mission statement, to create their own policies and, essentially, to take ownership of the program. Joyce was the peacemaker and the cheerleader among the group. She would accompany members to the housing agency, to the welfare office, or to the financial aid office, and advocate with them as needed.

In the meantime, Joyce met a man who also had graduated from the College for Public and Community Service (CPCS) and is a special education teacher. He had shared custody of two children. They combined their families and moved into an apartment in his mother's house. They had a daughter together, bringing the blended family to six children. They were married in 2000. Even though she is remarried, it is very important to Joyce that she continue to work and know that she is able to support her family if necessary.

Joyce feels that the impact of her education on her family has been positive. Her husband is motivated to continue his education, and her children are doing well in school. Joyce's mother-in-law has been a tremendous source of support; she is reliable and often watches the children. Throughout Joyce's college career she held positions with nonprofit agencies, and her brother or mother-in-law were available to assist with child care. She has been fortunate; not everyone has the level of family support she has had. Yet, working so hard at school, employment, and parenting has left her tired and torn among her many responsibilities and obligations.

Joyce completed her degree in June 2001, graduating with two awards: the Distinguished Student Award from the university and the Community Service Award from the College for Public and Community Service. Finding a job with some flexibility to meet the demands of her family was not easy. Through her WICD networks, however, she secured a position as an advocate in a program that provides case management to homeless women. Although Joyce has fulfilled some of her goals, she does not feel that she has fully realized her dream yet. She has been accepted into the master's degree program in mental health counseling at the University of Massachusetts and will start in the fall. She would like to move up the career ladder in the agency where she is currently working and become a supervisor. In another two to three years she will complete her master's degree and will look for more responsibility and higher pay. Her dream is to have a balanced life—managing career, family, and volunteer responsibilities.

Dora

Dora is an African American woman who is married and has three children, two adult children and a teenager, as well as a granddaughter who sometimes lives with her. Her educational journey has been a difficult one, beginning in the 1970s with forced busing, a court-ordered attempt to desegregate the schools in Boston. For Black students it was a scary and dangerous time as they were transported to White schools amidst hostility from adults and students alike. Dora focused on survival—classes were held in the auditorium for half the day, and Black students were unable to attend some other classes due to violence. After graduating from high school, with what she describes as a tenth-grade education, Dora enrolled at Bunker Hill Community College, located in the White neighborhood of Charlestown. There, many of the same racial hostilities continued, and after two semesters she transferred to a secretarial school and earned a certificate as a transcriber.

In the late 1970s Dora, married with three children, was working at a local utility company. Without a college degree, she was passed over for jobs. Due to health problems, her doctor told her she could not work a full forty-hour week. She left the company to earn licenses in cosmetology and barbering, thinking she could have a flexible work schedule. Health problems forced her to slow down again. Throughout this period of time, she was involved in her neighborhood organization, the Dudley Street Neighborhood Initiative (DSNI). She got involved in community organizing and was chosen to attend leadership training. Her involvement with DSNI led her to enroll in Roxbury Community College (RCC) with a focus on community organizing. While at RCC, she became active in a group called Welfare Education and Training Access Coalition (WETAC), spearheaded by Erika Kates at Brandeis University. After earning her associate's degree, she enrolled at CPCS at the urging of two WETAC members who were also WICD participants.

Since at CPCS, Dora has been the coordinator of a student-led organization, the ARMS center, which provides information and referral to low income students. She is active in the Survival Inc. organization, which does organizing for social justice. Since joining WICD, Dora has become a spokesperson in the organizations with which she is involved. She is also a speaker at her church, and her faith gives her daily inspiration. "WICD has been food for the support—to listen to other people and to seek resources."

Dora's concentration in school is community planning and adult education. She feels that there needs to be a focus on education for adults who have been out of school for a long time and believes that programs like the College of Public and Community Service and Women in Community Development ought to be expanded.

Jaquela

Jaquela is a gracious, middle-aged African American woman, and a very charismatic speaker. She is the mother of three girls, two adult twins and one teenager. A former welfare recipient, Jaquela decided to go back to school because her children were coming to her with questions that she could not answer. She graduated from Boston English High School, and then, after being out of school for ten years, attended Roxbury Community College and earned an associate's degree in social services. She is currently majoring in human services at the College of Public and Community Service at the University of Massachusetts, Boston. Her experience at CPCS has been positive.

Jaquela's family is very close and supportive. Her children recognize that it is time for her to better herself. Her two grown daughters have become helpmates. She has a supportive husband. Her youngest daughter is facing the challenges of adolescence. Jaquela tries to provide her daughter with love yet remain firm, to encourage but not push her. Her relationship with her youngest child is more work because she is no longer a stay-at-home mom and must make special time for her. Jaquela is also the primary caretaker for her mother, who is suffering from both Alzheimer's disease and cancer. Her mother requires full-time care, and it took Jaquela a long time to figure out how to manage her mother's illness; she compared taking care of her mother to the challenges of leaving welfare and going into the unknowns of the work environment. When she left welfare, she had to go into the new world of work. With her mother, she had to explore the new world of the health-care field and resources. Her older daughters are a lot of help, and they have worked out a schedule with their jobs to watch their grandmother, take her to appointments, and maintain the home. Encouraged by her academic advisor to explore adult day care, Jaquela went on the Internet and talked to doctors and other people to find the best resources for her mother. Now her mother goes to adult day care part time. Along with family support, this has made Jaquela's life more manageable and less stressful.

Jaquela also finds support in her church. She has been a devotional leader, a woman missionary, a minister, and a peer leader. Although these positions are volunteer positions, she was appointed to them. Her church helps her to support her life's goals and is an educational resource for her. Her roles in the church teach her to face challenges in her life that school does not necessarily deal with. Church and school together empower her. Because of these two supportive environments, Jaquela feels that she has the courage to tackle the seemingly impossible.

Leaving welfare and going into the workforce was a challenge for Jaquela. It meant developing a new set of skills but also abandoning full-time care of her children, and it was hard for her to focus on work when so many things were going on at home. She felt stigmatized as a former welfare recipient, and devalued by her co-workers and supervisors. According to Jaquela, "Class issues are a big barrier to job success for low income women. Class differences, mainly exposure to the professional world, technology, and the language of the job, exist. Low income women need the exposure in life to these things that can be learned. It is not a question of capacity to learn, so there shouldn't be barriers to growth on the job or in educational settings." Jaquela is not "permitting barriers on her growth" because she has taken control of her learning.

Jaquela has found that even within grassroots groups there is classism, and members will often not use the resources that minority and low income women bring to the table. They will, in fact, use outside resources. Jaquela felt that at first she did not possess the skills necessary to succeed in the nonprofit world. Having always been a leader, it was hard for her to be led instead of leading others. She felt that it was hard for her to shake off the stereotype of having been a welfare recipient. It wasn't until she came to CPCS and her present job at the ARMS center, where she works with two other WICD members, that she felt she had no barriers to her potential.

Theresa

Theresa is one of the newest WICD members. She was already a student at the College of Public and Community Service (CPCS) when a fellow student in the group recruited her. She found the group's purple pamphlet interesting. She was enticed by the content, which stressed grassroots leadership development and diversity of membership.

A former welfare recipient and mother of five children, Theresa has spent much of her adult life in the workforce. She worked for nine years as a nurse's aide in a nursing home. Although Theresa enjoyed her job, her wages were low. She became frustrated when her co-workers, who already had their high school diplomas or GEDs, were able to access a college scholarship to nursing school offered by the employer and eventually make a better wage. She felt that once her co-workers became her boss, their attitudes changed and they no longer thought of her as a friend but as a subordinate. Their attitude spurred her to finish her studies and with only one year left until she was eligible for retirement benefits, she completely changed the direction of her life. Although she had previously tried to finish her GED at Roxbury Community College, she was unsuccessful because she was working the graveyard shift and just could not concentrate on her classes after working all night. She then decided to continue her studies at Project Hope in Dorchester.

Theresa found Project Hope to be an amazing resource with numerous programs housed in one building right in the middle of the minority community. Theresa felt that the staff at Project Hope's adult education program made studying interesting. She found a mentor in Sister Margaret Leonard, director of Project Hope. Sister Margaret not only encouraged her to get her GED but also directed her to the College of Public and Community Service.

Many students at CPCS, like Theresa, are adult learners and have been active as advocates in their communities. Theresa has always considered herself a community activist. In the nursing home, she was always "standing up for her co-workers' rights," but she just didn't know what to call it. Theresa is active in her community. While at Project Hope, Sister Margaret saw Theresa's leadership potential and encouraged her to become a volunteer in the Annie E. Casey Foundation project called Connecting Communities. Located in eighteen cities, this nationwide program encourages local involvement in public policy by encouraging residents to become involved in politics in their neighborhoods. This project is connected with the McCormack Institute at UMass Boston, where staff hired Theresa as an outreach worker in her community. Theresa also works with the Dudley Street Neighborhood Initiative to encourage the community to develop strong bonds and to focus on issues that unite the community. She also works in a program called Student-to-Student, funded by the mayor's office. This program encourages students to stay in school. Theresa is a member of WETAC. She also has been hired by WETAC to document women's stories and to inform them of changes in policy that may affect them. As a member, she has testified at the State House on the behalf of human service programs that the legislators were considering cutting from the budget in the fall of 2001. She also testified against House Bill 4141 in which the governor proposed to increase the work hours of women on welfare because she feels this would leave very little time for welfare recipients to further their education.

Theresa believes that low income women should be encouraged to complete their education and that there should be no time limit on education. According to her, everyone learns at a different pace. Theresa pointed out, "What takes one student a year to do, may take another five years. It is difficult enough to concentrate on one's studies as it is, without the additional pressure of a time limit. Women should be encouraged as much as possible to advance themselves, because without the education they will never be able to make the next step up. Most countries have free education and free medical benefits. Since this is the wealthiest country in the world, why don't we have those benefits here?"

Theresa has been inspired by her experience at CPCS. She is a training assistant at the Competency Connection office at CPCS. She would especially like to help women her age, who have come into the college with a lifetime of learning experience, but are having trouble navigating the school system. Although she has never received official recognition for her role as training assistant, she knows she has made a big difference in the lives of the students she works with. When she graduates from CPCS, she hopes to continue on in a master's program in law.

COMMON THREADS

These stories of WICD participants illustrate the strengths of low income women and the challenges they face as they juggle education, work, family, and community involvement. Four major points emerge from these case studies. First, many women who receive welfare or work in low-wage jobs are highly motivated, as evidenced by the fact that they work very hard to maintain their families and improve their communities. All of these women worked hard to balance work, family, school, and unpaid voluntary activity in their communities. Their lives contradict the stereotypes many people hold of low income women.

Second, although these women were strongly inner-directed and highly motivated, each also required external moral, financial, and services support. Each woman had someone who recognized her potential and worked to help her realize it. The WICD program made a difference, as did supportive family members.

Third, among the group of women in the WICD program there is a high degree of community involvement and social capital. A recent study on social capital, sponsored by the Boston Foundation, showed that Bostonians volunteer less than their counterparts in forty cities.[4] The women in WICD, however, contradict this generalization; they volunteer in their churches, schools, and community agencies, perhaps more often than women with more economic resources. In addition, many women are caretakers of extended family members or assist friends and neighbors by babysitting.

Fourth, segregated racially and by class most of their lives, it is a challenge for low income women of color to be valued in the workplace and even in grassroots organizations. They might not possess the technical skills or speak the corporate talk, but that is not a reflection of their ability to learn. They also possess many skills that need to be recognized and valued—as leaders, mentors, teachers, negotiators, mediators. The stigma of welfare taints society's view of who they are and what they are capable of achieving.

CONCLUSION

The experience of Women in Community Development has been a powerful one, individually and collectively, for both participants and staff. The skills that the women learn, in the program and at school, not only empower and enrich their lives, but can be used to transform the communities in which they live and work. WICD, although a small program, can serve as a model for other college-access and leadership-development projects. Its advocacy for more general changes in access to education and training for low income parents plays a vital role in the community in which it is based. The women in our stories continue to struggle to improve their lives and encourage other women to reach their dreams. Women like Joyce, Dora, Jaquela, and Theresa live in every community and deserve the chance to further their education. Recognizing the skills and talents these women bring to the table would go a long way in producing a more positive image of low income women. A changed public perception that sees the assets of low income women could eventually change, for the better, policies that are premised on those negative attitudes.

Based on their experience, women who have successfully participated in WICD make several recommendations about how to improve low income women's access to and success in post-secondary education. First, they insist that college education must be made available to all low income women, including women receiving welfare and other women whose earlier education was compromised. The types of educational programs that they have found most valuable are: college-access programs (such as Women in Community Development) that provide peer support, financial assistance, and networking opportunities; informal educational opportunities in grassroots groups and churches that provide a chance to develop and exercise skills; and flexible college programs like the College of Public and Community Service, which is geared toward the nontraditional student (adults who have work and family responsibilities) and offers evening and weekend classes, is competency based, has computer and writing labs and tutors, is linked to community organizations, and counts prior learning and work experience.

Second, WICD women argue that public policy should provide family supports to low income women and their families in their journey to self-sufficiency. WICD is one example of a community-based program that adds support to a college program. It does so with limited resources. Quality child care and after-school programs are necessary so that women can manage school and work knowing their children are being well cared for; similar support systems for disabled elderly parents are also needed. Recognizing that women have family responsibilities, employers should offer flexible work schedules and opportunities to telecommute. Welfare policies should not make their lives more difficult with more requirements to meet and more demands on their time.

Third, WICD women think that government, nonprofit sector agencies, and private employers and organizations should remove barriers and penalties associated with going to work and increase supports available to those who are working. The women in WICD advise that welfare leavers should not be prematurely declared success stories and have their supports, such as Medicaid and other forms of health and disability insurance, child care subsidies, transportation assistance, food stamps, and tuition reimbursement cut off. In some cases, women report feeling more financially stressed once off welfare than when they were on. As earnings increase, supports such as housing subsidies decrease. Additional financial support, in the form of a supplement to earnings or an expanded earned income tax credit, could ease the financial stress while still encouraging work.

Fourth, WICD women argue that mentoring is critical to giving women the initial and ongoing, steady encouragement they need. Staff, co-workers, and educators are all potential motivators, mentors who can play an important role. Not all low income women attending college have a mentor, but efforts should be made to create such relationships. Colleges should link students with professional networks. Middle and upper income men and women use their affiliations in civic organizations, country clubs, sports groups, and so on to network, get customers, find jobs, and attain information; low income women need the same opportunities. Nonprofit organizations can link women to these associations, and professional groups can reach out and work with low income women. Likewise, employers can assist women with the transition to the work place and with their upward mobility within the company. Orientations and mentoring programs can help low income women make the transition to the work world. On-the-job training, career-ladder programs, and tuition reimbursement can help women move up the ladder.

Finally, the WICD experience suggests that society must value the contributions low income women make. Government agencies, employers, organizations, and churches can help create opportunities to involve low income women and provide leadership opportunities. Class differences and stereotypes too often prevent people from recognizing the talents and potential of low income women. Instead of focusing on deficits, employers and nonprofit organizations should take an asset-based approach that reveals skills that women bring to the work place or the organization.

NOTES

1. Jean Bacon and Laura Henze Russell, *The Self-Sufficiency Standard: Where Massachusetts Families Stand* (Boston: Women's Educational and Industrial Union, 2000).

2. Diana Pearce and Jennifer Brooks, *The Self-Sufficiency Standard in Massachusetts* (Washington, D.C.: Wider Opportunities for Women, 1998), p. 12.

3. Katherine Magnuson and Sharon McGroder, *The Effect of Increasing Welfare Mothers Education on Their Young Children's Academic Problems and School Readiness* (Evanston, Ill.: Joint Center for Poverty Research, Northwestern University, 2002).

4. Boston Foundation, *Social Capital in Boston: Findings from the Social Capital Community Benchmark Survey* (Boston: The Boston Foundation, 2001).

REFERENCES

Bacon, Jean, and Laura Henze Russell. 2000. *The self-sufficiency standard: Where Massachusetts families stand.* Boston: Women's Educational and Industrial Union.

Magnuson, Katherine, and Sharon McGroder. 2002. *The effect of increasing welfare mothers education on their young children's academic problems and school readiness.* Evanston, Ill.: Joint Center for Poverty Research, Northwestern University.

Pearce, Diana, and Jennifer Brooks. 1998. *The self-sufficiency standard for Massachusetts.* Washington, D.C.: Wider Opportunities for Women.

Roofless Women's Action Research Mobilization. 1997. *Lifting the voices of homeless women.* Boston: Women's Institute for Housing and Economic Development.

Women in Community Development (WICD). 1998. *Mission statement.* Boston: Women's Institute for Housing and Economic Development.

Chapter 10

Transcending Welfare

Creating a GI Bill for Working Families

Julie L. Watts and Aiko Schaefer

> I'm attending school, doing work-study, and also working a part-time job from 6:00 P.M. to midnight. This very tight schedule leaves me little time for my four-year-old son, maybe an hour or two a day (if any). Unless more financial help becomes available, I may have to quit school and work two full-time jobs in order to sustain my family. If I could get my AA degree in information technology, I could work one job, make more money and have more time as well as resources to care for my child.
>
> —Sarah, low income worker, and mother of one

Sarah is going to school because she knows what all the studies on education tell us: getting a college degree is the key to financial independence. However, thousands of women in Washington State like Sarah are forced to sacrifice time with their children to juggle employment obligations and coursework while pursuing the higher-education degrees they know can secure their economic futures. Many drop out. In the wake of welfare reform, the door to higher education has slammed shut, and those who stood at the threshold of a degree have had to turn on their heels and head into the low-wage workforce.

After years of trying to pry the door open, low income women and antipoverty advocates in the state of Washington have developed a policy proposal to allow women another way in. To ensure that Sarah and thousands of working poor women in Washington have a real chance to complete a degree, advocates have introduced new legislation—the Gaining Independence (GI) Bill for Families. Like the GI Bill passed in 1944, the Gaining Independence Bill expands access to college through financial aid: a Family Supplement partially offsets the costs of caring for children, which are prohibitive for working parents seeking higher education.

The difficulty in passing legislation that would allow for higher education for women on welfare has been compounded by another challenge: getting recipients referred to education programs. Even in situations in which the state has allowed parents limited opportunities for education and training, state agencies have been resistant to referring welfare recipients to programs other than job search. Caseworkers operate with a strong work-first orientation, and they are evaluated according to how many clients they place in jobs. The system offers no incentives for caseworkers to refer welfare recipients to job training or education.

Women on welfare, however, are not the only low income women who face barriers to post-secondary degrees. Thousands of working poor women who have left the rolls or earn just enough not to qualify also face significant obstacles in returning to school. The greatest challenge is finding the time and financial resources to care for children at home while pursuing a degree. How to juggle work, family, and school is first in the minds of low income mothers seeking education. Balancing classes, homework, and paid employment with home and family forces women to make tremendous sacrifices of time with their children. Of those who pursue education despite the barriers, many leave school before completing their degrees, overwhelmed by the demands on their time and financial obstacles.

The student financial aid system does not take into account the expense of caring for children. Correcting this inequity would not only help women on welfare get resources to support their families while going to school, it would help all working poor women who are struggling in the low-wage job market. This is the aim of the Gaining Independence Bill for Families.

This chapter will describe the post-welfare reform era in Washington State that motivated this proposal, the primary objectives of the Gaining Independence Bill for Families, the initial steps in the campaign for the GI Bill for Families, its recent legislative history, and the bill's future prospects.

THE CLIMATE FOR HIGHER EDUCATION FOR LOW INCOME PARENTS IN WASHINGTON STATE

I have learned that this so-called welfare reform is not about helping people become self-sufficient but just about shifting the statistics from those on welfare to those of the working poor. It is incomprehensible to me that a "successful" welfare story is someone who is earning $6.00 an hour and can't earn enough to support her children, doesn't have medical/dental insurance, can't afford quality and nutritious food for her children and will not be moving up the economic ladder out of poverty.

—Elena, welfare recipient, and mother of two

Low income women seeking higher education in Washington confront two systemic barriers to obtaining a degree: a welfare system that doesn't allow for education, and a financial aid system that doesn't account for the costs of caring for children while going to school. Both obstacles have stifled the potential of low income women seeking higher education and better paying jobs, and together they have kept nearly half of all single mothers among the ranks of the working poor (Klawitter 2001).

In the wake of federal welfare reform in 1996, the fight to allow women on welfare access to post-secondary education in Washington State has had little success. In 1999, advocates introduced the Independence through College for Achievers in Need (I-CAN) Bill. Based on Maine's Parents as Scholars program, it allowed Temporary Assistance for Needy Families (TANF) recipients to obtain post-secondary education. Given a political climate reluctant to grant access to four-year degree programs—something allowed in the Maine Parents as Scholars program—the Washington proposal sought only two years of post-secondary education for recipients at state community and technical colleges. Introduced in the Washington State Senate, the bill died before coming to a vote on the floor. Reintroduced in the 2000 legislative session, it again failed to gain the momentum necessary to pass. Two primary reasons led to I-CAN's failure. First, Democratic leadership deemed welfare reform a success, and shied away from supporting the bill because they did not see education for welfare recipients as a winning issue. Second, a costly fiscal note was attached, which was both unrealistic and guaranteed failure.

In the 2001 legislative session, advocates reinvigorated efforts to pass post-secondary education for women on welfare with a new policy initiative under a new name. The Higher Education for Lifelong Progress (HELP) Bill was also similar to the Parents as Scholars program and the previously introduced I-CAN Bill, and would have allowed two years of post-secondary education and training as well as child care assistance. Although businesses were reporting a lack of qualified applicants to fill positions that required two-year vocational degrees, this bill also failed, both in the 2001 session and again when it was reintroduced in 2002. The HELP Bill was introduced in the Senate while the GI Bill for Families was introduced in the House; neither bill was enacted in 2002.

Now more than ever, women in Washington need policy solutions that break down barriers to higher education. The state's economy is in recession, and Washington is facing one of the highest unemployment rates in the nation. As of this writing, the state's Office of Financial Management predicts that joblessness will remain high and Washington will remain in a recession even as the rest of the nation is recovering (Washington State Office 2002). Low-wage workers have little on which to fall back. Washington State's WorkFirst welfare program has done little more than move women on welfare into the ranks of the working poor. In fact, four years into the implementation of welfare reform,

55 percent of those leaving welfare for jobs in Washington State were living at or below the federal poverty line, and one out of three were returning to the rolls (Klawitter 2001). WorkFirst has put education last, and as a result, low income women are working, but working poor.

WORKING FIRST, BUT WORKING POOR

In 1997, Washington State implemented the WorkFirst welfare reform program in response to the passage of the Personal Responsibility and Work Opportunity Reconciliation Act (PRWORA). Women seeking state assistance would now need to comply with strict work requirements or face bitter sanctions. WorkFirst mandates that recipients move directly into job search and forces them to take the first job they're offered that pays at least a minimum wage. Those wanting to pursue vocational education can only be approved for up to twelve months, and recipients must be employed twenty hours a week in addition to time spent in school. Women on welfare may choose to pursue more than twelve months of vocational education; however they must also work twenty hours a week and cannot receive any assistance from the state for child care, tuition, or fees. By forgoing higher education, low income mothers in Washington have complied with the work-first mandate. In fact, in the first year of the WorkFirst program, state community colleges saw a 23 percent drop in enrollments of welfare recipients. An estimated 30 percent of the decline was attributed to changes in state welfare policy (Washington State Board 1998).

Working first, however, did not move low income women on to economic independence, but moved them directly into low-wage jobs that do not pay enough to support a family. In 1999, a survey of more than five hundred women who had been on welfare in the previous six months revealed that of those working full time, the average wage was $7.25 an hour, while part-time workers were making a mere $6.20 an hour. The median household income of families surveyed was only $1,100 a month, not nearly enough to lift a family of four above the poverty level (Statewide Poverty Action 2000).

The state's own longitudinal research reported similar wage trends during the same period. *WorkFirst Study: 3000 Washington Families* surveyed parents receiving welfare in March 1999 and found that those who were working earned, on average, $7.20 an hour, or slightly more than $1,000 per month. The study boasted that working mothers on welfare saw an increase in wages from March 1999 to June 2000; they report that employed women on welfare in June 2000 had an average hourly wage of $7.80 and monthly income of $1,200—an increase of sixty cents an hour, or $200 a month (Klawitter 2000). Even this improvement leaves a family of four living well below the federal poverty line. In fact, more than half of those families leaving welfare for employment were still living in poverty. Moreover, it is likely that the state's research did not fully reveal the reality of women's wages. When considering the results from the *WorkFirst: 3000 Families* study, it is important to note that the state reported the averages of the workers' wages, not their median wages or median income; the data actually give little indication of the range and spread of women's wages. Furthermore, the state soon lost track of the women it studied. When state researchers attempted to find their study participants one year later to interview them again, they were unable to locate nearly two-thirds of them. Such a high rate of attrition reveals a great deal about the instability of life for many low income, working mothers.

Without opportunities for education under the WorkFirst program, women have not been able to get jobs that pay enough to support a family. By not providing education and training, the state not only hurts these families but misses a unique opportunity to fill a growing gap in the job market. Since the implementation of WorkFirst, Washington businesses have faced a shortage of qualified workers to fill positions that pay a living wage. A study by the Washington State Workforce Training and Education Coordinating Board found that 64 percent of employers in the state had difficulty finding qualified job applicants (Washington State Workforce 2002). The most serious shortage was for individuals with post-secondary vocational education.

Although all women on welfare are forced to work first and work poor, the state's continued failure to invest in opportunities for women on welfare to obtain a post-secondary degree may also be compounding economic inequalities for communities of color. Although there have been few independent quantitative studies of racial equity in the wake of welfare reform in Washington State, a recent qualitative study based on focus groups (LaFrance 2002) indicates that women of color are facing unique challenges under WorkFirst to gain access to post-secondary education.

The majority of women who participated in the focus groups (56 percent) reported that a lack of job skills and education were major barriers to finding work. However, only about one-quarter said they had been offered assistance with this obstacle. Among the nonimmigrant groups, African American and American Indian women who participated in the focus groups tended to have less education and less work experience than White women. Despite their additional educational and skill needs, they were also less likely to be in education and training programs (33 percent, compared to 44 percent of Whites) and were more likely to be working than Whites (52 percent, compared to 22 percent of Whites.)

However, the most compelling finding from this study is that women across racial boundaries are asking for more opportunities to pursue a college degree to get their families out of poverty. When focus group participants were given the opportunity to voice what changes they would make to welfare policy that would help them move off welfare and into self-sufficiency, they overwhelmingly identified education and training as one of their highest priorities, second only to cash assistance to meet their basic needs (all respondents: 56 percent; African Americans: 75 percent; American Indians: 56 percent; Caucasians: 88 percent; and non-English-speaking immigrant groups: 40 percent). In fact, African American women identified education as a greater priority than cash assistance. The racist myth of the "welfare queen" has painted an ugly caricature of African American women on welfare as unmotivated check collectors; these focus group findings give evidence otherwise. Women on welfare across racial and ethnic boundaries know that education and training are key to moving out of poverty and becoming self-sufficient. Sadly, this is a fact that the state has not yet recognized.

HIGHER EDUCATION: A STEP UP ON THE CAREER LADDER

I believe that education can break the cycle of poverty. That is why I am getting my AA degree. I was married for eight years and have recently divorced. Now I'm the sole provider for my twin nine-year-old boys as well as a full-time student. I have a work-study position that will only last a few more months. I have such a strong desire to get an education and have a career that I have to give up precious time with my twins. Families like mine need financial support while going to school in order to be successful and get ahead.

—Rebekah, low income worker, and mother of two

The barriers facing women on welfare tell only part of the story of the challenges facing women seeking post-secondary education. Low income women who have chosen not to go on welfare despite being eligible, as well as those who make just enough not to qualify for benefits, are also struggling to get the post-secondary degrees that will help them get ahead. Student financial aid programs provide some assistance, but do not consider the additional expense parents face in caring for children while going to school.

Yet, completing a post-secondary degree is the surest way for families like Rebekah's to increase their income and become self-sufficient. Workers in Washington who obtain two years of post-secondary education earn, on average, $4,400 more each year than they would have earned without the degree. According to federal data, those with a bachelor's degree can earn up to $16,250 more each year than they would have without the degree (Pascall and Chase 2001).

Nonetheless, thousands of families are forced to forgo investments in education. Without additional financial support, families like Rebekah's may have to forgo the $4,400 a year raise they are working toward in favor of the $6.50-per-hour work that the low-wage job market offers. Over her employment career, the

$4,400 Rebekah would receive in additional earnings each year with her associate's degree would represent an 11.5 percent return on the cost of tuition, fees, and income forgone to pursue the degree itself. That is twice the rate paid on a Treasury bill, and better than the long-term growth rate of the stock market (Pascall and Chase 2001).

Making this investment in training and education for low income women does more than help working families to succeed. It also generates returns for the state. As low income single mothers move up the wage ladder into higher-paying jobs, they become greater contributors to the economic well-being of their communities, not only as consumers, but as taxpayers. In Washington State, students who have completed two years of college contribute, on average, $12,870 more in taxes to the state during their employment years as a result of higher earnings. Those who have completed four-year degrees pay as much as $150,000 in state taxes over the course of their working lives (Pascall and Chase 2001). Economic independence is more than just a benefit to low income parents—it is a fundamental part of creating and maintaining a strong community.

Yet despite the benefits of higher education, inequities in the financial aid system make it difficult for low income parents caring for children to have the same access to education as nonparent students. Eligibility for financial aid is the same whether or not one has children. Students with children have additional expenses, which make it difficult to achieve their post-secondary educational goal. The GI Bill for Families aims to make higher education attainable for low income parents.

THE STRATEGY TO PASS THE GAINING INDEPENDENCE BILL FOR FAMILIES

The GI Bill for Families, introduced in the House in 2001, would create a state-funded supplement for families, providing mothers with additional financial aid to help cover expenses they incur as parents. Eligible students would be able to use the Family Supplement to attend any two- or four-year college in the state, and would receive an additional cash benefit as a part of their financial aid package, to assist with the costs of caring for dependent children. To be eligible for the program, students must be custodial parents who qualify to receive financial aid, and able to attend school full time while receiving the supplement. The bill would also require the Washington State Higher Education Coordinating Board (HECB) to adopt rules to administer the Family Supplement in a manner that does not reduce the amount of current federal and state financial aid available to eligible students. (The details of these rules have not yet been worked out and would depend on the quantity of money involved and the number of students that could actually be served.)

By bolstering opportunities for parents to attend school without relying on state referrals to job training or the approval of agencies eager to purge the welfare rolls, the GI Bill for Families transcends the welfare system. It mitigates the circumstances that pit the educational needs of women on welfare against the opportunities of other working poor parents. Best of all, it honors the work that women are already doing in caring for children at home, and backs that up with real dollars.

The campaign for the GI Bill for Families was spearheaded by the Statewide Poverty Action Network. Created in 1996, the Statewide Poverty Action Network (then the Washington Welfare Reform Coalition) was organized in response to the passage of PRWORA at the federal level. An alliance of community members, welfare rights groups, immigrant and refugee groups, labor unions, faith communities, and other antipoverty advocates, this network addresses the root causes of poverty in Washington.

The 2002 legislative session in Washington State marked the first in a three-year campaign to pass the GI Bill for Families. The first year's goal was to introduce the bill and begin building support for the policy by recruiting key partners into the campaign. In addition, advocates wanted to raise the problem of access to education and training for low income parents in both houses of the legislature. One of the greatest challenges in moving policies that affect low income families through the Washington State legislature is that support for these initiatives repeatedly comes from the same camp: the human services lobby. The appearance of the "usual suspects" weighing in on a bill creates the impression that support is only coming from one sector of the community. The campaign for the GI Bill for Families sought support from constituencies that legislators were not accustomed to hearing on policies that affect low income women.

The first step was to bring together education and labor communities with human service advocates. By reaching out to these community partnerships, the campaign deepened and broadened the base of support. Of particular significance was the endorsement of the State Board of Community and Technical Colleges (SBCTC) as well as the Higher Education Coordinating Board (HECB). The backing of HECB was especially key because this body would be adopting rules to implement the program.

As the bill progressed through the House, campaign organizers needed to build support quickly. Organizers branched out and talked to community groups across the state. Many noted that the GI Bill for Families was the "easiest sell" they had ever made. People's basic sense of fairness was piqued when they learned about the inequities in the financial aid system. The message that the state must allow low income working parents the education they need to support their families instantly resonated whether it was heard in Spokane, Vancouver, or Seattle. Through an expanding network beyond the "usual suspects," support came from the leadership of such organizations as the Washington State Labor

Council, the Association of University Women, the Washington State Hospital Association, the League of Women Voters, the Washington State Student Lobby, and the Washington Association of Churches.

Yet the most persuasive voices were those of working poor mothers themselves. In the week prior to the bill's hearing in the House Higher Education Committee, each day legislators on the committee received a "Speak Out" sheet from someone who would be impacted by the passage of the GI Bill. Low income mothers from different parts of the state voiced their support for the program. Each sheet carried pictures of the family and their personal stories in their own words. Incorporating the voices of low income women was a vital part of the campaign. The greatest policy experts in legislative hearings proved to be those low income mothers who were already struggling to stay in school and get by.

THE CAMPAIGN CONTEXT: OPPORTUNITIES AND CHALLENGES

In 2002, Democrats controlled both houses of the state legislature though they held only a narrow margin in the Senate. Advocates surmised that the policy had the best chance for passage under Democratic leadership. The governor and legislature verbalized a strong commitment to education. However, both had, in the past, been reluctant to extend that commitment to women on welfare and the working poor, as illustrated by the failed I-CAN and HELP Bills.

One of the greatest assets in building the campaign for the Gaining Independence Bill for Families was the power wielded by women in politics: "Research has found that regardless of party affiliation, women officeholders are more likely than male officeholders to support women's agendas" (IWPR 1996, 7). In 2000, Washington ranked first in the nation for the number of women in elected office, including both U.S. senators. In fact, the Institute for Women's Policy Research (2000) in their *Status of Women in the States* report ranked Washington second in the nation for political participation of women. The strength of women in politics in Washington was potentially fertile ground for building support for policies that address poverty and increase access to postsecondary education for low income mothers. Although all female legislators do not necessarily support antipoverty bills, and often divide along class and racial lines, there is evidence for more family-friendly policies—including support for increased opportunities for women on welfare—from legislatures with more elected women (e.g., Deprez, Hastedt, and Henderson 1999).

Washington also has a strong and vital network of state colleges that not only connects students across the state, but also provides the necessary infrastructure to ensure low income mothers can take advantage of higher education opportunities in their home communities. Washington has six colleges and universities and thirty-five state community and technical colleges in rural and urban communities. Many of these campuses have organized groups of women students who are seeking to break down barriers to women's admission to and success in college programs.

Perhaps the greatest promise of advancing this policy comes from existing support for education programs to fight poverty. A recent national poll found that 82 percent of people support helping low income workers pay for career-related college programs (Jobs for the Future 2001). The public believes that education is a worthwhile investment. Public support for higher education has long been a driving political force in Washington State, and may prove to be a valuable asset in this campaign as well.

Although Washington has a number of strengths for organizing this campaign, advocates faced multiple challenges in moving this policy forward in the legislature. The most imposing was the state budget crisis. Declining revenues and short-sighted initiatives have led the state of Washington, which once boasted a luxurious surplus, into a deep budget crisis. Once awash in dollars for investment in state programs, the Washington State government faced annual budget pressures to the tune of over a billion dollars a year in 2002.

The budget problem is multifaceted. In 1993, voters passed Initiative 601, which placed a cap on state spending that only allows for increases due to a rise in the rate of inflation or population growth. Policy makers soon found that the state's actual expenses increased based on factors that far outpaced these arbitrary standards, including the rising rate of inflation for health care, the rising prison population, and growth in the aging population. The state's budget surplus diminished rapidly as voters passed initiatives that simultaneously cut taxes and allocated spending. Entering into a debate on increasing access to postsecondary education in the legislature, advocates were thrust head-on into this budget struggle in 2002. The inescapable question from every corner of the state capital was, "How will we pay for it?"

THE 2002 LEGISLATIVE SESSION AND BEYOND

Indeed, how to respond to the budget challenge emerged as the defining question hovering over the GI Bill for Families' life in the 2002 legislative session. The debate over how to fund the program led the policy through numerous changes, including one that weakened the bill's effectiveness in fighting poverty. The prime sponsor of the bill in the Washington statehouse was Representative Phyllis Kenny (D), chair of the House Higher Education Committee. The measure had support from both parties, with nineteen sponsoring members, sixteen of whom were Democrats, and three of whom were Republicans.

Concern over how to fund the program during a tense budget-cutting session led advocates to agree to an amendment to the bill that restricted funding to private sources. Advocates' intent in supporting this amendment was to ensure that the bill would not die in the Appropriations Committee, as did many worthy programs that session. The ultimate hope was that state funding could be restored in conference if the bill could pass the Senate in its original form. It soon came to a vote on the floor, where it passed with ninety-eight yeas and no nays. Unfortunately, the Senate bill was also amended to include the same restrictions. Concerned that if the bill passed both houses in this form it would hurt future attempts to pass the bill as intended, with state funding attached, advocates quickly, and successfully, moved to kill the bill.

Nonetheless, the first year of the campaign provided evidence that many community members and lawmakers support the GI Bill for Families and its approach to expanding access to post-secondary education for low income parents. During the interim between 2002 and 2003 legislative sessions, advocates decided on a new, multiyear strategy. After first securing commitment for the concept of the bill, they would then seek increasing budget allocations. The model for their strategy was the successful Washington State Housing Trust Fund. Established in 1989 by the legislature in response to mounting pressure from housing advocates, the fund began with a modest state allocation of $1 million in 1989 and allowed for private funding sources. In each successive year, the fund grew, and it is now backed by $80 million in state funds.

With this strategy in mind, the GI Bill for Families was again introduced in the 2003 legislative session in both houses, but without state funding attached. The bill gave the Higher Education Coordinating Board (HECB) authority to create a private funding stream. In this form the bill neither required a fiscal note nor had to pass through an appropriations committee. Advocates from human services, education, labor, and faith communities again mobilized to support the bill. Members of the Statewide Poverty Action Network organized students across the state to engage in campus letter-writing campaigns. Over two hundred people submitted handwritten letters to their representatives, and many more called, e-mailed, and faxed their concerns. With broad popular support, the bill unanimously passed both houses of the legislature and was signed by the governor on April 16, 2003.

The next stages of the campaign may be the most challenging. As advocates prepare for the 2004 legislative session, it will be critical to identify a funding source and build political support to appropriate state money. Like most states in the nation, Washington has faced a dramatic fiscal crisis in recent years. In 2002, while the GI Bill was moving through the legislature, policy makers cut $2.2 billion from state services, many of which serve the poor.

Although identifying funding is a challenge, opportunities exist to generate revenue. Tax loopholes are robbing the state of potential sources of funding. Even as policy makers continue to gut services for the poor, they have proposed tax cuts to the rich by eliminating the state's estate tax. By whatever means the governor and legislators choose to address the revenue problem, this situation will dictate the future of the GI Bill for Families. Efforts to generate revenue and bring tax reform to the state of Washington will be a vital part of ensuring that the money is there to provide the state services on which residents depend and to create opportunities for new initiatives such as the GI Bill for Families.

Furthermore, gloomy projections for the Washington state economy may yet shine the light on the need for worker retraining. As unemployment rises steeply, the need to move displaced workers into jobs that pay has become essential. Local governments, labor unions, and legislators are all eager to ensure that workers have the job skills they need to manage in the recession. A rapidly changing economy has underscored the need for workers to periodically update their skills to stay competitive in a changing job market. Convincing legislators and the public that the GI Bill could have a significant role in ensuring that such opportunities exist for workers to acquire new skills in both good economic times as well as bad will be key in the next legislative session.

The presence and visibility of public support is the most important asset in persuading lawmakers to allocate state dollars. Bill sponsors from the 2003 legislative session will seek between $1 and $2 million in state funding in the supplemental budget in 2004. As the campaign continues, it will be critical to convene the same base of supporters and mobilize communities to take action to ensure that adequate funding is dedicated to the program, and that it grows over time.

It will also be vital that students and low income women play a central role in the campaign, speaking out about their personal experience and keeping the needs of their families at the forefront of the debate. Also, to ensure that the program arises as a funding priority for policy makers who are worried over the bottom line, advocates must show why education for low income women is a sound investment.

The campaign plans to continue to demonstrate that it is not only low income families who benefit from higher education, but that businesses, the economy, and the state benefit as well. Advocates will continue their outreach to new partners and to build new alliances that include members of the business community, to support policies that address the root causes of poverty in Washington State.

Conclusion

When I think about the future, I think about having a good enough job that pays enough for me to spend more time with Kaiya. I've missed out on so much of her life trying to work and go to school, just so we can get ahead. She's grown a lot in that time. Getting a degree is really all about spending more time with her, being there as she grows up.

—Joanne, welfare recipient, and mother of one

By expanding educational opportunities for women in poverty, Washington State can open up a door that slammed shut behind welfare recipients in 1996. When welfare reform denied low income women the ability to decide whether to work or go to school it denied them something essential that all women, all people, value: a choice for the future of their families. Breaking down barriers to higher education holds the promise of restoring that choice for women on welfare. For many other women raising children in poverty, it could open that door for the first time. The GI Bill for Families has tremendous potential for providing opportunities to a portion of Washington State's population that has faced constrained choices in the past.

To win real policy change, advocates must build a movement to address the root causes of women's poverty. The potential to win real change is there, and to tap it, the struggle for a just economy for low income women must become every woman's fight. Regardless of age, race, or economic background, all women must see that the inequities facing working poor women undermine the rights and opportunities of us all. Ultimately, the future of community organizing to address poverty will require advocates to lift up the voices of women struggling on the edges of our economy, and to engage communities in a meaningful dialogue that generates the political will for change. The GI Bill for Families can be a vehicle for just such a discussion given that greater access to post-secondary education clearly benefits all levels of society: individuals, families, communities, and the state.

NOTE

The names of the women quoted in this chapter have been changed to protect their privacy.

REFERENCES

Deprez, L., C. Hastedt, and M. T. Henderson. 1999. Parents as Scholars: A model higher education program for low-income women in the new welfare landscape. In *Women's progress: Perspectives on the past, blueprint for the future. Proceedings of the Fifth Women's Policy Research Conference*, ed. Institute for Women's Policy Research (IWPR), 195–199. Washington, D.C.: IWPR.

Institute for Women's Policy Research (IWPR). 1996. *The status of women in the states: Politics, economics, health, demographics.* Washington, D.C.: IWPR.

———. 2000. *The status of women in the states 2000.* Washington, D.C.: IWPR.

Jobs for the Future. 2001. *Public views on low wage workers in the current economy.* Boston: Jobs for the Future.

Klawitter, M. M. 2000. *WorkFirst study: 3000 Washington families: Employment report.* Seattle: Daniel J. Evans School of Public Affairs, University of Washington.

———. 2001. *WorkFirst study: 3000 Washington families: TANF experience, exits and returns.* Seattle: Daniel J. Evans School of Public Affairs, University of Washington.

LaFrance, J. 2002. *The missing voices in WorkFirst: Discussion in diverse communities.* Seattle, Wash.: Poverty Action Network.

Pascall, G., and R. A. Chase. 2001. *The economic impact of community and technical colleges in Washington State.* An analysis commissioned by the Trustees Association of the Community and Technical Colleges. Olympia, Wash.: Trustees Association of the Community and Technical Colleges.

Statewide Poverty Action Network. 2000. *Reality check: The reality of welfare reform for families in Washington State.* Seattle, Wash.: Statewide Poverty Action Network.

Washington State Board for Community and Technical Colleges. 1998. *Welfare enrollments in Washington community and technical colleges: Fall quarter 1997.* Olympia: Washington State Board for Community and Technical Colleges.

Washington State Office of the Forecast Council. 2002. *Washington's economic picture.* Retrieved August 15, 2002 from http://www.ofm.wa.gov/budget02/highlights/waeconomy.htm.

Washington State Workforce Training and Education Coordinating Board. 2002. *Washington's economy.* Olympia: Washington State Workforce Training and Education Coordinating Board.

Chapter 11

Securing Higher Education for Women on Welfare in Maine

Luisa Stormer Deprez, Sandra S. Butler, and Rebekah J. Smith

INTRODUCTION

The passage of the Personal Responsibility and Work Opportunity Reconciliation Act (PRWORA) in 1996 brought an end to welfare as we knew it. Never before in the history of this country had such harsh and punitive restrictions and sanctions been imposed on low income parents raising children—parents who were mostly lone women, poor enough to need government financial support to help them raise and maintain their families. Among the most noteworthy features of the act were the repeal of the sixty-year-old financial assistance program, Aid to Families with Dependent Children (AFDC), and the creation of the Temporary Assistance for Needy Families (TANF) program; the establishment of a five-year lifetime limit on receipt of federally funded benefits, regardless of recipient need or cause; the ability of states to curtail benefits to additional children born to women while on welfare—the "family caps" (a state option); the implementation of the "states' rights" approach to funding state programs—block grants tied to work-participation rates; and the rescission of access to post-secondary education for low income parents on welfare.

These changes reflected a commitment to a "work-first" ideology that sought to reduce welfare rolls by, among other things, institutionalizing work requirements for participants, demanding work in exchange for benefits and, the focus of this chapter, restricting access to higher education. The act's intent, "to end the dependency of needy parents on government benefits by promoting job preparation . . . and . . . to enable them to leave the program and become self-sufficient" (Personal Responsibility, 1996), was in direct conflict with the means employed to achieve it. A plethora of research studies confirmed the relationship between higher education and increased earnings potential, yet the restrictions on access to higher education were justified on

217

the grounds that "the discipline of work, rather than, say, more education, does most to help recipients keep full-time jobs" (Will tinkering bring the building down? 2002, 29).

Aggressive campaigns to counter the powerful antiwelfare sentiment embedded in this act dotted the country in 1996. In Maine in the early 1990s, a coalition of groups representing women, low income families, religious and labor organizations, and social service agencies had formed the Women's Economic Security Project (WESP). When passage of PRWORA seemed certain, WESP escalated their activities and took their campaign on the road, engaging news media boards, legislators, and community groups in dialogues about welfare, women, and the economy. Campaign representatives challenged traditional stereotypical claims about welfare receipt by placing welfare programs in the broader context of gender inequality, unemployment, low-wage jobs, and poverty. Everywhere they went the same message was reiterated: *Welfare reform must be about raising families out of poverty, and this won't happen until we change the economic position of women in the labor market.* Securing access to post-secondary education for low income families was high on the list of necessary outcomes.

While it is difficult to evaluate the impact of such a campaign, it is clear that the public debate about welfare in Maine was broader than it was in many other states. WESP's determined and systematic effort to change the terms of the debate by insisting on the crucial connections among women's economic security, labor market access, income-generating capacity, occupational success, and post-secondary education created a political climate receptive to legislation that honored these connections.

Maine emerged as a national leader in implementing federal welfare mandates by passing legislation creating the Parents as Scholars program, a state-funded student aid program for welfare recipients. Parents as Scholars, developed in response to restrictions on access to higher education imposed by the federal law, formed the basis of a coherent policy that not only maintained an obligation to women's education but could more successfully accomplish PRWORA's avowed claim to "end dependency" and secure "self-sufficiency."

This is the story of women activists intent on ensuring that low income Maine women would have a better chance to succeed in the new economies of the twentieth and twenty-first centuries. It is a story of hope, opportunity, and political activism. It describes how Maine women, in coalition with other groups aspiring to secure social and economic justice for Maine citizens, carried out this campaign in the 1990s and once again coalesced to address the reauthorization of 2002. Then, as now, their vision of the centrality of securing access to post-secondary education for low income families is key. All pathways point to the promise, prospect, and irrefutable importance of higher education.

THE PARENTS AS SCHOLARS PROGRAM:
AN ENACTMENT OVERVIEW

In 1997 the Maine legislature rejected the route prescribed by PRWORA. As one of only two states (Wyoming is the other) to recognize the necessity of including higher education in its welfare plan, it enacted the Parents as Scholars (PaS) program after hearing testimony from many welfare recipients about the value of education and about their difficulties in obtaining it. Maine's approach presumed that when PaS families (usually headed by single mothers) leave welfare, they will earn higher wages, be more likely to have employment-based health insurance, and be less likely to return to welfare than their TANF counterparts. The state chose the bold step of enacting a law to provide access to post-secondary education for low income parents under TANF rather than relying on the more punitive federal approach that led most states to abandon programs offering post-secondary education to welfare recipients.

Parents as Scholars is not a part of the TANF program, but a separate, state-funded student aid program limited to two thousand TANF-eligible participants (about 10 percent of the total TANF caseload in 1997). PaS enrollees in two- or four-year post-secondary education programs get the same cash benefits they would have received through TANF and the same supportive services they would be eligible for in Additional Support for People in Retraining and Employment (ASPIRE), Maine's welfare-to-work program: assistance with child care, transportation, car repairs, auto liability insurance, eye care, dental care, books and supplies, clothing and uniforms, occupational expenses, and other services as necessary. They also receive a range of services available from the post-secondary institutions they attend: personal counseling, on-campus health care, job opportunities, job-search assistance, campus housing, child care, financial aid, support groups, academic advising, wellness facilities and programs. Because PaS is state funded, the federally mandated five-year time limit does not apply. Students are required to "work" but can count both school and study time toward these hours. For their first two years of participation, they must take part in twenty hours of class and study time each week, with work or volunteer hours making up the balance if necessary. Beyond the first two years of participation, PaS recipients must take part in forty hours of class, study, work, or volunteer time. The definition of work in Maine's law is much broader than in PRWORA: school-related volunteer activities, practicums, tutoring, internships, and work-study all count toward the required work hours. Students are expected to complete their programs in one-and-one-half times the normal matriculation time and maintain at least a 2.0 grade-point average.

What caused Maine to take a path different from so many other states? The answer involves a mix of historical, technical, and political factors. Ironically, it was the same ideological view that brought the welfare block grant with its animus toward education that also provided the technical opening to create the PaS program.[1]

In the early fall of 1996, two Washington-based policy groups, the Center on Law and Social Policy and the Center on Budget and Policy Priorities, argued that a state could use its maintenance-of-effort (MOE) dollars to create a separate state program apart from its TANF-funded program and that by doing so could continue to provide access to post-secondary education for low income parents. Such a program would count toward the state's maintenance-of-effort obligation but participants in the program would not be considered in the calculation of the state's work-participation rate nor be subject to PRWORA's five-year time limit. This analysis was approved by the federal Department of Health and Human Services early in 1997.

While it was possible to continue to provide access to education without legal penalty, most who had fought this battle knew that persuading policy makers was only the first step in a challenging political battle. Advocates in Maine had three points in their favor when they began efforts to enact the PaS legislation in early 1997. First, Maine had a tradition of providing access to two- and four-year post-secondary education in its welfare-to-work programs,[2] which was intact at the time that PRWORA was implemented. The fact that post-secondary education had been part of the welfare-to-work landscape for a long time enabled a group of articulate spokespersons, who had either benefited from the program directly or had otherwise come to recognize its value, to emerge. These spokespersons, able to act on their own and others' behalf, were positioned to promote an agenda that would enable them, and others like them, to access the means of assuring their own economic security.

Second, as mentioned earlier, a coalition of groups representing women, low income families, religious and labor organizations, and social service agencies had organized in the early 1990s. The Women's Economic Security Project (WESP) conducted an aggressive campaign to counter the powerful antiwelfare sentiment sweeping the country. The goal of the campaign was to shift the terms of the welfare debate from a focus on behavior to a broader understanding of how the economy keeps women, and particularly single parents, poor: "In particular, WESP's goal was to develop a 'real' welfare reform agenda that acknowledged the economic difficulties encountered by single parents at home and in the labor market, and that gave voice to the concerns, aspirations, and trials of women currently on welfare" (Butler and Nevin 1997, 29).

In 1994, WESP surveyed three thousand AFDC families. Stephanie Seguino, an economist then at the Margaret Chase Smith Center at the University of Maine, was asked to place the experiences of survey respondents into the context of a labor market analysis for all Maine women. The report, *Living on the Edge: Women Working and Providing for Families in the Maine Economy* (1995), was groundbreaking in its description of the labor opportunities available and not available to low-skilled working women; it identified who in

Maine was receiving welfare and why. It received wide coverage from a Maine press hungry for concrete, state-specific data related to welfare. Replete with evidence that nearly two-thirds of single parents with young children lived below the poverty level and that the average wage of welfare recipients was $5.37 per hour, the report dramatically reinforced the point that "real" welfare reform had to focus on the condition of women in the labor market.

With this evidence, members of WESP made visits to the editorial boards of every major Maine newspaper, held a series of educational lunches for legislators, and dispatched volunteer members of a speaker's bureau throughout the state to engage community groups in dialogue about welfare, women, and the economy. Dozens of women came to the statehouse to oppose stereotype-based legislation calling for "family caps," "learnfare," and time limits. WESP's determined and systematic effort to change the terms of the debate helped to create a responsive political climate.

In late 1996, another event occurred that had a significant impact on the PaS legislation. An employee from a community action program in the Portland area organized a "Walk-a-Mile" project, pairing legislators with welfare recipients throughout the state. The purpose of this project was to help lawmakers better understand welfare by spending a month sharing experiences with a partner who was on welfare; over fifty legislators participated. By sheer coincidence, the ranking Republican member of the legislature's Health and Human Services Committee was paired with a young woman who was struggling to overcome bureaucratic obstacles that prevented her from enrolling in college. The young mother realized that college was her only hope of escaping poverty, and together they worked to get her enrolled with the services she needed. That experience made a lasting impression and the legislator became a strong ally of the PaS effort.

Thus, by the time that the PaS legislation was presented to legislators in early 1997, a considerable amount of political groundwork had already been laid. A broad coalition of groups and individuals, including representatives from the university and technical college systems, quickly organized in support of the bill. After hearing from dozens of people, including powerful testimony from many past and present welfare recipients, the bill won strong bipartisan support from the Health and Human Services Committee. The remaining obstacle was the Department of Human Services' reluctance to take the untested step of using its MOE dollars, set aside pursuant to PRWORA, to create a separate state program. The department was eventually persuaded and an agreement was reached that would allow them to opt out of the program if the federal Department of Health and Human Services (DHHS) did not permit them to count state dollars spent in PaS toward the MOE obligation. (This was eventually allowed.)

A final advantage that cannot be ignored is the active role that the bill's sponsor played in its success. At the same time that this bill was introduced, the

Maine legislature made history by electing a majority of women to legislative leadership. One of those leaders, Senate Majority Leader Chellie Pingree (D-Knox), was the sponsor of the Parents as Scholars legislation. She lobbied tirelessly in support of the bill with her colleagues, in the press, and with Maine's Commissioner of Human Services, emphasizing her interest in seeing the PaS bill pass. Her commitment to the goal of helping low income women escape poverty through access to education never faltered, and her tenacity paid off. Maine women have benefited tremendously from the work of legislative leaders who understand the significance of women's economic roles in families today and are committed to bettering their economic status. The Parents as Scholars program exemplifies the state's promotion of a welfare-reform strategy that in its judgement would best serve the goal of moving families out of poverty and empowering them to secure their own futures.

EVALUATING THE PARENTS AS SCHOLARS PROGRAM

The significance and benefits of higher education opportunities for poor women cannot be overstated. Findings from two surveys of PaS program participants, which we conducted in 1999 and 2001, affirm the positive correlations between access to higher education, well-being, empowerment, and enhanced relationships with children. For the purposes of this chapter, we will review the results of those surveys briefly; fuller discussions of the survey findings are presented elsewhere (see Butler and Deprez 2002; Smith, Deprez, and Butler 2002; and Deprez and Butler 2001).

In July 1999, a nineteen-page survey was sent to all 848 participants in the PaS program. The instrument was composed of questions about the participants' current and past educational experience; work and welfare receipt history; health and the health of their children; current financial situation; children and child care circumstances; time use in their daily lives; experience in the PaS program and with their post-secondary educational institution; and beliefs about how PaS had impacted their lives. Most questions were closed-ended or short-answer, although there were several places for respondents to explain their answers more fully. The last several pages of the survey included open-ended questions exploring how PaS had impacted the respondents' feelings about themselves, their relationships with family members, and their future plans. We received 222 completed surveys, a response rate of 26.2 percent. Given the length of the survey and the multiple responsibilities borne by respondents, we were pleased with this rate of return.

We invited these respondents to participate in a longitudinal study: 192 (86.5 percent) of the respondents said that we could contact them again in the future. Two years later, we queried this group of 192 about their continued participation in our study: nearly two-thirds of the original respondents (n = 127,

66.1 percent) were located and replied affirmatively to our inquiry. A second survey was mailed to this subset of respondents in November 2001.

One of the primary purposes of the second survey was to see how participants who had graduated were faring in the labor market. We knew these data would be particularly important in the federal TANF reauthorization debates and in state legislative discussions about the future of the PaS program. While shorter than the first survey, it followed the same format of asking about employment, education, finances, child care and health, and again included open-ended questions about the respondents' overall experiences with the PaS program and attending college. We received sixty-five completed surveys in this second round, giving us a response rate of 51.2 percent. We attribute this relatively high response rate to participants' eagerness to report on their successes and their interest in participating in the state discussion on the future of the PaS program. We present findings from each of the surveys in the following section.

In the 1999 survey, all but seven of the respondents were women (96.8 percent) and most were either single (36.9 percent) or divorced (34.7 percent). The survey respondents ranged in age from twenty to fifty-six with a median age of thirty. All respondents had biological children living with them; 43.2 percent had one child, 34.2 percent had two children, and the remaining 22.6 percent had three or more children. Forty-five respondents (20.3 percent) reported they had a disability and fifty-six (25.2 percent) had a child with a disability. In the three years prior to entering the PaS program, the vast majority of respondents (81.4 percent) had been employed in either full-time or part-time work at a median hourly wage of $6.50.

Most respondents (83.6 percent) had received traditional high school diplomas before entering post-secondary education; the remainder had completed their general equivalency diploma (GED). Respondents were fairly evenly split between pursuing two- and four-year degrees, although slightly more were in four-year programs (56 percent). Respondent grade point averages (GPAs) ranged from 1.83 to 4.0—five respondents reported 4.0 averages—with a mean GPA of 3.21. Respondents seemed happy with their post-secondary education (PSE) institutions, with 92.5 percent rating their institutions as either good or excellent.

As part of the longitudinal study, the second survey allowed us to see how sixty-five (29.3 percent of the original sample) respondents were doing two years later: many of them had graduated and moved into the labor market. Their profiles, while similar to the original group of which they are a part, differ slightly from the original sample: all respondents were women ranging in age from twenty-three to forty-four with a median age of thirty-one. Twenty-five respondents (38.5 percent) indicated that they were partnered; twenty-one (32.3 percent) were single; fifteen (23 percent) were divorced or separated, and not re-partnered; and four (6.1 percent) were married or remarried. All the respondents had children: fifty-two respondents (80.0 percent) were sole caretakers. Slightly over half (50.8 percent) had children under the age of six living in their households.

At the time of the second survey, fourteen respondents (22.2 percent) were still in school and participating in the PaS program; thirty-five (53.8 percent) had graduated and were working; six (9.5 percent) had graduated, but were not working; six (9.5 percent) were still in school, but no longer in the PaS program; and four (6.2 percent) had left school and PaS. Most of the respondents who were still students, but not in the PaS program (66.7 percent), were making too much money in their jobs to qualify for PaS. Among the four students who had left school and PaS, three appeared to have terminated their studies for employment, while the fourth needed to take disability leave although she hoped to return to school soon. Among the respondents who graduated but were not working, a variety of circumstances caused their unemployment: one had just been laid off and was about to start her own business; another had lost day care two months earlier, causing her to lose her job; one had an intermittent disability and was looking for appropriate work; one did seasonal summer work and was taking continuing education classes; one was pregnant and had taken disability leave; and the sixth had left work one year earlier to have a child and continued to suffer from depression.

Survey Findings

Both of the surveys included several open-ended questions that allowed respondents to share, in a narrative format, their experiences, insights, struggles, and prospects for their futures. We analyzed these questions to determine if any themes emerged from participant responses. A number of significant themes emerged that we examine later. Findings are reported for both the first survey (1999) and the second survey (2001).

Change in Self-Concept

A question in the first survey asked "Has your participation in a post-secondary program affected your feelings about yourself?" Nearly all the respondents answered that it had and wrote comments describing changes in their self-concept. A thematic analysis revealed three dominant themes: empowerment, self-esteem, and well-being. Respondents experienced overwhelming positive transformative experiences on returning to school. While many cited initial nervousness and insecurity as they began classes, nearly all reported that this melted away as they met the challenges of higher education and often exceeded their own expectations.

Many respondents (57.5 percent) in 1999 reported a feeling of independence and liberation as a result of their participation in post-secondary education. For example, some women spoke specifically of how they would no longer
allow abusive men to push them around and tell them what to do. A thirty-
year-old divorced mother of three children—a third-year sociology student
with the career goal of being a teacher—formerly in an abusive relationship,
spoke of her increased feeling of empowerment in the following way:

> I feel confident in my ability to face challenges. I have ambition. Before
> I used to crumble in the face of adversity and wait for someone to "res-
> cue" me—either my parents or a boyfriend. Now I know I can make it
> on my own. I don't have to "settle" anymore.

Over 55 percent of the 1999 respondents answering this question reported
increased self-esteem, greater confidence, and strengthened self-respect as a result
of going back to school. One respondent, a thirty-nine-year-old senior majoring
in political science, said:

> My self-esteem has greatly improved. For most of my life I believed I
> was not intelligent enough to go to college. When I began school I was
> very nervous and stressed about whether I could succeed; I have! I now
> feel confident in my ability to think, process and produce answers both
> academically and personally.

This mother of two teenagers maintained a 3.7 GPA and hoped to go on to law
school.

Effect on Lives

A second open-ended question in the first survey asked respondents whether
they thought post-secondary education had changed their lives or enhanced
their opportunities. Almost all of the respondents (99.5 percent) indicated that
college had changed their lives. The three themes that emerged were opportunity, goals, and enrichment. Narratives reflected a mood of anticipation and ex-
citement. They believed their hard work in school would pay off in terms of
opening doors to employment that would be personally satisfying and financially lucrative, and that would bring them respect. Being in school had introduced them to new ideas, new friends, new ambitions, and new ways of looking
at the world.

Seventy-five percent of respondents in 1999 wrote about the increased opportunities that post-secondary training afforded them by opening doors to better jobs, increased pay, and more stable employment. This theme is illuminated

by the words of a senior nursing student, a twenty-five-year-old mother of two children with severe health problems—one with epilepsy and the other with asthma—who maintained a 3.4 GPA:

> Without the education I have received I would still be cocktail waitressing for $2.13 per hour and tips until 3:30 A.M.; with a BSN I will have the opportunity to provide for my children, work for good pay, receive employee benefits, and have a marketable career, especially since I chose the field of nursing.

Nearly a quarter of the 1999 respondents (23.1 percent) indicated that college had broadened their horizons, enriched their lives, and allowed them to see things in new ways. This theme of enrichment is illustrated by the words of a senior in behavioral sciences, a mother of four children, ages six to ten, who hoped to pursue a master's degree in occupational therapy on finishing her undergraduate degree:

> I became a senator on student government. I learned about politics when once I hadn't a clue. I've learned so much about so many different things. I'm really excited about the spectrum of opportunities open to me and the easy availability of learning opportunities to do those things I want to. Life sure is good these days.

Not surprisingly, the changes in self-concept and life goals impacted the relationships respondents had with their children, partners, parents, and friends: as one element of the system shifts, other elements must adjust.

Effect on Relationships

About one-third of the respondents (33.0 percent) in the first survey spoke about how their return to school modeled good decisions and behavior for their children. Some spoke of doing homework together with their children, others said their children were doing better in school, and others said their children now spoke of going to college themselves. A thirty-seven-year-old student of business management said her return to school had impacted her two children—ages nine and ten—in the following manner:

> It has inspired them to get a good education and has shown them that they can aspire to be what they want to be career-wise. It has shown them that to be self-sufficient they must work towards their careers and that education is a lifelong journey.

This respondent, who had a 3.85 GPA, had never worked before returning to school; she claimed she had never had enough education. Her career plans were to own her own business after completing her degree.

Similarly, over one-quarter of the respondents (26.2 percent) of the first survey wrote about the enhanced understanding they had of their children, and the increased amount of quality time they were spending together: they had learned more about child development, enhanced their parenting skills, and gained patience. They spoke of enjoying their children more, talking with them more, and having more fun with them. The following quote from a sophomore in criminal justice speaks to this theme:

> My daughter and I do our homework at about the same time each night. I am less stressed about everything in my life, therefore I am more pleasant to be around. My daughter and I get along a lot better.

This thirty-five-year-old respondent maintained a 3.8 GPA and hoped to be a probation officer once she graduated; prior to returning to school she had been a waitress and had made about $5.00 per hour.

Effect on Self, Family, and Life Opportunities Two Years Later

After seven pages of short-answer questions, respondents of the second survey were also given the opportunity to write in narrative form about how their participation in a post-secondary education program had affected their feelings about themselves, their lives, their opportunities, and their relationships. Forty-six respondents (70.8 percent) provided narrative responses to this question. Among these responses, over two-thirds (69.6 percent) reiterated the themes of the first survey: their self-esteem was greatly improved, they felt empowered, they had far more opportunities, and their relationships were enhanced. Seven respondents (15.1 percent) felt good about their school experiences and the possibilities that lay ahead, but felt they needed some transitional assistance as they moved from school into the labor market. A few (6.5 percent) were ambivalent about whether all the sacrifices they had made would be worth it in the end, and four respondents (8.7 percent) said they did not think they would be financially secure even with a college education.

Respondents of the second survey who wrote about the possible lack of financial rewards (i.e., adequate wages) for all their hard work in school described the depressed economies and lack of jobs in many parts of rural Maine. The response of one twenty-nine-year-old respondent who had received a bachelor's degree in social services, lived in a small town in a rural region of the state, and was currently unemployed, illustrates the situation faced by respondents seeking work during an economic recession:

> Receiving a degree was fulfilling; however, I cannot find a good pay-ing job in my area. The job market is horrible. On a single income without child support, I need a job paying at least $10 per hour in order to be self-sustaining. Those kind of jobs just simply are not available. I am seriously considering leaving the state of Maine due to the current job market.

Similarly, a twenty-six-year-old respondent of the second survey, with two children under six, reflected on whether all she had given up to obtain her de-gree would pay off in the end. She was working on a bachelor's degree in social sciences at the time of the survey. Her words document the multiple demands faced by student parents and exemplify the ambivalence described by a small number of other respondents (16.5 percent):

> My college experience has had a profound effect on my life and my family. I would like to say it has been a good experience as going to school has benefited me but it has been a hard road. The demands of the work expected for my courses, the demands of my children, and the need for a more stable financial situation cause more stress and hardship than I wonder if it's worth. I'm scared as I approach my final semester before obtaining my degree, about acquiring a job that will support my family comfortably as well as pay back my educational loans. I know it's good for my girls to see me getting an education and trying to better myself and give our family a promising future but the cost of less time with my girls especially when they are young I often feel is too high. . . . School itself has been rewarding and I know I have gained priceless knowledge. I just haven't concluded if all the sacrifices have been worth it.

This respondent's oldest child (age five), for whom she received Supplemental Security Income (SSI), had epilepsy. In the preceding year, the family had ex-perienced many financial hardships such as needing to skip meals to save money and falling behind on utility and car payments.

Most respondents of the second survey (nearly 70 percent) wrote about their experience in glowing terms and described how going to school had helped them turn their lives around in very positive ways. One thirty-one-year-old respondent, with four children under six and a bachelor's degree in the so-cial sciences, described what a different person she was compared to when she first started school:

When I started college, I was in an abusive relationship. . . . I had no self-esteem, but wanted desperately to make life better. He'd sabotage the car and offer to baby-sit but then not be around. I prayed and prayed for him to die or go back to jail. I couldn't make him go away no matter what I said or did. Finally my prayers were answered. He went to jail. I had tremendous difficulties focusing on my studies and critical thinking. I was PTSD and didn't realize it. I figured I was an educated woman; this stuff shouldn't happen to me. I kept plugging away and was amazed when I got good grades. . . . My life has changed significantly because of school. I used to have trouble in social situations. I'd blank out completely if I had to interact or share my thought and opinions in class. . . . I was also very angry and didn't like being a mom. Now, I'm a school-based educator with my local rape crisis center. . . . I would never have imagined myself doing this. I love my family now and do my best to provide for their emotional needs. I'm a Girl Scout leader for a third year. The town I live in calls me whenever there's a social function, to help out. . . . If you had known me when I first started school, you'd understand just how much life has changed for me as well as [for] those who are with me daily.

This respondent had not only become financially self-sufficient, but spoke of being a better mother and a more involved member of her community. A desire to give back to the community was mentioned by numerous respondents in both the first and second surveys. Post-secondary education appears to provide the necessary tools for some of these respondents to meet their potential as active citizens.

One thirty-five-year-old graduate in sciences, who was pursuing further classes in a teacher-education program, reiterated this desire to make a difference in her community, and believed that her degree would make that possible. According to this respondent of the 2001 survey, post-secondary education was her protection against destitution for herself and her children:

Completing my degree has had a tremendous impact on my self (image, self-esteem, etc.) and my future. When I received my degree this past spring I finally felt that I had achieved something worthwhile in life. That many more jobs would be available to me. At the same time I want to be able to give back to my community. I decided to go into teaching and am working on getting state certified. . . . My family is proud and supportive and my child has a positive role model for the effort one must make when working toward a goal. I will always be grateful to have had the opportunity to complete my education. That is the one factor that can keep me from sliding into hopeless poverty. In completing my degree I know that I can do whatever it takes to go after my dreams.

Sources of Stress

Despite these overwhelmingly positive effects of returning to school, some reported negative consequences resulting from the very full lives they had chosen. Going to school, raising children, and often holding down a job left a portion of the respondents stretched to their limits. For example, twenty-eight respondents (13.6 percent) in the first survey reported that their relationships were negatively affected by going to school. They wrote of being stressed and not having enough time for their children or other family members.

Securing child care was also a source of stress for some respondents in both surveys. While PaS participants receive financial assistance with child care, nearly half of the respondents in each survey who needed help with child care (45.5 percent in 1999 and 40.5 percent in 2001) reported problems in securing it. For example, in 2001, twelve respondents (32.4 percent of those needing child care) had trouble finding affordable care; nine respondents (24.3 percent) could not secure safe, quality care; nine (24.3 percent) had problems accessing care; and four respondents (10.8 percent) could not find child care to fit their work schedules.

Another source of stress for some respondents involved their interaction with the Department of Human Services (DHS). Although some respondents praised PaS caseworkers for the emotional support and assistance they provided, other respondents ran into barriers and unsupportive attitudes in their interactions with the department. In 1999, we asked respondents to rate their experience with DHS: 61.5 percent gave a good or excellent rating and 38.5 percent said their experiences were fair to poor.

Wages and TANF in 2001

As mentioned earlier, one of the primary purposes of the second survey was to see how graduates of the PaS program were faring in the labor market and whether they were earning wages that allowed them to escape poverty. Four-fifths (or fifty-two) of the sixty-five respondents in the second survey were working at the time of the survey: thirty-five had graduated, seventeen had not. The mean hourly wage of the primary job for all respondents was $10.61, but graduates were earning significantly higher wages than respondents who had not yet graduated: $11.75 versus $8.26 per hour. Moreover, when comparing the highest wages respondents had earned prior to graduation—something we asked those respondents who had graduated—with their current wages, there was, on average, a significant increase: for the thirty respondents who answered this question, the average wage increased from $8.63 to $12.13. Furthermore, employed respondents who had graduated had a significantly higher probability of working in a job that offered benefits than did employed respondents who had not yet graduated (83.3 percent vs. 31.2 percent).

Eight respondents (12.3 percent) still received TANF at the time of the survey. Of these, five had graduated but were only able to secure part-time or seasonal work and thus still qualified for TANF to supplement their wages. So, while post-secondary education clearly increases one's earning potential and the ability to secure work with benefits, a post-secondary degree does not provide total immunity from disability, economic recessions, underemployment, or other life circumstances that could result in inadequate earnings and the need for government assistance. Nonetheless, the vast majority of respondents of the second survey, like those two years earlier, wrote at length about the positive impact post-secondary education had had on all aspects of their lives.

Some respondents (15.1 percent) were generally positive about their experience in school and the opportunities a degree opened up for them, but wished there were more transitional benefits as they worked toward economic self-sufficiency. Exemplifying this sentiment was one graduate with a bachelor's degree in social services who was employed as a case manager; her salary was about $24,000 and she had full health benefits. Prior to going to school, her highest hourly wage had been $8.50.

> It definitely has affected my entire life in a positive way. Self-esteem has increased as well as opportunities. The relationship with my children is great and I'm proud for them to know I completed my education. It's hard because I can't spend near enough time with them. My main issue now is housing. Living in subsidized housing, they charge 30 percent of your gross income. For me this is $600. I am paying so much in rent I'm unable to save money for a home. . . . I think PaS is an excellent program. Very helpful in helping people better their lives. Though I'm off the welfare system (except Medicaid), I am no better off financially with rent going up and losing all benefits, especially food stamps.

SUMMARIZING SURVEY FINDINGS

In summary, the findings from these two surveys demonstrate that pursuing higher education while raising children—often by themselves—was personally satisfying, financially rewarding, and beneficial to family relationships for many respondents. The stress, described by a small portion of the sample, of demanding academic work on top of other parenting responsibilities is not an unexpected finding; it merely strengthens the case for assuring that adequate supports such as child care and transportation assistance are provided for these families as they work toward economic security.

In an extensive literature review focused on women, welfare, and higher education, Center for Women Policy Studies analyst Erika Kates (1992, 2) affirms these findings: "low income women who have engaged in higher education experience several tangible advantages: their incomes improve, their levels of satisfaction with their own lives and their children's improve; they become more productive citizens; and they become prime motivators in improving the lives of others closely connected to them." Our own discussions with the Maine Department of Human Services' (DHS) staff and Parents as Scholars program participants reveal similar findings: participants have increased self-esteem and confidence, fewer family crises, and experience positive family interactions around issues related to education. Children of participants experience a heightened quality of life and have elevated aspirations and comfort with higher education. DHS staff find that participants require fewer support services and less employee time and energy. Employers have access to a better educated and more well-rounded workforce. And the state of Maine sees the genuine prospect of higher earning power and a stronger tax base as well as a more viable citizenry.

PREPARING FOR WELFARE REAUTHORIZATION

When the reauthorization of PRWORA loomed on the horizon at the beginning of 2002, the activists who had convened the Women's Economic Security Project in the mid-1990s recognized that once again grassroots activism and coalition building was essential to ensure that Maine's experience was heard in the national reauthorization debate. They invited together a host of groups from around the state—organizations representing women, children, low income families, religious groups, labor interests, families with disabilities, domestic and sexual abuse victims, and social service agencies. The coalition, formed in January 2002, was named the Alliance for Family Success.

The alliance created an ambitious agenda for Maine to take its reauthorization message to the national arena. Maine had created some very humane and successful approaches to welfare that needed to be championed at the national level. It had implemented many innovative and successful programs with state funds and central to this approach was the conviction that states should be allowed to use federal funds to continue the programs lest they be jeopardized by tight state budgets combined with difficult federal requirements. A critical component of the message was the success of the Parents as Scholars program and its potential to move low income women not just off welfare but out of poverty. Other successful aspects of Maine's welfare plan had included specialized programs to help families with multiple barriers to employment, methods to ensure that families who went to work maintained a floor of assistance under low wages, and transitional aid for families leaving welfare for work.

The alliance's mission was to provide information and education to policy makers to encourage a reauthorization effort that would respect the basic dignity of families and enhance their access to supportive assistance, necessary to meet their basic needs and improve their opportunities for economic security. Among the chief principles of the alliance were increased funding for TANF, food stamps, and other supports for low income families, including subsidized child care; support for education and training, including vocational education and post-secondary degrees; reduction of the punitive aspects of welfare reform such as sanctions and time limits; design of TANF-related activities that recognize the individual characteristics of families and rejects a one-size-fits-all approach, including accommodating physical and mental health problems; and restoration of benefits to legal immigrants.

Several of the recent plans swirling around Congress, the president's proposal among them, did not support most of the alliance's principles, including access to post-secondary education. President Bush's welfare reauthorization proposal discouraged states from using federal funds to help low income families go to college: post-secondary education was not a "countable" TANF activity for families receiving TANF, and any family not involved in a "countable" activity jeopardized a state's ability to meet its required participation rate. The president's plan also limited a family's ability to access GED or vocational education to three consecutive months every two years; outside that three-month period, a family would have to work or volunteer for at least twenty-four hours per week before being able to undertake GED or vocational education as a "countable" activity.

To implement its agenda, the alliance devised a multifaceted approach. It began by organizing biweekly meetings to move the campaign forward and provide structure to its agenda. Members shared information about TANF individual reauthorization activities and engaged in broader alliance-driven activities. One such activity was focused on the Parents as Scholars program. Cognizant that members of the public, as well as many politicians, were not aware of the success of PaS, the alliance joined with the educational community in making the case for Parents as Scholars. Based on the longitudinal surveys previously discussed and other state-specific data on low income families, we created a booklet called *Parents as Scholars: Education Works* (Smith, Deprez, and Butler 2002), which was widely distributed to the media, to Maine's congressional delegation, and to the public.

The booklet highlighted the positive outcomes of participants and explained the dangers of relying entirely on state funding to support the program. Positive outcomes of PaS graduates were compared to the findings of a Maine Center for Economic Policy survey of individuals who had been on welfare in

1997 (Pohlmann 2002). Findings from that survey found that individuals who had left welfare without a post-secondary education were not faring at all well: median wages were only $7.50 per hour and it was unlikely they would secure benefits. Further, among all survey respondents, 30 percent had cycled back on to welfare at some point since 1997.

Armed with these telling data, alliance members undertook a series of editorial board visits with newspapers around the state to enlist their assistance in educating the public, as well as policy makers, about the success of the PaS program. These meetings resulted in a series of newspaper editorials explaining the positive impact that PaS had made on low income families. Several papers also undertook to report on a local individual "success story," a Parents as Scholars graduate doing well and escaping poverty. Articles also appeared in national newspapers such as the *Christian Science Monitor*.

Another facet of the alliance's approach was to convene groups of current and former TANF recipients from around the state to educate them about the reauthorization proposals circulating in Congress and ask them how they felt certain proposals would affect them. Many of those who attended were current or former PaS participants; they were especially alarmed at the possibility of less, not more, support for education for low income, especially single, parents. These families mobilized to undertake a letter-writing campaign to explain to their local newspapers as well as to their congressional representatives how the president's proposals would hurt Maine families. In addition, the alliance developed a second booklet highlighting the hardships faced by both low-wage workers who had left TANF but were still struggling, and by those who remained on TANF, many of whom were experiencing severe barriers to employment such as health problems in their families (Hastedt and Smith 2002). This booklet culminated in a series of "success stories" and comments on how to improve welfare programs at the state and national levels.

The final prong of the alliance's campaign was to ensure that Maine's congressional representatives and senators knew of Maine's welfare reform successes and would help ensure that they would not be jeopardized. To begin, the alliance held a series of meetings with Maine's Department of Human Services wherein together they created a "Common Ground" of principles critical to Maine's continued success in TANF reauthorization. Among them were increased funding to support TANF programs, improved support for education, realistic participation rates, and reinstatement of federal funds to help legal immigrants. The alliance and the Department of Human Services then presented this "Common Ground" statement to Maine congressional delegation staff in a day-long meeting.

As we go to press, members of the alliance continue to educate Maine's congressional delegation about particular aspects of welfare reauthorization and specific plans being proposed in Congress. The alliance continues its campaign to make education a "countable" activity for families receiving TANF to preserve the important path to economic stability that it has forged for Maine's low income mothers. A major victory has already been won: Maine's Senator Olympia Snowe introduced legislation in the 107th Congress, "The Pathways to Self-Sufficiency Act," modeled on Maine's PaS program, that would allow states to include access to post-secondary education as a work activity for up to 10 percent of its TANF families. In discussing the bill in the Senate Finance Committee in 2002, Senator Snowe quoted statistics from the surveys of PaS participants and spoke eloquently of the group of PaS graduates and students she had met. Senator Snowe's bill was included as part of the welfare reauthorization package approved by the Senate Finance Committee in 2002 with overwhelming support.

Unfortunately, the Senate did not vote on this bill before the end of the 107th Congress. The Senate of the 108th Congress, under Republican leadership, is less likely to pass as "progressive" a bill as would have been possible in 2002. On September 10, 2003, the Senate Finance Committee voted on a new TANF Reauthorization Bill that will require consideration by the full Senate. While this bill is more punitive than its previous version, it still contains Senator Snowe's proposal that states be authorized to enact programs like Maine's PaS program. But because this proposal is not contained in the even harsher House bill (HR 4), it is unclear whether Snowe's proposal can withstand a Conference Committee even if it does pass in the Senate. TANF once again faces an uncertain future; it has been extended until March 2004. As such, the fate of low income mothers seeking to provide for their families by pursuing higher education remains unclear.

CONCLUSION

Maine's Parents as Scholars program provides welfare recipients with access to post-secondary and higher education programs that can increase their prospects of a life without poverty. The National Campaign for Jobs and Income Support's recent report "praised Maine for developing an education . . . component of public assistance" (*Portland Press Herald* 2001). While the program is not an absolute guarantee of a life without poverty, low income women and their families face greatly enhanced chances of secure living when their opportunities for obtaining and maintaining successful, supportive, and fulfilling work are increased. Parents as Scholars models one way in which the long quest to reduce poverty among poor families can be achieved and affords low income women who are parents the same access to higher education that the public at large believes is essential for the rest of society to succeed in the new economy.

NOTES

1. Fundamental to the idea of a block grant is the notion that states will have greater flexibility to operate their program as they see fit. Although the federal restrictions in

PRWORA, such as limits on education and the five-year time limit, belie that notion—these restrictions apply only to federal block grant funds; they do not apply to state dollars. PRWORA required states to continue to spend a percentage of the funds they spent in the former Aid to Families with Dependent Children program in the new program. These state funds, referred to as "maintenance-of-effort" (MOE) dollars, can be used to avoid the more undesirable provisions of PRWORA.

2. In 1982 when the first Work Incentive Demonstration (WIN) projects were announced by then president Reagan, advocates persuaded the Maine Department of Human Services to take this opportunity to demonstrate the antipoverty impact of providing access to post-secondary education to welfare recipients. This program, originally called "WEET," was eventually renamed "ASPIRE." Throughout the 1980s, the program enjoyed considerable popularity, but as the recession of the early 1990s took hold and the national attitude toward welfare began to shift dramatically, it came under criticism for being "too generous."

REFERENCES

Butler, S. S., and L. S. Deprez. 2002. Something worth fighting for: Higher education for women on welfare. *Affilia* 17:30–54.

Butler, S. S., and M. K. Nevin. 1997. Welfare mothers speak: One state's effort to bring recipient voices to the welfare debate. *Journal of Poverty* 1(2):25–61.

Deprez, L. S., and S. S. Butler. 2001. In defense of women's economic security: Securing access to higher education under welfare reform. *Social Politics* 8:210–227.

Hastedt, C. B., and R. J. Smith. 2002. *Welfare, work and raising children: Conversations with twenty-one Maine families.* Augusta: Maine Equal Justice Partners.

Kates, E. 1992. *Women, welfare and higher education: A selected bibliography.* Washington, D.C.: Center for Women Policy Studies.

Personal Responsibility and Work Opportunity Reconciliation Act of 1996. 1998. Public Law No. 104-193, 110 Stat 2105 [codified at 42 U.S.C. sec. 601 (1998): 42 U.S.C. sec. 601(a)(2) and 602 (a)(1)(A)(i)].

Pohlmann, L. 2002. *Welfare reform: Lessons from Maine.* Augusta: Maine Center for Economic Policy.

Portland (Maine) *Press Herald.* 2001, March 12. Welfare transition is failing, study finds, p. 10.

Seguino, S. 1995. *Living on the edge: Women working and providing for families in the Maine economy 1979–1993.* Orono, Maine: Margaret Chase Smith Center for Public Policy.

Smith, R. J., L. S. Deprez, and S. S. Butler. 2002. *Parents as Scholars: Education works.* Augusta: Maine Equal Justice Partners.

Will tinkering bring the building down? 2002. *The Economist* 2 March:29.

Afterword

The Editors

Higher education matters. For low income mothers with children, a college degree may be the only secure pathway out of poverty, ensuring access to economic self-sufficiency and family stability. The narratives of low income mothers' lives in this book depict the psychological impact and the personal and social empowerment that take place when single mothers gain access to a college education. The transformation from "welfare mothers" to determined and capable student parents and activists mobilizing the resources of the communities in which they live, dramatically demonstrates how higher education builds social capital in a previously stigmatized and disenfranchised constituency. Low income single mothers' own sense of the value of higher education confirms the data about post-secondary education and employment outcomes—both in terms of the gender divide between women and men's earnings, as well as the dramatic difference that accrues when women complete a bachelor's degree, with substantially higher monthly earnings and greater job stability than for those with two-year college or high school degrees (U.S. Census Bureau 2002).

The chapters in this volume were written just as the six-year life span of the 1996 Personal Responsibility and Work Opportunity Reconciliation Act (PRWORA) was drawing to a close. With its combination of punitive and short-sighted Work First requirements, PRWORA sharply undermined the ability of low income mothers to pursue post-secondary education. Many states, with their new autonomy under the act, increased the barriers beyond those erected in the federal legislation, although a small number of states (as documented here) developed notable and innovative ways of supporting education. Among these policy barriers to post-secondary education were onerous work requirements; refusal to permit education as a legitimate work activity; age-of-youngest-child rules (which in several cases required mothers of three month olds to work forty hours a week); time limits on welfare receipt; inadequate provision of child care resources for work and educational activities; misinformation

237

to clients; and multiple, complex, difficult-to-navigate welfare bureaucracies. Several chapters have depicted the impact of these hurdles and often insurmountable obstructions in the lives of women, particularly in New York City and Michigan.

Despite ample evidence that most of the three million mothers who left welfare since 1996 have continued to work intermittently in low-wage jobs, leaving them no better off financially than they were while receiving benefits, the Bush administration and other policy makers have proclaimed the Work First model, with its marginalization of education and training, a success. Reducing the welfare rolls continues to take precedence over education and training and poverty alleviation in most of the current welfare reauthorization proposals. The Bush administration's reauthorization plan introduced in 2002 includes increased work requirements (forty hours with almost no exemptions) for a greater number of recipients (70 percent of the state caseload) than the 1996 law. Most aspects of the Bush proposal—including a marriage promotion component—were enacted in the House of Representatives both in the 107th Congress (HR 4737) and in the 108th Congress (HR 4). Proposed restrictions on post-secondary education are even more severe than under current law. The 1996 PRWORA allowed vocational education as a core activity for up to one year, but the House reauthorization bill eliminates this provision, requiring recipients to be employed for twenty-four hours per week before any access to education or training is permitted, for the remaining sixteen hours of required work activities. Funding for child care has decreased proportionately, and future funding is now in jeopardy. The dominant rhetoric of welfare reauthorization continues to blatantly disregard both the research and the evidence pointing to the importance of higher education as a pathway out of poverty; rather the Bush administration and the Republican-dominated Congress continue to promote the "marriage cure" as the antidote to so-called welfare profligacy and single mother poverty. While touting the moral and economic benefits of marriage, such policies coerce large numbers of single mothers into dead-end jobs—no matter how low the pay and how dismal the future prospects for advancement, further trapping women and their children in poverty.

During the 107th Congress, advocates and organizations for low income families organized a national campaign to counter these harsh and discriminatory proposals. Lobbying efforts, focused in particular on the Senate Finance Committee, met with some success. The bipartisan bill reported out of committee in 2002 was an improvement on the House bill. In addition to including increased funding for child care and work exemptions for mothers with disabled children, more recipients of Temporary Assistance for Needy Families (TANF) would be permitted to satisfy their work requirements in post-secondary education activities. Republican Finance Committee member Senator Olympia Snowe from Maine, introduced wording that would allow states to include access to post-secondary education as a work activity for up to 10 percent of its caseload—a model similar to Maine's successful Parents as Scholars Program. However, the Finance Committee's bipartisan bill never came to the floor for a full Senate vote before the 107th Congress ended. As we write, the bill proposed by the Senate Finance Committee in the Republican-controlled Senate of the 108th Congress, ironically entitled Personal Responsibility and Individual Development for Everyone (PRIDE), closely mirrors the punitive House bill; the provisions of the 107th Congress's Senate bill have been stripped away, and any opportunity for post-secondary education has disappeared. We anticipate that reauthorization, together with state budget cuts and crises, will severely constrain the space available for advocates and recipients to maneuver in the coming year.

Such policies, if implemented, presage a bitter and contested future for poor women and their children—regulating their personal and family lives, diminishing their autonomy, and severely restricting their educational opportunities; and all is publicly framed in the Orwellian doublespeak of "Personal Responsibility and Individual Development."

Shut Out has presented the stories of low income mothers' struggles to overcome the economic and political oppression of their lives and has documented the mobilizing actions of advocates and community organizers and the responses of educational institutions. Throughout the country both established and new innovative programs for low income mothers continue, and we believe it is essential that the fight for low income mothers' access to education becomes a visible and mobilizing political issue. Activist research and advocacy play vital roles in critically analyzing, exposing, confronting, and resisting policies that continue to violate the rights of low income mothers.

D. F. (see chapter 2 in this volume), who has graduated from college after twenty-five years on public assistance and now holds a good job at a community college reflects on how education changed her life:

> I don't understand why anyone wouldn't want anyone to get an education. I mean if you want productive citizens out there, they *need* education. If they don't have no education, how do you expect them to be productive? . . . Education to me is just always the key. It's given me energy. It's given me a whole new outlook on a lot of things. I feel so good with the knowledge that I've absorbed . . . I think I've changed tremendously . . . I try to drum into my daughter's head all the time "you've got to get that education because you can't get nowhere . . . you need to stay in school so you can get an education so you can decide what you want to do, you can have a choice. But if you don't go to school you have no choice. You have to accept whatever it is that they give you. . . ."

It is precisely that choice and opportunity, the right to build and live an autonomous life with one's children, that all women deserve. Higher education still offers that promise.

September 2003

REFERENCES

U.S. Census Bureau. 2002, July. *The big payoff: Educational attainment and synthetic estimates of work-life earnings.* Washington, D.C.: United States Census Bureau.

Contributors

Stefani A. Bjorklund is a Ph.D. candidate in Higher Education at the Pennsylvania State University. Ms. Bjorklund is a research assistant at Penn State's Center for the Study of Higher Education and a research associate at Rankin & Associates Consulting. Her research interests include the interplay of federal, state, and institutional policies affecting access and retention of underrepresented college students, staff, and faculty; welfare reform and student financial aid policies; and campus climate for diversity. Prior to returning to graduate school, Ms. Bjorklund was a social worker and administrator of a federally funded demonstration project funded by the National Center on Child Abuse and Neglect.

Sandra S. Butler, Ph.D., is Associate Professor in the School of Social Work at the University of Maine. She received her M.S.W. from George Warren Brown School of Social Work at Washington University and her Ph.D. at the University of Washington. From 2001 to 2003, Dr. Butler was a Hartford Geriatric Social Work Faculty Scholar and the Resident Scholar at the UMaine Center on Aging. Dr. Butler is the author of *Middle-aged, Female and Homeless: The Stories of a Forgotten Group*, and co-editor with Lenard Kaye of a volume forthcoming in 2004: *Gerontological Practice in Small Towns and Rural Communities*. In 2001, she received the Feminist Scholarship Award from the Commission on Women of the Council on Social Work Education for her research regarding post-secondary education for women on welfare. Dr. Butler sits on the editorial board of the *Journal of Poverty: Innovations on Social, Political & Economic Inequalities* and is a consulting editor for *Health & Social Work*. She teaches graduate and undergraduate courses in social-welfare policy, policy practice, gerontology, and macro-practice methods.

241

Deborah Clarke is employed as the Outreach and Processing Coordinator for the Soft Second Loan Program, a state-subsidized mortgage program in Massachusetts for low and moderate income first time homebuyers. She was able to continue her education as an adult by participating in a research project on women's homelessness in the state of Massachusetts called RWARM (Roofless Women's Action Research Mobilization). The program was a partnership between government agencies and nonprofits, and was based at the College of Public and Community Service of U/Mass Boston. Participants received help with tuition and fees. When the project ended, she completed her education with the help of a spin-off of the program called Women in Community Development, also based at U/Mass Boston. As a graduate of the program, she sits on its steering committee. Deborah has served on numerous boards and committees. In 2001, she was able to purchase a home with the help of the Family Self-Sufficiency Program at Community Team Work in Lowell, Massachusetts.

Luisa Stormer Deprez is Interim Dean of the College of Arts and Sciences, former Director of the Women's Studies Program, and Associate Professor of Sociology at the University of Southern Maine. She has a B.A. in Sociology, an M.S.W. in Community Organization from Rutgers University, and a Ph.D. in Social Policy from the Heller School at Brandeis University. Her scholarly interests and publications center on the broad arenas of social-welfare policy including the politics of policy-making; the impact of ideology and public opinion in policy; poverty; women and welfare; and women, welfare, and higher education. She lives in Portland with her two children, Réal and Esmé.

Donald E. Heller is Associate Professor and Senior Research Associate in the Center for the Study of Higher Education at the Pennsylvania State University. He earned an Ed.D. in Higher Education from the Harvard Graduate School of Education, and holds an Ed.M. in Administration, Planning, and Social Policy from Harvard and a B.A. in Economics and Political Science from Tufts University. Before his academic career, he spent a decade as an information technology manager at the Massachusetts Institute of Technology. Dr. Heller teaches and conducts research on issues relating to higher education economics, public policy, and finance, as well as academic and administrative uses of technology in higher education. The primary focus of his work is on issues of access and choice in post-secondary education, examining the factors and policies that help to determine whether or not individuals attend college, and what type of institution they attend. Dr. Heller has consulted on higher education policy issues with university systems and policy-making organizations in California, Colorado, Massachusetts, Michigan, New Hampshire, Tennessee, and Washington, D.C., and he has testified in front of state legislative and congressional committees. He is the editor of the books *The States and Public Higher*

Education Policy: Affordability, Access, and Accountability (Johns Hopkins University Press, 2001), and *Condition of Access: Higher Education for Lower Income Students* (ACE/Praeger, 2002).

Peggy Kahn teaches in the Political Science Department and Women's and Gender Studies Program at the University of Michigan-Flint. Recently her research, publication, and advocacy have focused on the access of low income women to post-secondary education; single-parent families and the 1996 welfare law; low-wage women and the workplace; and public policy and women's employment. She has received the UM-Flint David M. French Professor Award in recognition of her outstanding achievement and the University of Michigan Academic Women's Caucus's Sarah Goddard Power Award in recognition of service and contributions to the status of women on campus and in the community. She is co-author (with Deborah Figart) of *Contesting the Market: Pay Equity and the Politics of Economic Restructuring* (1997) and co-editor (with Elizabeth Meehan) of *Equal Pay/Comparable Worth in the United Kingdom and the United States of America* (1992). She is co-author (with Norman Lewis, Rowland Livock, and Paul Wiles) of *Picketing: Industrial Disputes, Tactics and the Law* (1983).

Erika Kates is currently Research Director at the Center for Women in Politics and Public Policy at the University of Massachusetts, Boston. Since 1986 she has been involved in advocacy and research on access to education for low income mothers, and has written extensively in this area. Previously, she was a senior research associate at the Heller Graduate School of Social Policy, Brandeis University, where she co-founded and directed the Welfare Education Training Access Coalition (WETAC). In March 2002 she testified before Congress on the importance of including education and training in the reauthorization of the Responsibility and Work Opportunity Reconciliation Act (PRWORA).

Anita K. Mathur is a doctoral student in Sociology at the University of California, Berkeley. She has worked with the California community colleges over the past several years to ascertain the economic outcomes of welfare-recipient students. In addition to her work with the California community colleges, Ms. Mathur is also a researcher with the University of California Data Archive and Technical Assistance (UC DATA). At UC DATA she was part of the team that evaluated the Cal-Learn demonstration program in California, and she is currently completing a project that measures the impact of welfare reform on California's immigrant families.

Christiana Miewald is a Research Associate with the Community Economic Development Centre at Simon Fraser University. She received her Ph.D. in 2000 in Applied and Medical Anthropology from the University of Kentucky.

Her dissertation examined the effect of welfare reform and economic restructuring on women's care work in Appalachian Kentucky. She also worked with welfare rights organizations in the region to improve access to education. Papers from this research can be found in *Urban Geography and Environment and Planning A*. She is currently examining issues of urban planning and food security in Vancouver, British Columbia.

Lynn Peterson, Co-Director, Center for Supportive Communities, develops new programs and partnerships for the Women's Institute for Housing and Economic Development. In her role as senior housing project manager, she consulted with a number of community groups, assisting them in the development of service-enriched housing. She also developed programs at the Women's Institute including Roofless Women's Action Research Mobilization and Women in Community Development. Previously, Ms. Peterson facilitated neighborhood-planning efforts with the city of Boston, and managed congregate housing for the elderly in the Merrimack Valley. She is active in housing in her town where she serves as the chair of the local housing partnership. She holds a B.A. in Human Services and Urban Affairs from Northeastern University and an M.A. in Urban Policy from Tufts University.

Valerie Polakow is Professor of Education and Director of the Center for Child and Family Programs at the Institute for the Study of Children, Families and Communities at Eastern Michigan University. She has been active in local, state, and national advocacy organizations that support post-secondary educational access and child care for low income women. She has written extensively about women and children in poverty, homelessness, and welfare and child care policies in national and international contexts. She was a Fulbright scholar in Denmark in 1995, and the recipient of the Ronald W. Collins Distinguished Faculty Award for scholarly activity in 2002. She is the author and/or editor of six books including *The Erosion of Childhood, Lives on the Edge: Single Mothers and Their Children in the Other America* (which won the Kappa Delta Pi book of the year award in 1994), and *The Public Assault on America's Children: Poverty, Violence and Juvenile Injustice*. She is currently working on a forthcoming book about the crisis of child care for low income families in the United States.

Lizzy Ratner worked as a welfare-rights advocate in a community-based Brooklyn law office throughout the late 1990s and early 2000s. During that time, she began an oral history project to document the often devastating impact of New York City's welfare "reform" policies on low income New Yorkers. Several of the stories from that project are published in this book. Lizzy Ratner is currently a journalist living in New York City.

Judy Reichle was CalWORKs Unit Coordinator at the California Community Colleges Chancellor's Office from 1999–2003, providing oversight and technical assistance to this $81M program that serves 45,000 students at 108 community colleges. She holds a Master's Degree in Rehabilitation Administration, University of San Francisco, and has been employed in the fields of education and employment services for twenty-five years.

Frances J. Riemer is an Associate Professor at Northern Arizona University, where she teaches graduate level classes in ethnographic research methods, educational anthropology, and educational sociology. She conducted field research on welfare-to-work programs in 1992 and 1993, funded in part by a grant from the Spencer Foundation. *Working at the Margins: Moving off Welfare in America*, an ethnography based on that research, was published by SUNY Press in 2001. Frances is currently completing ethnographic research on literacy as social practice in Botswana with partial support from a Fulbright research award.

Aiko Schaefer is the Director of the Statewide Poverty Action Network, an alliance taking action on the root causes of poverty with real solutions by informing the public debate, organizing communities, and influencing public policy. Aiko has been a community organizer for over fifteen years, and has worked on a variety of candidate, initiative and issue campaigns around the country. Aiko received her B.A. from the College of Wooster in Ohio. She has a Master's of Social Work degree from the University of Washington, where she also is currently a lecturer in their graduate program. Aiko lives in Seattle, Washington.

Sally Sharp earned her Ph.D. from the University of Michigan's Center for the Study of Higher and Post-secondary Education. Her research on the experiences of low income mothers in college was inspired by the women she met while volunteering at the Fernside Center for Grieving Children in Cincinnati, Ohio. Sharp has over twenty years of administrative experience working in a variety of post-secondary and independent-school settings.

Rebekah J. Smith, J.D., is a Policy Analyst at Maine Equal Justice, where she focuses on issues impacting low income families. She received her undergraduate degree in Economics and Government from Bowdoin College and her law degree from the University of Maine School of Law. After clerking for Chief Justice Daniel Wathen of the Maine Supreme Judicial Court and Senior Judge Frank M. Coffin of the United States First Circuit Court of Appeals, she was awarded a two-year Skadden Fellowship to assist welfare families in Maine seeking access to post-secondary education. Her publications have focused on welfare reforms and their impact on families. She is currently researching the negative impacts of family caps in state welfare policies.

Julie Strawn is a Senior Policy Analyst in the areas of workforce development and welfare reform, with a particular focus on job advancement and access to post-secondary education for low income adults. From 1993 to 1996, Ms. Strawn developed policy and legislative positions for the National Governors' Association in the areas of workforce development and welfare reform. She has also worked on these issues at the Center on Budget and Policy Priorities, at the U.S. Department of Health and Human Services, and in the U.S. House of Representatives. She has authored numerous publications and provided technical assistance to antipoverty organizations, legislators, and program administrators.

Julie L. Watts, M.S.W., is Advocacy and Communications Coordinator for the Statewide Poverty Action Network, an alliance taking action on the root causes of poverty with real solutions by informing the public debate, organizing communities, and influencing public policy. During the period of the campaign to pass the Gaining Independence Bill for Families, Ms. Watts was the Church & Public Policy Associate for the Washington Association of Churches, a fellow organizational partner working on the legislation. Ms. Watts holds a Master's Degree in Social Work from the University of Washington. Prior to working for policy change in Washington State, Ms. Watts worked for several years in social services in homeless and women's shelters, hospitals, and foster care homes. She lives in Seattle.

W. Charles Wiseley (Chuck) has worked in the California Community College (CCC) system since 1982. While at Southwestern College in San Diego, California, in the early 1980s, much of his work examined factors involved in student success using student outcomes as measures of success. He developed a program evaluation system at Southwestern that included student employment and transfer outcomes. His work at the CCC Chancellor's Office continued to incorporate student outcomes in the evaluation of educational programs with the criteria that student outcome measures developed must be useful to prospective students, faculty, and policy makers. His policy research in welfare reform and vocational education has continued to use student outcomes as the basis for understanding the successes and shortcomings of community colleges.

Index